D1036982

199 WAYS
TO REVIEW A BOOK:

A Librarian's Readings in
the Novel of the Sixties

by

JOHN C. PINE

The Scarecrow Press, Inc.
Metuchen, N.J.   1971

For My Mother

My Best and Dearest Critic

Contents

Introduction

The title of this collection of book reviews written during the decade of the 1960's is not meant to be facetious, even though as a librarian myself I know how much importance librarians attach to "how-to" books on every conceivable subject from arts and crafts to how to write a novel in ten easy lessons. As a matter of fact, one of the few nonfiction books assigned to me for review by the Library Journal in the sixties was a "how-to" book by the well-known literary agent, Paul R. Reynolds, entitled The Writing and Selling of Fiction. "Most novels are divided into sections," Mr. Reynolds aptly noted. "If the sections number six or eight or more, they are usually called chapters. If there are only two to four sections, it is customary to call them parts. Some novels have both chapters and parts." Now this is the kind of book we librarians relish and understand!

Mr. Reynolds recognized that a novel is much more than the sum of its parts. "Anyone of reasonable intelligence can learn to write publishable non-fiction," he wrote. "About fiction no such statement can be made. Success as a musician or as a painter requires talent. The same is true of a novelist. What the talent consists of is a mystery." As a successful literary agent and author, Paul Reynolds is perhaps being excessively modest in renouncing the critic's role, but it does seem to me that anyone who undertakes to review current fiction has an obligation to do

more than summarize the plot.   Is the novel good, bad or
indifferent?   This is the question that pursues him inde-
fatigably from the beginning, the final irrevocable judgment
he cannot escape.   In explaining why he considers the novel
to be good, bad or indifferent he is fulfilling his critic's responsibility to the best of his ability.   And if in the process
(as seems likely) he tells us something about the creative
process and the mystery of artistic genius, so much the
better.

   And so, in complete seriousness, I have named this
collection 199 Ways to Review a Book.   I have done so in
respectful awareness of the diverse and complicated nature
of the creative process as manifested in the literary form
called the novel.   There are literally ninety-nine or 199
or 999 ways to review a novel; in fact, almost as many
ways as there are novels to be reviewed.   To the extent
that each novel, whether good or bad, is a unique artistic
creation, to that extent it calls for a fresh and individual
response on the part of the critic or reviewer.   Of course,
not all novels are unique artistic creations, good, bad or
indifferent.   The celebrated author of The Carpetbaggers,
Harold Robbins, merely writes the same formula novel over
and over again.   It would be manifestly impossible to
respond in a fresh and individual way to each Robbins' novel
as it comes off the press.   One should not even try.   I have
done my duty by reviewing The Carpetbaggers and doubt if I
will ever again read or review a book by Harold Robbins.

                                2

   In a sense, book reviewing is the ultimate critical
act, since the reviewer must respond directly to the specific
work of art and cannot easily avoid a final evaluation.   It is

undoubtedly true that many so-called book reviewers do
manage to avoid evaluating the work at hand and, indeed,
simply use the book as a convenient starting point from which
to launch their own theories and ideas.   Let us insist that
the book reviewer has a solemn obligation to deal directly
with the work being reviewed.   If he shirks this fundamental
responsibility, no matter how brilliantly he writes, what he
has written may be an essay but it is not a review.   Book
reviewing is considered by many to be the most menial of
critical pursuits, and yet I suspect that the opposite is more
nearly true; that in so far as the review represents a direct
interplay and exchange of human sensibility and intelligence
between the work of art and the beholder, it offers the greatest challenge and opportunity to elucidate the nature of art
and life.

In this connection, I am reminded of a remark made
by Philip Rahv in his essay, "Notes on the Decline of
Naturalism," reprinted in his recent book, Literature and
the Sixth Sense (a work I heartily recommend to critics and
librarians).

> The art of critical evaluation is best performed in
> a state of ideal aloofness from abstract systems.
> Its practitioner is not concerned with making up
> his mind about the ultimate character of reality
> but with observing and measuring its actual pro-
> portions and combinations within a given form. The
> presence of the real affects him directly, with an
> immediate force contingent upon the degree of
> interest, concreteness, and intensity in the impres-
> sion of life conveyed by the literary artist.   The
> philosopher can take such impressions or leave
> them, but luckily the critic has no such choice.

Philip Rahv's eloquent defense of the eclectic method
of criticism appeals to me enormously and I have attempted
in a modest way to apply this method in the reviews
contained in this book.   Although each review is different

and there are literally 199 ways to review a novel, certain
principles and criteria do emerge from the criticism as a
whole, and it is even possible to generalize about specific
attributes and qualities that distinguish the good novels from
the bad.   I would like to discuss briefly a few of these attributes and qualities in the hope that the discussion will help
to prove that talent or genius, as manifested in specific works
of art, consists of something more tangible than a mystery.

        The one quality that stands out in these reviews, even
more than "characterization" or "plot" or "prose style, " is
compassion and love of humanity.   Perhaps this should not
be too surprising, since the novel by definition ("a fictitious
prose narrative of considerable length portraying characters,
actions, and scenes representative of real life in a plot of
more or less intricacy") is the most human of art forms.
" . . . the sun has the power of a million-watt searchlight
focused on Mexico City, " writes José Romero in A Million
Pesos.   "And while that light makes no hissing sound, its
golden rays generate the energies of young couples so they
can fulfill their destiny; love in its purest form. "

        In a review of Joan Williams' Old Powder Man, Robert
Penn Warren wrote that the author "has . . . that last and
greatest gift: to move the heart. "   The first book reviewed
in these pages, John Updike's The Centaur, is noteworthy
for its compassion and love of humanity.   The late Edward
Lewis Wallant (tragically dead at the age of thirty-six) is an
even better example of a writer whose nobility of spirit and
sympathetic awareness of the human condition permeates his
whole work.   An example of this is half-crazed Sammy's
remark in The Children at the Gate about old Lebidov
(arrested for criminally assaulting a little girl in one of the
wards of the state hospital): "He's a human--that's all there

should be.   There shouldn't be anything but people on this
earth. "   It is one of Sammy's more lucid moments.

Conrad Richter, Georges Simenon, Josephine Johnson
and Shirley Ann Grau are a few of the other novelists represented in this book whose work is characterized by compassion and love of humanity.   Conversely, William Golding's
The Spire suffers grievously from a lack of human sympathy
and understanding.   As I noted in my review, Golding uses
the phrase, "a purely human prerogative. "   "It is precisely
this purely human prerogative, " I wrote, "that is so conspicuously absent from William Golding's fiction.   There
are no real human beings in The Spire, only human attributes.   There are no individuals, only vast impersonal
armies swept with alarms of struggle and flight. "   In
Sybille Bedford's A Favourite of the Gods I also found "a
lack of human sympathy that is positively fatal. "

Novels are never set in heaven, nor are they often
set in some mythical kingdom.   For better or worse, they
are set here on earth.   Characters in novels are earthlings
like ourselves, committed to some specific place at some
specific moment of time.   Before preparing this manuscript
for publication, I do not think I was aware of just how
powerful a force love of place really is in the modern novel.
It shines through the' pages of Shirley Ann Grau, Conrad
Richter, William Faulkner and, yes, John Updike, whose
Yoknapatawpha County is southeastern Pennsylvania and the
"great Middle Atlantic civilization, bounded by New Haven
in the north and Hagerstown in the south and Wheeling in
the west. "   It is a peculiarly American world of gas stations, Y. M. C. A. 's and high school athletic banquets.   In
The Grandfathers it seems to me that Conrad Richter has
written the classic novel of Appalachia.   The intense love of

place is inseparable from the plot.   Take away that affinity
for the land and people of Appalachia and the novel would
dissolve into nothingness.   Shirley Ann Grau's <u>The Keepers</u>
<u>of the House</u> is, in essence, the story of one piece of blood-
stained earth, the American South.   Consider even a writer
as difficult and symbol-laden as Günter Grass.   Much of the
effectiveness of his allegorical <u>Cat and Mouse,</u> translated
from the German, can be attributed to the author's poignant
recreation of a boy's growing up in Danzig during the
Second World War.

A quality that can perhaps best be described in a
single word as "passion" is another important attribute that
characterizes many of the outstanding novels I have reviewed
during the last decade.   Nikos Kazantzakis, Edward Lewis
Wallant, Claude Simon and John Fowles (to name just a few)
have it in abundance.   It gives their work a vitality that
makes it almost impervious to the petty vicissitudes that
affect lesser writers.   As far as John Fowles' <u>The Collector</u>
is concerned, the entire novel takes place within the narrow
confines of Frederick Clegg's country house, and yet it is
imbued with such passionate intensity that interest never
flags or falters.   It is truly a tour de force.   In the case
of Wallant (and I am thinking particularly of <u>The Tenants of</u>
<u>Moonbloom</u>), passion is combined with compassion in such a
way that it is difficult to know where the one begins and the
other ends.   One of the things I found deficient in John
O'Hara's <u>Elizabeth Appleton</u> was just that quality of passion
that could make an Elizabeth Appleton a real flesh-and-blood
creature instead of simply a case history out of <u>The Status</u>
<u>Seekers</u> and <u>Kinsey Report</u>.   I disliked <u>The Birthday King</u> by
Gabriel Fielding because it seemed bloodless and academic,
an exercise in which the author set out to prove he could

recreate the dying, infamous German Third Reich without
actually having been there.   It is conspicuously lacking in
just that passion that could make it believable.   Stephen
Crane did not have any personal experience of war when he
wrote The Red Badge of Courage.   He had something infinitely more valuable, a passionate belief in what he was
doing that made it all come vividly alive.

3

Literary criticism is undoubtedly more of an art
than a science.   Of all the reasons cited in these reviews
for writing unfavorably about a novel, two stand out among
the rest.   These are implausibility of plot and pretentiousness
of style or content.   What is implausible or pretentious to
me, of course, might well strike someone else as quite
plausible and unpretentious.   In these circumstances, all
one can do is be as specific as one can and provide the
reader with enough information so that he can form his own
opinion, no matter how tentative or incomplete.   The
Andromeda Strain soared to the top of the best-seller list
and remained there for weeks, so apparently hundreds of
thousands of readers found it quite plausible.   I personally
thought this banal saga of why a sixty-nine-year-old Sterno
drinker with an ulcer resembles a two-month-old baby was
altogether preposterous.   Fail-Safe is another best-seller
that belongs in this same category.   Certainly we live in a
perilous world.   All the more reason, then, for the Messrs.
Burdick, Wheeler and Crichton to appeal to our reason and
intelligence as well as to play upon our fears of Armageddon.
Pretentiousness is admittedly a rather vague word
that covers a multitude of sins   Mary McCarthy's The Group

is probably one of the most pretentious novels of the decade
because of the wide gap between what the author set out to
do (sum up an entire generation between the covers of a
book) and what she actually accomplished (eight characters
in search of a theme).   John Updike is pretentious in a different way.   Updike has been called the most brilliant prose
stylist of his generation so often that it may be affecting his
work.   In The Centaur, the first novel reviewed in these
pages and one that I liked very much, I noted a tendency
toward over-elaboration in the prose that inevitably runs
counter to the simple and effective story line (a boy perched
on the top of a stack of folding chairs in the school gymnasium is "riding on this rickety raft the ocean of tumult").
I hesitated to use the term pretentious.   Reviewing Of the
Farm several years later, I no longer hesitated, but commented that this was pretentious writing at its worst.   Of
the Farm can scarcely be considered a novel at all (a novel
says something), but rather a self-conscious vehicle for
Updike to exploit those stylistic gifts with which he is so
richly blessed.

        Prose style is not the be-all and end-all of fictional
prose anyway, although a writer of genius such as Nabokov
can almost make it seem that way.   In another perceptive
essay from Literature and the Sixth Sense, entitled "Fiction
and the Criticism of Fiction," Philip Rahv points out that
style is but one facet of a novelist's fictive world, and
indeed that two of the greatest novelists who ever lived,
Tolstoy and Dreiser, are indifferent prose stylists.   Obviously their greatness must reside elsewhere.   The late
author of The Sand Pebbles, Richard McKenna, who is
definitely not one of the greatest novelists who ever lived
and who writes a competent but not inspired prose, is a good

example of how a small talent can be nurtured and developed through hard work and dedication to the writer's craft. As I mentioned in my review of The Sons of Martha and Other Stories, the outstanding characteristic of McKenna's small body of work is its absolute authenticity. He wrote about what he knew best, and what he knew best was the United States Navy in the Far East and, in particular, the engine rooms and refrigerator plants of numerous naval vessels. This authenticity cannot be faked, although representatives of what I call the "Fab Soap School of Realism" try very hard, by dwelling on the trivial detail (a particular brand name, for example), to cover up a fundamental lack of authenticity. Surely the example of Richard McKenna should be an inspiration to all aspiring writers of modest talent.

4

In my review of a first novel by Joanna Crawford called Birch Interval, I wrote as follows:

> Creativity is truly a mysterious phenomenon. There is no telling where it will strike nor whom it will suddenly fail. Saul Bellow can pour everything he knows into a long, complex, stylistic, philosophical novel--I am thinking of Herzog--and still leave one feeling vaguely disappointed at the result. How much is art and how much is sheer literary bombast and pretentiousness? On the other hand, an unknown writer will suddenly come along and write an unpretentious first novel of barely 180 pages on the age-old theme of a young girl awakening to the joy and terror of life in an adult world, and her artistry literally leaps from the printed page.

Perhaps I was being overly harsh on Herzog--it is a novel I must read again--and yet it is not the only "major" novel that disappointed me in the sixties, nor is Birch Interval the only novel by a relatively unknown writer to

strike me with such freshness and power. Joanna Crawford's book is an example of one of the great joys of reviewing (or simply reading books, for that matter): to be able
to make such discoveries and to share them with others.
As far as Herzog is concerned, it seems ironic to me that,
of all Bellow's novels, this particular one should have had
the greatest impact on the reading public. Mary McCarthy's
The Group, a far lesser achievement than Herzog, is
another example of a disappointing "major" novel by a gifted
writer that immediately catapulted to the top of the best-
seller list. The Group was not only disappointing; for a
writer whom Time called "quite possibly the cleverest writer
the U. S. has ever produced," it was downright dull. One
searches in vain for the author's celebrated wit. The pages
follow one another in dreary, solemn succession, and not
until page 351 is there a real laugh in the book.

     John Cheever is another popular novelist whose suc-
cess with the critics is something I will never be able to
understand. Quite frankly, The Wapshot Scandal, a sequel
to The Wapshot Chronicle (1957), is a scandal. Maudlin
and inane, it is all put down in such a tired, finicky style
("It was a harsh and an ugly light. . .") that it almost lulls
one to sleep. Having recently read Cheever's Bullet Park,
which has received extravagant praise in some quarters and
which also rose high on the best-seller list, I am more
mystified than ever about the popular and critical success of
a talented short story writer who reached his zenith some
years ago writing slight, sardonic stories for the New
Yorker. In fairness to Cheever, it is certainly possible that
the critics who praise him are right and that his work represents a blind spot in my own critical arsenal. To be a
critic, it is not necessary to claim greater infallibility than

the Pope. I did not like Joseph Heller's Catch-22 either,
and yet look at the history it has made less than ten years
after its publication. Not only has it become a symbol for
a whole war-sick generation, but the Vietnam War has since
managed to confirm much of what the author had to say and,
in retrospect, made Catch-22 a prophecy of things to come.
In view of all this, I must certainly reread the book, but I
am not yet convinced that I will like it any better than
before.

It is more pleasurable to write about authors that
one especially admires than to write about those in whom one
has been disappointed. Without any question, Elie Wiesel is
my "author of the decade." Certainly he is one of the few
contemporary novelists of undoubted genius. Reviewing
The Accident in Library Journal in 1962, I wrote:

> The author of this short, bitter novel is of
> course the author of the widely acclaimed Night.
> In that work (which unhappily was not fiction),
> Mr. Wiesel told the horrifying story of his and
> his family's personal tragedy in the concentration
> camps of Nazi Germany and his reluctant loss of
> faith. Everything he has since written has ap-
> parently been an attempt to come to terms with
> this searing and catastrophic experience.

Four years later, I reviewed Elie Wiesel's fourth
novel, The Gates of the Forest, in the Smithtown Messenger.
It is one of the most moving and eloquent novels I have
ever read. "Elie Wiesel carries a terrible weight on his
shoulders," I wrote, "a weight such as few men have lived
to bear. This terrible weight, this knowledge, gives to his
utterance a passionate intensity almost unique in modern
literature." I pointed out that, in trying to alleviate this
terrible burden, Elie Wiesel goes right to the point and
asks the fundamental question of God and man. "And
Auschwitz?" the main protagonist, Gregor, asks the Rebbe

in America. "What do you make of Auschwitz?" "Auschwitz proves that nothing has changed," the Rebbe replies,
"that the primeval war goes on. Man is capable of love
and hate, murder and sacrifice. He is Abraham and Isaac
together. God himself hasn't changed." Gregor is angry.
"After what happened to us," he shouts, "how can you believe in God?" With an understanding smile on his face,
the Rebbe answers, "How can you not believe in God after
what has happened?"

5

Librarians are told so often by disgruntled older
readers of Faith Baldwin and Taylor Caldwell that the novel
is not what it used to be that, if they were not such an indomitable breed, there is considerable danger that they
would begin to believe it themselves. Even bright young
critics go on record as saying that the novel is a dying
form. In these circles, the novel has been dying for a
long time, but to my knowledge no one has ever discovered
the corpse. I do not believe for a moment that the novel
is dying or is likely to die. On the contrary, the evidence
of the 1960's indicates to me that the novel is thriving as
never before.

The traditional novel with its emphasis on plot and
character development is still being practised successfully
by such novelists as John Braine (The Jealous God), Vance
Bourjaily (The Man Who Knew Kennedy), Graham Greene
(The Comedians), Richard Jones (The Three Suitors), and
L. Woiwode (What I'm Going to Do, I Think), to name just
a few. Even the naturalistic novel, made famous by Frank
Norris around the turn of the century (McTeague), still
shows considerable vitality, as witness the success of two

recent novels, Don Carpenter's Blade of Light and Leonard
Gardner's Fat City.

In a more experimental vein, the novels of John
Hawkes (Second Skin), James Purdy (Cabot Wright Begins),
James Merrill (The (Diblos) Notebook), Abram Tertz (The
Trial Begins and The Makepeace Experiment), Anais Nin
(Collages), and Uwe Johnson (Two Views), are all powerful
reminders that the novel is far from dead. The "New
Realism," a French import, is represented by Claude Simon
(The Palace), a novelist who combines the "New Realism"
technique with his own intensely passionate lyrical quality.
The satirical novel is well represented by Günter Grass (The
Tin Drum and Cat and Mouse), Elliott Baker (A Fine Madness), and Kurt Vonnegut, Jr. (Slaughterhouse-Five), all
writers of authentic genius of whom one can confidently say
that if the novel form did not exist they would have to invent
it. And if anyone truly believes that the novel is dead, he
should consider the furor Abram Tertz' The Trial Begins
occasioned inside and outside the Soviet Union when it was
smuggled out of Russia almost a decade ago. Reverbera-
tions from that historic book are still being felt today. Can
anyone seriously doubt that the pen is mightier than the
sword?

What follows now is a list of first novels published
during the 1960's and reviewed in these pages. This
impressive catalogue does anything but document the death
of the novel: Captain Cat by Robert Holles, Night by Francis
Pollini, Saturday to Monday by Ruth Rehmann, Revolutionary
Road by Richard Yates, The Benefactor by Susan Sontag,
The Messenger by Charles Wright, One Hundred Dollar Misunderstanding by Robert Gover, The Collector by John
Fowles, The Tin Drum by Günter Grass, A Fine Madness by

Elliott Baker, Birch Interval by Joanna Crawford, The Last
Gentleman by Walker Percy, Norwood by Charles Portis,
Crazy February by Carter Wilson, Landscape in Concrete by
Jakov Lind, Moss on the North Side by Sylvia Wilkinson,
Blade of Light by Don Carpenter, What I'm Going to Do, I
Think by L. Woiwode, Cowboys Don't Cry by L. J. Davis,
and Fat City by Leonard Gardner.

"The novel is at the present time universally recognized as one of the greater historic forms of literary art,"
writes Philip Rahv in "Fiction and the Criticism of Fiction."

> Its resources and capacities appear to be commen-
> surate with the realities and consciousness of the
> modern epoch, and its practitioners, having in-
> herited a good many of the functions once exer-
> cised by poetry and the drama, no longer feel
> the slightest need to engage in the kind of
> apologetics that were quite common even as late
> as a hundred years ago, when in respectable
> quarters novel writing and novel reading were
> still looked upon as activities falling below the
> level of true cultural aspiration.

Surely these words will remain just as true for the
decade of the seventies as they were for the decade just
past.

6

The best (or at least the most practical and concise)
advice I know of on the subject of how to write a book review was given by the distinguished late scholar-critic,
F. O. Matthiessen, in an article entitled "The Winter
Critic" which appeared in the October 1952 issue of the
Atlantic. "Challenged by the ghost of Poe," Matthiessen
wrote, "I would submit that what he called 'a critical
notice' should at the minimum do three things. It should
furnish exposition and description; it should enable you to

feel concretely what is described; and it should give you in the process an evaluation. " Matthiessen then continued as follows:

> The first of these three functions cannot be satis-
> factorily discharged by, say, making a digest of
> the plot of a novel or the chapter headings of a
> book of history.   That will use up all your space
> and leave you with the compendium without judg-
> ment against which Poe so rightly objected.   In-
> stead you must interweave your three functions.
> If the book at hand is a piece of literature, you
> can best suggest its quality by concentrating your
> exposition upon a few significant episodes, and by
> letting your reader feel for himself that quality,
> not through some illustrative quotations tacked on
> mechanically at the end, but through the force of
> a few deftly foreshortened examples woven into
> your exposition.   And if that weaving has been
> really skillful, you won't be faced with the neces-
> sity of a heavy-handed summary for your
> evaluation.   You will have painted it out lightly,
> by analytical insights, as you went along.

I know there are librarians who actually believe that fiction cannot be evaluated at all, presumably because of its subjective nature.   In their opinion it is presumptuous for librarians to decide for their patrons which novels they should or should not have available for them to read.   To reject The Carpetbaggers, say, on the basis of literary standards is, in their view, to indulge in a subtle but un-mistakable form of censorship.   In a letter published in the February 1, 1970, issue of Library Journal, one of these librarians stated that "the same criteria which are used for nonfiction cannot be applied to the purchase or consideration of fiction.   The differences in the definition of terms should make the distinction quite apparent. " Now I certainly do not say that the same criteria necessarily apply to fiction and nonfiction alike, but this does not mean (as this librarian implies) that no criteria apply to fiction.   I think

librarians are on solid ground in rejecting <u>The Carpetbaggers</u>,
no matter how great the demand for it is.   Although I cannot prove it, I strongly suspect that F. O. Matthiessen would
agree.

    By way of supplementing Matthiessen's remarks on
the "critical notice," from my own experience as a book
reviewer, I would like to emphasize that it is not enough to
say why a novel is good or bad; the reviewer should back up
his critical points by offering <u>specific examples</u> from the
work itself.   This will provide the reader with something
more than the reviewer's word to go on and make it possible
for him to evaluate the critic who is evaluating the novel.   I
know that it is quite possible to praise a novel or castigate
it simply by quoting from the book itself.   The review of
<u>Images</u> by Paul Young in this book is a case in point.   Let
the book speak for itself and this will accomplish more than
all the vague critical pronouncements put together.   Of
course, one must be alert to the opportunities at hand (read
everything, skip nothing), must select carefully from among
all the thousands of sentences, and must know how to exploit these opportunities to maximum advantage.   Obviously
a good critic possesses a "killer instinct" which is really
the obverse of his special love and enthusiasm for what is
truly good in literature.   An inept performance literally
fills him with rage at the performer for sullying that ideal
image he holds in his mind's eye of (no matter how obscene)
the true and the beautiful.

                                7

    A reviewer subjects himself to criticism every time
he evaluates or criticizes a book.   Only once has an author

taken exception to a review of mine in writing. This was in
regard to a novel by Al Hine called Lord Love a Duck. I
had said that for sheer vulgarity it would be hard to surpass
this book. Mr. Hine raised a very pertinent question. Without disputing my right to my own opinion, he wondered if I
knew the difference between a novel of sheer vulgarity and a
novel about sheer vulgarity. He said that he was trying to
write the latter, but conceded that apparently he had failed.
Otherwise I would see in it more than a vulgar novel.

As I have said, a reviewer must be ever alert to
the opportunities at hand. In an article in Esquire magazine, Hiram Haydn explained why he had gone into partner-
ship with Simon Michael Bessie and Alfred Knopf, Jr. to
form the new publishing firm of Atheneum. "I like to make
my own mistakes," Mr. Haydn wrote. I seized upon this
(that old killer instinct no doubt) in my review of Lord Love
a Duck, one of the first books published by the brave new
firm of Atheneum Publishers. "In a recent article in
Esquire magazine," I wrote, "Mr. Hiram Haydn of Atheneum is quoted as saying, 'I like to make my own mistakes.'
This is one of them." Now Hiram Haydn is a scholar and
a gentleman and he responded wryly and good-naturedly to my
review, even though the joke was more or less on him. He
astutely commented on the similarity of the names Hine and
Pine and noted that they rhymed. Al Hine is also a gentleman. His letter was polite and reasonable. It is difficult
to distinguish a vulgar novel from a novel about vulgarity.
It is one of the most difficult areas in criticism. Perhaps
I made a mistake in calling Lord Love a Duck a vulgar
novel. As I suggested before, critics are not more in-
fallible than the Pope. Let us retain a measure of
humility. Al Hine is such a nice man that, ten years later,

I would like to give him the benefit of the doubt. Incidentally, Lord Love a Duck was later made into a movie, and the critics were unanimously of the opinion that it was a vulgar film. I do not think Mr. Hine had anything to do with it, however.

The nicest thing that can happen to a book reviewer is to receive a letter of thanks from an author whose book he admired very much. This happened to me once. In a review of Josep Maria Espinas' By Nature Equal (translated from the Catalan by Anthony Bonner), I wrote:

> This novel could have been merely sentimental, but it is not. The author writes with a sure sense of the complicated nature of the human condition, of the subtle differences that separate men as well as the similarities that bind them together. His use of symbolism (the working man's café is on the harsh level of the street, the rich man's three steps down "below the level of life") is excellent. Furthermore, he has humor and deep poetic insight. In short, By Nature Equal is that rare book (but not so rare as we might think?) that touches something deep in all of us.

Some weeks later I received the following letter from Barcelona:

> Dear Sir, I have seen your critic about my book, By nature equal / Pantheon /. Excuse me my english, it is rather poor, but I want to show you my gratitude for your commentary. Like you can understand, it is very important to me. Your pleasing words are for me a far and cordial fellowship. Many thanks, that is all. Yours sincerely, J. M. Espinas. "

I fervently hope this brave man, this artist, is alive and well somewhere in the world today. We need him very much.

PART ONE

REVIEWS AND COUNTERVIEWS

All reviews in Part I originally appeared in the Smithtown <u>Messenger</u> and are reprinted here with grateful acknowledgment to the publishers of that newspaper.

THE CENTAUR

By John Updike (Knopf, 1963).

Born in 1932, John Updike is considered by many to be the most brilliant writer of his generation. The Centaur, his third novel, will certainly not detract from this reputation. In what is perhaps his most ambitious work to date, he retells the myth of Chiron, the noblest centaur of them all, who consents to die so that Prometheus might live. The myth, in Mr. Updike's novel, is set in a small Pennsylvania town in 1947. Chiron becomes George W. Caldwell, a fifty-year-old high school general science teacher, and Prometheus his fifteen-year-old son Peter.

The narrative covers three days during which Caldwell and his son become marooned in a blizzard and undergo a number of unexceptional adventures before returning home safely to the family farmhouse. Harassed by the minor trials and tribulations of his teaching position and suffering from nervous indigestion, George Caldwell still manages to persevere and to give his talented son, as well as all those dependent on his labor, the gift of life. "He thought of his wife's joy in the land," Updike writes, "and Pop Kramer's joy in the newspaper and his son's joy in the future and was glad, grateful, that he was able to sustain these for yet a space more."

In telling this story of a modern Chiron, the author of Rabbit, Run and The Poorhouse Fair has never written with greater compassion or love. George Caldwell is that extraordinary ordinary man whose life is made up of good deeds. Is it merely a coincidence that his name resembles that of the adolescent hero of J. D. Salinger's The Catcher in the Rye? Superficially the two novels would seem to have much in common, but Salinger's Holden Caulfield inhabits a world in which the accent is definitely on the "phony," a world of pimps and perverts, dear Phoebe notwithstanding. John Updike's world is different. The evil still exists in the person of a Deifendorf or Minor Kretz, but it does not seem quite so appalling as long as a George Caldwell is around to counteract it in his humble, unpedagogic way.

Not only is there love of humanity in this novel but love of a particular place as well. Southeastern Pennsylvania

is John Updike's Yoknapatawpha County, and the small ugly
cities of the East, the "great Middle Atlantic civilization,
bounded by New Haven in the north and Hagerstown in the
south and Wheeling in the west," is his special preserve. It
is a peculiarly American world of gas stations, Y. M. C. A. 's
and high school athletic banquets.

A word must be said about the style. John Updike
is unquestionably a brilliant stylist, a writer who can simultaneously remind one of James Joyce and Dylan Thomas, but
there is a nagging suspicion of excess, a tendency toward
over-elaboration in the prose that inevitably runs counter to
the simple and effective story line. A boy perched on top
of a stack of folding chairs in the school gym is "riding on
this rickety raft the ocean of tumult. "

One hesitates to use the word pretentious. And in
one who, describing a snowstorm, can write a passage such
as the following, even this must be forgiven: "A yellowness
broods low in the sky; above Alton in the west a ruby glow
seeps upward. From the zenith a lavender luminosity hangs
pulseless, as if the particular brilliance of the moon and
stars had been dissolved and the solution shot through with
a low-electric voltage. The effect of tenuous weight, of
menace, is exhilarating. "

The effect is exhilarating indeed. Who knows? Perhaps John Updike is the most brilliant writer of his
generation.

THE BIRTHDAY KING

By Gabriel Fielding (Morrow, 1963).

The English novelist Gabriel Fielding is well known
in this country for such fine novels as Through Streets
Broad and Narrow and In the Time of Greenbloom. Now, in
The Birthday King, in what has been called "an astonishing
feat of empathy for an English novelist," he has attempted
to recreate the Nazi regime in Germany from 1939 to 1945
through the fortunes of an aristocratic family of part-Jewish
steel magnates.

The Weidmann Group flourished long before Hitler
and expected to continue flourishing long after he was gone.
To most of them it was a question of simple survival. Political innocents, they first ignored Hitler and then used him
to further their own interests. Only young Alfried, heir to
the Weidmann fortune, seems to realize what is at stake in
collaborating with the Nazis. And not surprisingly, it is
Alfried who alone survives to carry on the family business.

This novel received excellent reviews when it was
published in England last year. Although recognizing Gabriel
Fielding's superb gifts as a novelist, this writer must
reluctantly confess to some disappointment. "Sometimes we
can believe we are reading an exceptionally good translation
of an exceptionally gifted liberal German author," one reviewer observed. Perhaps this is the trouble. The novel
seems somewhat bloodless and academic, as if the author
had set out to prove he could successfully recreate the dying
Third Reich without actually having been there. Until the
final superb chapters depicting the suicide pact between
Kommandant Grunwald and his wife and Alfried's release
from a concentration camp, the novel lacks that passion and
personal involvement that we associate with the greatest
works. In this respect, Heinrich Böll's recent Billiards at
Half-Past Nine, also about modern Germany, is a greater
achievement. But then Böll was not trying to prove a point.
He was there.

COAT UPON A STICK

By Norman Fruchter (Simon and Schuster, 1963).

"An aged man is but a paltry thing," wrote the Irish
poet W. B. Yeats, "a tattered coat upon a stick." In this
highly acclaimed first novel by Norman Fruchter (it was
published last year in England where its American-born
author lived for three years) the old man is an impoverished
New York Jew living in a furnished room on the lower East
Side. A humble shamos at the local synagogue, he clings
to his Jewish faith even while being tormented by feelings
of guilt towards those whom he has wronged in the past.

As in so many novels by Jewish writers (Bernard
Malamud's The Assistant springs immediately to mind),
guilt and how to atone for it is the principal theme of Coat
Upon a Stick. In this respect it is that rare thing, a truly
religious novel. The old man is not alone in his guilt.
His son Carl also feels guilty about the strained relationship
with his father. Now married and with a son of his own, he
has fled the lower East Side and escaped to the suburbs.
"Why have you forsaken me?" the old man complains bitterly
throughout this unusual novel.

And indeed this is a bitter novel, relieved by only
occasional flashes of mordant humor. It is bitter the way
Zola is bitter or Frank Norris in that classic of American
naturalism, McTeague, "Every day another headline somebody's done something mean and rotten to somebody else,"
muses the sweeper employed by the New York Transit
Authority, leaning on his pushbroom. The world that Mr.
Fruchter writes about is one in which people steal from
the halt, lame and blind. This brooding pessimism, misery
piled upon misery, threatens, and perhaps more than
threatens, to smother what little story there is.

And yet there is Zitomer, the eccentric idealist,
thrown out of the synagogue for preaching the uncomfortable
doctrine that life should be lived according to the Ten Commandments. The climax of the novel comes when Zitomer
tries to imbue the embittered old man with the fruits of
his own hard-won philosophy. "So what can I tell you?"
he exclaims. "You got to have faith, that's all I know.

Listen, there are millions and millions of us, we can't all be bad people. We got to help each other, and we got to have faith." It isn't a great deal but on this relatively optimistic note this somber and pessimistic novel comes to an end.

AFTER THE BANQUET

By Yukio Mishima (Knopf, 1963).

Translated from the Japanese by Donald Keene,
After the Banquet tells what happens when two utterly in-
compatible and unyielding personalities clash headlong in
marriage.   Although the novel is Japanese in style and
feeling, the theme is so universal that it will be enjoyed
by discriminating readers everywhere.

At the age of fifty Kazu Fukuzawa, the proprietress
of the luxurious Setsugoan Restaurant, is still beautiful and
blazing with vitality.   She has been in love many times
in the past, but is convinced that she will never fall in
love again.   As the novel begins, Kazu is peacefully smok-
ing a cigarette and contemplating her beautiful garden.   "As
she smoked her cigarette," we are told, "Kazu felt as if
the garden's exquisite perfection had completely enveloped
all her memories."

Despite Kazu's good intentions, she does fall in love
again.   The Kagen Club, an association of former ambassadors, decides to hold its annual meeting at the Setsugoan.
Kazu presides over the affair as hostess and is immediately
struck by the distinguished presence of Yuken Noguchi, a
former cabinet minister and now leading adviser to the
Radical Party.   The aristocratic elder statesman, who is
ten years older than Kazu, is an idealist, a man of unbend-
ing principle.   Kazu, on the other hand, sensual and flam-
boyant, lives for the moment according to the dictates of
her emotions.   Although obviously mismatched, the two
are drawn to each other.   A woman of humble origins,
Kazu earnestly desires the security and prestige marriage
to Noguchi will being.   More than anything else, she
desires a place in the Noguchi family grave.

The ensuing marriage is shortlived, of course, and
it is the breakup of this unlikely union that the author,
Yukio Mishima, delineates with all the conciseness and
inevitability of a Greek tragedy.   The trouble begins when
Noguchi is chosen to be his party's candidate in the guber-
natorial election.   Kazu throws herself energetically into
the campaign without bothering to observe all the proprieties.

She considers the election her "Heaven-appointed task"
and even mortgages the Setsugoan to raise money to carry
on the illicit campaign.   Noguchi, who is a model of decorum and the very incarnation of the old moral virtues,
is furious when he learns of his wife's activities.   It is
only a matter of time before the debacle is complete.

If Noguchi does not emerge as a very sympathetic
character, Kazu certainly does.   She is impulsive and
uneducated, but there is real blood flowing through her veins.
Undoubtedly she is a character in the tradition of Madame
Bovary and Molly Bloom.   The full genius of Yukio Mishima
is realized in the creation of this extraordinary woman.

LORD OF THE FLIES

By William Golding (Capricorn Books, 1963).

According to a recent survey in the New York Times, the number one best seller among the paperbacks is William Golding's Lord of the Flies. What is this amazing novel that has become a publishing phenomenon since it first appeared in England in 1954? What is the spell of this modern fable that outrivals even J. D. Salinger's The Catcher in the Rye in popularity among college students?

"The greatest ideas are the simplest," the author says, and perhaps he will not mind if we borrow his words and apply them to his own masterpiece. He has taken the classic theme of boys cast adrift on an uninhabited island -- a theme with all the beautiful simplicity of Robinson Crusoe and Treasure Island -- and turned it into a parable of man's dilemma on earth, the loss of innocence that comes with the revelation of evil at the center of things.

It is never made clear in the book (and it is the author's intention not to do so) the circumstances surrounding the boys' captivity on the island. All we know is that they have been mysteriously dropped from an airplane which could not land. The time is the vague indefinite future and the earth is being wracked by atomic war. The boys are fairly divided between "biguns" and "littluns" (ranging in age from six to twelve) and there is not a single adult to tell them what to do.

The question the author is posing, of course, is whether children are really the innocents we (and Mr. Salinger) like to believe, trailing Wordsworth's "clouds of glory" in their wake, or whether the evil in the universe is inherent in them as well as in their elders. In short, what will they make of their idyllic tropic island, a paradise or merely another wasteland?

The answer is not long in coming and it is worked out in wonderfully appropriate symbolic terms. The boys are divided into two hostile groups. The group let by Ralph desperately tries to impose law and order as represented by the conch and a pair of spectacles belonging to

"Piggy," the intellectual of the group who suffers from
asthma. The group led by Jack the hunter believes in the
law of the jungle and their symbol is the Lord of the Flies,
an old sow's head hung on a stick. The dramatic climax
of the book occurs when the sensitive and introspective
Simon confronts the Lord of the Flies and perceives in the
pig's half-shut eyes "the infinite cynicism of adult life."
The shattering of "Piggy's" spectacles and all the horrow
that follows is as inevitable as the black blob of flies
buzzing around the pig on his stick.

WHO SHALL LIVE, WHO SHALL DIE

By Daniel Stern (Crown, 1963).

What happened in the Nazi extermination camps a
mere two decades ago is something most of us would like
to forget.   Even though we may not feel personally responsible, we are children of the twentieth century and must
share a certain complicity in the horror.   In Who Shall
Live, Who Shall Die, Daniel Stern raises "the silence curtain" to reveal "the twentieth century in action: absolute
negation of existence, the era of the uncity, the unperson,
of possibilities of subtraction down to zero."   In this bitter
and disturbing novel he will not allow us the luxury of for-
getting.

Jud Kramer, a survivor of the camps, is a successful Broadway director.   Happily married to a talented
Hollywood actress and the father of a little girl, he would
seem to have all that anyone could possibly desire.   Moreover he is engaged in the most exciting project on Broadway, a Theater Workshop production of At the Gates, under
the membership of his old teacher and father confessor,
Paul Rovic.

Ironically, At the Gates is a European play about the
concentration camps written by the late Maurice Bolet, a
survivor of Auschwitz and Dachau.   Although Jud Kramer
has lowered "the silence curtain" over his past, he is
irresistibly drawn to direct the play.   And into his life and
literally onto the set comes Carl Walkowitz, like Lazarus
back from the dead.   Walkowitz knows more about Jud
Kramer than Jud will even admit to himself.   And unlike the
successful younger man, he comes "wearing his wounds like
decorations, wearing his humiliated past like honor."

In what Jud comes to think of as "the Walkowitz
winter," Carl Walkowitz comes bearing a bitter grief and
is obsessed with it.   "My good friend Kramer," he says,
"I have subtractions prepared for you.   Let us see how
you'll survive them."   "What do you want from me?"   Jud
answers.   "What do you want?"

This is a deeply philosophical novel because it deals with the problems of guilt and responsibility in a world in which "everything is possible." Although some of the minor characters and incidents seem somewhat contrived (the plot is perhaps unnecessarily complicated and has elements of implausibility -- did Jud's wife have to be a movie star?), there is nothing contrived or implausible about Carl Walkowitz with his burden of grief. The final confrontation between the two protagonists is both dramatic and true. Obviously Daniel Stern feels deeply about what happened in the concentration camps and he has the power and skill to make us feel it, too.

THE TIN DRUM

By Günter Grass (Pantheon, 1963).

Brilliantly translated from the German by Ralph Manheim, The Tin Drum is the sensational novel by Günter
Grass describing the adventures of Oskar Matzerath, the
hunchbacked anarchist, who, with the aid of a red and white
lacquered drum and his twin masters Goethe and Rasputin,
attempts to "harmonize chaos and intoxicate reason."

Oskar is only three feet tall, for he stopped growing
at the age of three rather than grow to normal adulthood
and have to take over his father's grocery store.   His
mother has made him a present of a tin drum, the kind you
can buy in the dime store.   When the grownups try to take
away his drum, Oskar develops a glass-shattering voice
which can demolish everything from a forty-watt electric
light bulb to a plate glass window.

And so the "eternal three-year-old drummer" observes the doings of the adult world from the time of his
birth in 1925 until his thirtieth year when he is confined
to a mental hospital, convicted of a murder he did not commit.   His angry drumming is a cry of protest at the atrocities of the grownup world which make murderers of us
all, guilty and innocent alike.   The Tin Drum, as ludicrous
as it is (Günter Grass has affinities with Rabelais, James
Joyce and our own exemplar of the absurd, Edward Albee),
is a most appropriate book for the century of Dachau and
Auschwitz.   Only Oskar's grandmother, Anna Bronski, who
sits in the Kashubian potato fields in the October rain, her
four skirts billowing protectively around her, represents
peace and security in a world gone berserk.

At the close of this unique autobiography Oskar recapitulates his history: "What more shall I say: born under
light bulbs, deliberately stopped growing at age of three,
given drum, sang glass to pieces, smelled vanilla, cough-
ed in churches, observed ants, decided to grow, buried
drum, emigrated to the West, lost the East, learned stone-
cutter's trade, worked as model, started drumming again,
visited concrete, made money, kept finger, gave finger
away, fled laughing, rode up escalator, arrested, convicted,

sent to mental hospital, soon to be acquitted, celebrating
this day my thirtieth birthday and still afraid of the Black
Witch."

At one point Oskar admits that his famous glass-
shattering voice is "probably beginning to bore the lovers
of novelty among you." The Tin Drum is almost six hundred
pages long and this reviewer has to admit that he occasionally wearied of Oskar's antics. But let us not confuse
Günter Grass with Herman Wouk. Rabelais and James Joyce
are sometimes boring too, but we still know a genius when
we see one. And if anyone doubts that Günter Grass is a
genius let him read the chapter entitled "Faith, Hope, Love"
(pp. 196-206) and judge for himself.

INSIDE DAISY CLOVER

By Gavin Lambert (Viking Press, 1963).

That glorious nymphet Lolita, fertile girl-child that
she was, has given birth to an amazing progeny in the few
years since she cavorted through the pages of Vladimir
Nabokov's famous book.   Two recent additions to this precocious progeny are Kitten, the fourteen-year-old colored
prostitute of Robert Gover's One Hundred Dollar Misunderstanding and Daisy Clover, the female Elvis Presley, who
parlays a talent contest into Hollywood stardom.

Gavin Lambert's first book, a collection of short
stories entitled The Slide Area, earned the plaudits of such
distinguished writers as Christopher Isherwood and Kingsley
Amis, but Inside Daisy Clover is a distinct disappointment.
Mr. Lambert is a talented writer (he has an extraordinary
feeling for locale and brings the Hollywood scene vividly to
life), but Daisy Clover completely eludes him.   The title
notwithstanding, we remain securely encased inside Gavin
Lambert.

Who is Daisy Clover?   She is this "fantastically talented kid" who drinks vodka out of Dixie Cups and whose
favorite adjective is FANTABULOUS.   While living with her
mother (known as The Dealer because she is always playing
solitaire) in a ramshackle trailer camp overlooking the
Pacific Ocean, Daisy enters a talent contest sponsored by
the Bay Area Markets in association with Magnagram Studios.
She is only fourteen, but quickly rises to stardom in the
Zombiland that is Hollywood.

Actually Daisy is in Hollywood but not of it, and she
soon finds herself at odds with Raymond Swan of Magnagram
Studios.   When she marries Wade Lewis, a misfit actor,
Daisy Clover has had it.   The marriage is never consum-
mated (Wade turns out to be a homosexual) and Daisy goes
through a very difficult period that culminates in divorce
and a nervous breakdown.   "Goodbye, you few millions of
the millions I made laugh and cry and identify with me,"
says Daisy to herself.   "I'm going out of your lives and
it won't make the slightest difference to you!   You'll wake
up in the morning as if I'd never happened."

Talent and spirit will out, however, and at the ripe
old age of twenty-four Daisy Clover moves to New York
(a much healthier moral climate) and makes a comeback.
The "new Daisy Clover" opens the season at Atlantic City
and is a big hit.   All her old friends come backstage to con-
gratulate her and the only person missing is Ralph Edwards
with a script that reads, "This Is Your Life, Daisy Clover."

In conclusion, this reviewer recommends <u>One Hundred
Dollar Misunderstanding,</u> a most original and touching first
novel by a thirty-three year-old son of a Kentucky hillbilly,
which has been acclaimed on both sides of the Atlantic for
its sincerity and power of expression.

WHAT'S BECOME OF WARING

By Anthony Powell (Little, Brown, 1963).

The English novelist Anthony Powell has become well
known in this country for his brilliant dissection of English
upper-class society in "The Music of Time" series.   Now
his American publisher has brought out <u>What's Become of
Waring,</u> one of Powell's early novels never before published here.

Although not part of his ambitious "The Music of
Time" series, <u>What's Becomes of Waring</u> clearly anticipates
this remarkable project.   Here is the same spoiled Englishman in his prewar habitat.   Here is the same devastating
eye and ear for the comic and absurd.   Here is the saving
compassion that refuses to cast a cold eye on human ec-
centricity.

The narrator of <u>What's Become of Waring</u> is a reader
for the publishing firm of Judkins & Judkins.   The firm's
best-selling author is the noted writer of travel books, T.
T. Waring.   T. T. Waring is a mysterious character whom
no one has actually seen.   He reports from such exotic
places as Ceylon and Cambodia.   We do not have to read
very far before realizing that the legendary Waring never
did exist and that the person who assumes this name has
perpetuated an elaborate hoax.

But although Waring turns out to be a fraud, the
other characters are all too real.   There are the Judkin
brothers, Hugh and Bernard, who are thrown into a frenzy
at the news of Waring's reported death.   There is the reserved Captain Hudson with the bristling mustache and buck
teeth, who undertakes to write a biography of the late
author.   And there are the various friends and relatives
who form a composite picture of pre-war English society,
a picture which is not exactly flattering but which possesses
a certain eccentric charm.   And if London seems no larger
than a small village (there are some wonderful coincidences
in this book), it is no doubt all part of the author's intention
for London society was highly stratified and family con-
nections all-important.

The narrator of the novel (I am not sure we are ever told his name) is working on a book called "Stendhal: and Some Thoughts on Violence" in his spare time. Although he never quite completes it, what Mr. Powell seems to be saying is that one need not go to Cambodia or the pages of Stendhal to discover the exotic, the ridiculous and the sublime. Many of us have discovered this, too.

It is amazing how much this early novel resembles a recent novel by another Powell, our own Dawn Powell. Dawn Powell's The Golden Spur, a contender for last year's National Book Award, stands in approximately the same relation to her best work as What's Become of Waring does to "The Music of Time" series.

ONE HUNDRED DOLLAR MISUNDERSTANDING

By Robert Gover (Grove Press, 1963).

Recently this reviewer briefly mentioned Robert Gover's One Hundred Dollar Misunderstanding, a most original and touching first novel by a thirty-three year-old son of a Kentucky hillbilly that has been acclaimed on both sides of the Atlantic for its sincerity and power of expression. The novel has also achieved a considerable amount of notoriety since its publication and Henry Miller's enthusiastic endorsement ("What a find! I've been recommending it to everyone") has not had a deleterious effect in this regard. Henry Miller aside, the spectacle of fully-grown and supposedly intelligent people shrinking in disgust from this innocuous little fable gives one pause to thing. How much do people get from the books they read anyway? Do they read, as we like to believe, to broaden themselves, to learn the other person's point of view, or do they merely read to confirm their own prejudices and beliefs?

The protagonists of One Hundred Dollar Misunderstanding are a fourteen-year-old colored prostitute named Kitten, and a pompous college sophomore who cautiously assumes the name of James Cartwright Holland. At semester's end, failing three subjects and inadvertently caught without car or date for the big frat formal, JC seeks solace by fleeing with one hundred dollars (a belated birthday present from his aunt) to what, with characteristic bombast, he calls "a house of ill repute."

It is here that the "one hundred dollar misunderstanding" begins. Kitten sees in this fay College Joe a profitable long-term investment ("This baby lo-o-o-o-did! Ooh-wee!") or, at the very least, the one hundred dollars. For his part, JC naïvely believes that Kitten, whom he constantly underestimates, is impressed by his manhood and loves him for himself alone. In alternating chapters Kitten and JC tell the story in their own words, each from his own vantage point. There is of course no real communication between them and their relationship is destined to end in failure.

Kitten is undoubtedly the literary discovery of the

year.   As warm and human as JC is calculating and cold,
she wholeheartedly endeavors to reeducate her "drum in-
vessment." "I try agen.   I try teechin him.   Talkin t'him
jes like he was a lil chile.   Yeah!   I gotta Un-learn him,
an then I gotta Re-learn him."   Alas, it is too big a job,
even for Kitten.

Although many readers will not bother to read between the lines, <u>One Hundred Dollar Misunderstanding</u> is
more than the simple encounter between a fourteen-year-old
colored girl and a pompous college sophomore.   It is an
allegory for our times depicting the spread of violence in
the modern world ("They alla time killin somebody, them
whitefolks on tee vee.   They shootin and fightin an playin
lawman, an they killin an killin") and its terrible counterpart, the absence of love.

THE UNICORN

By Iris Murdoch (Viking Press, 1963).

The Unicorn, Iris Murdoch's seventh novel, is a
dazzling religious allegory, a kind of twentieth century Pilgrim's Progress. If it seems rather murky and overwrought
compared to John Bunyan's immortal classic, it must be
remembered that the author of Pilgrim's Progress did not
have to take into account the work of Sigmund Freud and
his disciples. For in addition to being a religious allegory,
The Unicorn is also (to borrow a term from the novel itself) a "psychological masquerade." Add to all this Iris
Murdoch's own vivid imagination and it is perhaps not surprising if the novel is murky and overwrought.

The setting is an old castle in a desolate region of
northern England (this is Wuthering Heights country) surrounded on one side by the sea and on the other by a treacherous peat bog. As this strange novel begins, a young
woman named Marian Taylor is on her way to Gaze Castle,
having accepted a teaching position there. Upon arriving
she is surprised to learn that her pupil is to be none other
than the mistress of Gaze Castle, the still beautiful but
mysterious Mrs. Hannah Crean-Smith.

Before long Marian discovers that everybody at Gaze
Castle is under a spell -- master and servant alike -- and
that Hannah Crean-Smith is a virtual prisoner in her own
house. It seems that, a long time ago, she fell in love
with Pip Lejour, the owner of Riders across the valley.
The lovers were caught and as a result Hannah was kept
under constant surveillance. But one day she escaped and
headed for the cliffs. Peter Crean-Smith ran after her.
Apparently there was a struggle and Peter fell over the
edge of the cliff. Miraculously, he lived. Now seven years
have passed and Hannah still remains beleaguered in her
castle. "I know one mustn't think of her as a legendary
creature, a beautiful unicorn-," says Effingham Coop, one
of Hannah's admirers. "The unicorn is also the image of
Christ," replies scholarly old Max Lejour. "But we have
to do too with an ordinary guilty person."

"What is the matter with this place?" poor Marian

wants to know. No one can seem to allay her fears for Hannah and so she plots to rescue this modern Sleeping Beauty and spirit her away. The plot is foiled by sinister Gerald Scottow, however, and Marian is more bewildered than ever. She even wonders whether the world of Gaze Castle is a "world of good or of evil, a world of significant suffering or a devil's shadowplay, a mere nightmare of violence." This reviewer must humbly confess that he doesn't know either.

But although the symbolism borders on the farcical, there are some superb scenes in this novel. The author's description of a man caught in quicksand and slowly going under is a piece of realistic writing that prosaic souls who do not like heavy-handed symbolism can admire unreservedly.

THE REIVERS

By William Faulkner (Random House, 1963).

It seems almost as strange to this reviewer that William Faulkner's The Reivers, a pleasant enough tale but nothing more, should win the Pulitzer Prize for fiction as that Edward Albee's mordantly striking play, Who's Afraid of Virginia Woolf, should fail to win the Pulitzer Prize for drama. No one disputes the fact that the late novelist and short-story writer was one of the greatest, if not the greatest, creative geniuses of our time. But in The Reivers he was obviously in a relaxed and nostalgic mood. And the fact that the book is subtitled "A Reminiscence" indicates that Faulkner himself did not consider it a very important work.

The story relates the "hilarious" (and I am afraid quotation marks are necessary) adventures of eleven-year-old Lucius Priest who in the year 1905 absconds with two older friends in his grandfather's Winton Flyer, one of the first automobiles in Yoknapatawpha County, Mississippi. The two friends are Boon Hogganbeck, who is part Indian, and Ned William McCaslin, a Negro youth. Together they drive to Memphis eighty miles away, where they put up at Miss Reba's, the brothel made famous in Sanctuary.

Ned is a born gambler and he takes it upon himself to trade the automobile for a dubious race horse, with the idea that he can win it back fair and square in a race. The reivers soon find themselves in trouble with the law, but still manage to take part in one of the most bizarre horse races in the annals of fiction.

The story is mildly amusing provided one succeeds in penetrating the almost impenetrable thicket that is Faulkner's prose. This is how he describes Grandfather's car being pulled out of a mudhole by two mules: "There was something dreamlike about it. Not nightmarish: just dreamlike -- the peaceful, quiet, remote, sylvan, almost primeval setting of ooze and slime and jungle growth and heat in which the very mules themselves, peacefully swishing and stamping at the teeming infinitesimal invisible myriad life which was the actual air we moved and breathed in, were not only un-alien but in fact curiously appropriate,

being themselves biological dead ends and hence already
obsolete before they were born; the automobile: the expensive useless mechanical toy rated in power and strength by
the dozens of horses, yet held helpless and impotent in the
almost infantile clutch of a few inches of the temporary
confederation of two mild and pacific elements -- earth
and water -- which the frailest integers and units of motion
as produced by the ancient unmechanical methods, had cop-
ed with for countless generations without really having
noticed it: the three of us, three forked identical and now
unrecognisable mud-colored creatures engaged in a life-and-
death struggle with it, the progress -- if any -- of which
had to be computed in dreadful and glacier-like inches. "

Poor courtly William Faulkner, the Southern Gentleman as Genius, is dead.   Miss Reba's brothel is no more
and the Memphis of frolicking and dancing, where Ned sleeps
with the cook, has given way to the sit-in demonstrator,
the fire hose and the police dog.

THE PUMPKIN EATER

By Penelope Mortimer (McGraw-Hill, 1963).

It should be said at the outset that The Pumpkin Eater by Penelope Mortimer, the English author of Saturday Lunch with the Brownings, should ideally be reviewed by a woman rather than a man. The reason for this will soon become apparent.

The narrator of the story, an intelligent, attractive and capable woman who never reveals her name, is married to the successful writer-producer Jake Armitage. (Mrs. Armitage would be even more intelligent and capable except for the fact that Jake is her fourth husband.) As the novel begins, Mrs. Armitage has undergone an emotional breakdown and is consulting a psychiatrist. Her problem, or at least one of them, is that she has a family so large that when they play netball they are spread out over a quarter of a mile of playing field. Actually we are never told the precise number of her offspring, but they linger ominously in the background like some huge Greek chorus.

Although the doctor advances several theories to account for his patient's childbearing proclivities ("Could it be that in spite of what might be called a very full life, it's sex you really hate? Sex itself you are frightened of?"), this reviewer has read the book two times and still cannot seem to relate the narrator's emotional breakdown to her vast horde of children. Apparently it is not the children themselves who are causing the trouble, but rather the mother's compulsive need to have children. (As I said, a woman would understand these things better than a man.)

Even disregarding the horde of children, the heroine's problems are big enough to lead to a breakdown. "You hate ...messes, don't you?" the doctor admonishes. And indeed it is clear that, up until now, she has led a very protected life and has never had to face the real world of evil and of men and women not so gifted and perfect as she. It might even be that her incessant reproduction is her way of insulating herself from this imperfect world. At any rate, this aspect of the novel is quite beautifully and adroitly delineated.

But if our heroine is not altogether convincing to a mere man, Penelope Mortimer is still an extremely talented writer who seems to have learned a great deal from James Joyce's <u>Portrait of the Artist as a Young Man</u>. As a matter of fact, she too writes "epiphanies," to borrow the term made famous by Joyce to refer to a sudden spiritual manifestation which an object or action achieves as a result of the observer's apprehension of its significance. Such a concise style demands a lot from the reader.

But if it demands much, it has much to give. And perhaps the best compliment that any reviewer could pay to Mrs. Mortimer's novel is that he read it twice and liked it better the second time.

ELIZABETH APPLETON

By John O'Hara (Random House, 1963).

      The heroine of John O'Hara's latest book sounds like a character in a novel by Booth Tarkington. And indeed Mr. O'Hara, for all his naïve sniggering over sex, is as old-fashioned and sentimental a novelist as the author of Alice Adams and Presenting Lily Mars. Once he wrote a book called Appointment in Samarra, but that was a long time ago. Elizabeth Appleton is soap opera disguised as fiction. It is also going to be on the best-seller list, if it isn't already there.

      Lately all of John O'Hara's novels have tended to blur together indistinguishably and this one is no exception. The setting is a small Pennsylvania town called Spring Valley and Mr. O'Hara loses no time impressing us with his intimate knowledge of what constitutes the best society in such a town. "In this block alone," he has Jarvis Webster say, "I've seen two Scotties and two Sealyhams. They cost money. A Lincoln. Two Cadillacs, and two Ford station wagons. And the women dress just the same as the women in any good suburb of New York. If they have a country club here, these are the people that belong to it." If it sounds like The Status Seekers, it is undoubtedly true that Vance Packard could not do it better. What is missing, of course, is the passion that distinguishes a major writer from a minor entertainer. Like Booth Tarkington before him, John O'Hara emphasizes accuracy of detail to hide the fact that he really doesn't have much to say.

      He does say one thing, however, and this is where Elizabeth Appleton fits into the picture and Booth Tarkington leaves it. In the exact center of almost every O'Hara novel the heroine commits some shocking act which is completely out of character with her upbringing. Usually she makes love in the back of a car and cruelly emasculates her husband in the process. Everything leads up to this act of defiance and nothing much follows it. The theme of Elizabeth Appleton, then, is adultery, and apparently what keeps John O'Hara turning out one novel after another (besides the need to earn money) is some deep-seated need to expose the modern American woman as some

kind of bitch goddess.   Although this is certainly a legiti-
mate enterprise, he lacks the passion and insight to make
an Elizabeth Appleton a real flesh-and-blood creature instead of simply a case history out of <u>The Status Seekers</u>
or the <u>Kinsey Report.</u>

What else is there to say?   Elizabeth Appleton (nee
Webster), an alumnus of Miss Chapin's Finishing School,
becomes the wife of a history professor at Spring Valley
College.   After a while she grows bored with her role of
"tweed-skirted faculty wife" and has an affair with the confirmed bachelor and nonconformist, Porter Ditson.   Finally she terminates the affair and goes back to her husband,
with the profound realization that there is no such thing as
a perfect marriage.   Who besides Elizabeth Appleton and
Our Gal Sunday ever thought that there was?

THE MESSENGER

By Charles Wright (Farrar, Straus, 1963).

Charles Wright's The Messenger is the remarkable
first novel about the subterranean junkie world of New York
that has already received high praise from Lucy Freeman,
Kay Boyle and James Baldwin. "And, no matter what the
city fathers may say," Baldwin writes, "this is New York;
this is the way we live here now."

In a way The Messenger is even a more impressive
performance than Baldwin's own Another Country. No one
excels James Baldwin as an essayist, but the didactic
brilliance of his essays does not always carry over to the
novel form. Charles Wright, on the other hand, is under
no compulsion to preach. He is committed to nothing except recording what he has truly seen and felt. " 'I am
the future,' I once wrote in a passionate school-boy essay,"
his protagonist, Charles Stevenson, exclaims. "Now, at
twenty-nine, I am not expecting much from this world.
Fitzgerald and his green light! I remember his rich, mad
dream: 'Tomorrow we will run faster, stretch out our
arms farther.' But where will this black boy run? To
whom shall he stretch out his arms?" Charles Wright
has no illusions about himself or the world in which he
lives, and that is why we instinctively accept what he has
to say, as shocking as much of it is, at face value. The
novel has the cold, frightening ring of utter authenticity.

But who is Charles Stevenson? He is a messenger
whose job takes him to all parts of the city and even beyond the city's boundaries to the strange green world of
the suburbs. It is an ideal job for one who, like Charles
Stevenson, aspires to be a writer, as it puts him in contact with every conceivable aspect of humanity. Actually
it is the subterranean junkie world with which he is most
familiar, the world of dope addicts, prostitutes and homo-
sexuals. The Messenger is a chronicle of the lower depths,
and the symbolism of the title is clear: Charles Wright
is sending a message in the form of this book and it says
quite simply, "This is New York; this is the way we live
here now."

Obviously this book is going to shock a lot of people. Many of us would prefer not to know anything about the underworld described in <u>The Messenger.</u> Oh, we will tolerate an occasional sentimental fable like <u>The Catcher in the Rye</u> which is, after all, about a youth much like ourselves who inadvertently stumbles on evil. But <u>The Messenger</u> is no sentimental fable. It is <u>The Catcher in the Rye</u> turned inside out.

One final comment. There are some wonderful flashbacks in which the narrator tells of his childhood in Sedalia, Missouri, and of his Grandmother sitting on the vine-covered porch who asks: "Sonny do you still say your prayers?" When Charles returns to Missouri for his Grandmother's funeral, we realize that a profound connection has been broken. All that is left is a "cluttered, yellowing room" in the heart of Manhattan. And at the end, he is even forced by the Housing Authority to leave this. But no matter what becomes of Charles Stevenson, there can be no doubt that he has delivered his message.

THE GIFT

By Vladimir Nabokov (Putnam, 1963).

In a review of Vladimir Nabokov's <u>Pale Fire</u>, Mary
McCarthy remarked that it is not only "one of the very
great works of art of this century," but is also a "trap to
catch reviewers." This reviewer suspects that these same
words could be applied to Nabokov's sensational and contro-
versial novel, <u>Lolita</u>. "I want to keep everything as it were
on the very brink of parody," says the hero of <u>The Gift,</u>
written in the author's native Russian in Berlin during the
thirties and now translated into English for the first time.
"...And there must be on the other hand an abyss of serious
ness," he adds, "and I must make my way along this narrow ridge between my own truth and a caricature of it."
With these words in mind, we can begin to see why Nabokov
is so often misinterpreted and has become such a notorious
"trap for reviewers." He is a master at skirting on the
brink of parody (his own artistic version of "brinksmanship"),
but the same cannot always be said for his earnest and lit-
eral-minded readers.

The hero of <u>The Gift</u> is Fyodor Godunov-Cherdyntsev
an impoverished Russian poet living in Berlin, and the book
he dreams of writing is not <u>Lolita</u> (interestingly enough,
there is a passage on page 198 that suggests the genesis of
that infamous book), but <u>The Gift</u>. Like Vladimir Nabokov
himself and thousands of other members of the Russian
aristocracy, Fyodor emigrated to Berlin after the revolution where he now lives the rootless life of an expatriate in
an alien country.

Actually the real hero or heroine of Mr. Nabokov's
book is Russian literature. Pushkin, Gogol and the revolutionary critic and novelist, Nikolay Gavrilovich Chernyshevski
figure as importantly in the narrative as Fyodor himself.
Like most geniuses, Vladimir Nabokov felt compelled to
measure himself against the great creative geniuses of the
past ("these raids on the past of Russian thought") and to
come to terms with their achievement before he could fully
commence on his own.

If The Gift is difficult, then, it is because it demands
of the reader at least some knowledge of, and interest in,
Russian literature.   One entire chapter, for example -- it
is really a book within a book -- is devoted to Fyodor's
Life of Chernyshevski.   Now Fyodor doesn't think much
of the obscure author of Aesthetic Relationship between
Art and Reality.   In fact, he believes him to cut quite a
ridiculous figure.   But whether we are interested in Chernyshevski or not, it is obviously important to the understanding of Fyodor Godunov-Cherdyntsev to know where he stands
in relation to him.   No, this is not an easy book, but it
is certainly a rewarding one.

And over everything the author's marvelous style
glimmers and scintillates like the early mist in China
which, according to Fyodor's father, the noted explorer of
Central Asia, "caused everything to vibrate."

The Gift may well be a "trap for reviewers," but
it is not to be avoided for that reason.

EHRENGARD

By Isak Dinesen (Random House, 1963).

Ehrengard is one of the last tales of the great Danish novelist Isak Dinesen, the nom-de-plume of Baroness Karen Blixen of Rungstedlund, who died in 1962 at the age of seventy-seven. The tale begins simply, "An old lady told this story," and from this modest beginning until the very last word the famed writer holds us completely enthralled under the spell of her genius. "Look up and down, right and left, with your most critical eye," says the artist Herr Cazotte, "you will not find a single tone which be not harmoniously tuned into the harmony of the whole." Herr Cazotte happens to be referring to Schloss Rosenbad, but the same words could be used to describe the consummate artistry of Isak Dinesen.

The story which the narrator calls "my small sonata" falls into three parts, a prelude, a pastorale and a rondo. The setting is the lovely country of Babenhausen, a small principality of Germany, and the time is 120 years ago.

When young Prince Lothar of the house of Fugger-Babenhausen courts the beautiful Princess Ludmilla of Leuchtenstein everyone is relieved and delighted. The threatened extinction of the dynasty is not to be. As a matter of fact, the ducal heir is to make his entry into the world a full two months ahead of schedule.   To avoid a scandal it is decided to remove the Princess to a secluded country resort.   Surrounded by a small trustworthy court sworn to secrecy, the Princess would give birth to the ducal heir in the middle of May.   Two months later a hundred-and-one gun salute from the old citadel of Babenhausen would officially proclaim the great and happy news.

The instigator of this delicate plot is Johann Wolfgang Cazotte, the celebrated artist, who at the age of forty-five is "persona grate at a dozen courts." The place of confinement is left to Herr Cazotte and after various expeditions he chooses the little chateau of Rosenbad, charmingly situated on a mountain slope and suitably isolated from the rest of the world.

But the most important and delicate task of all is
the choice of a maid-of-honor to the Princess. And once
again Herr Cazotte proves his worth and nominates the
beautiful and virginal Ehrengard von Schreckenstein, the
daughter of General von Schreckenstein. "A very stern,
indeed Puritan breed," the Grand Dutchess acknowledges.
"All military people. "

Now in addition to his other talents, Herr Cazotte
is also celebrated as the conqueror and seducer of fair
ladies, the "irresistible Don Juan of his age. " He immediately sets out to conquer Ehrengard whom he calls "my
youthful victim," but not in the "orthodox and old-fashioned
manner. " For above all Herr Cazotte is an artist and he
intends to obtain a full surrender without any physical touch
whatever.

The ending is a surprise and not at all what Herr
Cazotte had in mind. His sole objective had been to bring
a blush to the cheeks of Ehrengard, a blush in which her
past, present and future would be thrown before his feet.
But in the end it is Herr Cazotte who blushes, his blood
drawn upwards as from "the profoundest wells of his being,
till it colored him all over like a transparent crimson veil. "

THE PRINCIPAL

By Benjamin Siegel (Harcourt, Brace and World, 1963).

        Benjamin Siegel, the author of three historical novels, has chosen as the theme of his new book the very immediate and pressing problem of education in a democracy. The Principal is manifestly a "thesis novel" without literary pretensions. It is instruction under a very thin coating of fiction, which as a matter of fact are the very words one reviewer used to describe the author's A Kind of Justice.

        Considering its limited objectives (and granted the author is no Vladimir Nabokov), this is not really a bad book. Mr. Siegel does pretty much what he sets out to do. He appears to be well informed about the public schools. He is as concerned about school problems as any member of the P. T. A.

        Robert Evans has just been appointed to succeed the retiring Johnny Loomis as principal of the high school in Pine Hills, New York, a fast-growing suburb some fifty miles from New York City. Although Johnny Loomis is greatly loved in the community, the situation at the school has deteriorated badly in recent years. When the new principal arrives, he finds students roaming the corridors at will, a secretary who can neither spell nor take dictation, and complete chaos in assembly hall. "I will not be politic, pleasant and safe," Robert decides. "I will be crotchety, sharp, and disliked. If, eventually, they fire me, I will be able to live with the notion that, although stupid, I resisted hypnosis."

        And so he suffers through a whole school year, fighting everyone and everything in sight, irate parents, incompetent teachers protected by tenure, bureaucratic gobbledegook and a superintendent of schools firmly committed to mediocrity. It is a good fight, but the odds are enormous. He may win a few battles, but how can he possibly win the war? This reviewer (forgetting for the moment that this was a "thesis novel") thought that the only honorable way the book could end was for Robert to either resign or be fired. But no, the ex-principal, popular Johnny Loomis (remember him?) comes to Robert's defense in the very last chapter.

And thus Robert does win the war, after all.   And to round
things off with an added flourish, he even marries Johnny
Loomis' daughter, an English teacher at Pine Hills.

And this reviewer couldn't help thinking of another
novel about a harried schoolteacher, Bernard Malamud's
A New Life.   Mr. Malamud's teacher, S. Levin, does not
get reappointed.   Instead, he becomes involved in an affair
and runs off with another professor's wife.   But then Malamud, unlike Benjamin Siegel, was not writing a "thesis
novel."   He was composing a work of art.

THE COLLECTOR

By John Fowles (Little, Brown, 1963).

"A young Englishman named John Fowles," announces Granville Hicks in the July 27th issue of The Saturday Review, has just written a first novel, The Collector, that is so ingenious that its considerable merits may be overlooked." Overlooked by whom, Mr. Hicks? The Collector is not a book whose merits are so easily overlooked.

An obsequious little clerk named Frederick Clegg whose hobby is collecting butterflies, conceives the horrible idea of kidnapping a lovely young girl, whom he secretly worships from afar, and putting her in his killing-bottle along with his other rare specimens. Miranda Grey is everything that Frederick Clegg is not, and he entertains the mad notion that he can thus force her to acknowledge his presence. The collector buys an old country house (he has won some money in a soccer pool) and proceeds to carry out his diabolical plan. For two months he holds Miranda -- a beautiful butterfly fluttering against the glass -- imprisoned in his killing-bottle. It would of course spoil the book to reveal the macabre denouement, but I can assure you that Alfred Hitchcock could not do better.

Almost the entire book takes place inside the narrow confines of Frederick Clegg's country house (the story is first told in Clegg's own words and then in the form of a diary kept by Miranda during her ordeal), and at first this reviewer was frankly doubtful that the author could sustain interest for over three hundred pages. Perhaps the most remarkable thing about this novel is that what might so easily have been an ambitious failure turns out to be a powerful tour de force.

Obviously the author felt this book deeply. It has the passion of D. H. Lawrence (Miranda's diary reads like Lawrence's famous Studies in Classic American Literature) and the nightmarish Mad Hatter quality of Alice in Wonderland.

How John Fowles despises Frederick Clegg ("He's a collector, that's the great dead thing in him") and all

that he represents! And such is his talent that the collector
does not exist merely as an abstract principle of evil, but
as an all-too-real, flesh-and-blood person. This is how
Miranda describes him in her diary: "Gangly. Hands too
big, a nasty fleshy white and pink. Not a man's hands.
Adam's apple too big, wrists too big, chin much too big,
underlip bitten in, edges of nostrils red. Adenoids. He's
got one of those funny inbetween voices, uneducated trying
to be educated. It keeps on letting him down."

And of course Miranda represents all the goodness
and joy in life that the Frederick Cleggs of this world would
utterly destroy and stuff in their ghastly killing-bottles.
(Actually she thinks too highly of Salinger's The Catcher
in the Rye, but then she is only twenty-years-old and can
be forgiven this youthful failing.) There is one entry in her
diary that reads like a litany and will suffice for her epitaph: "I hate the uneducated and the ignorant. I hate the
pompous and the phoney. I hate the jealous and the re-
sentful. I hate the crabbed and the mean and the petty
... I love honesty and freedom and giving. I love making,
I love doing. I love being to the full, I love everything
which is not sitting and watching and copying and dead at
heart."

NIGHT AND SILENCE WHO IS HERE?

By Pamela Hansford Johnson (Scribner, 1963).

         This novel by Pamela Hansford Johnson has received
such flattering notices that I thought it might be a good
book to review, even though I must confess to a personal
bias against women authors who insist on using all three
names (Grace Livingston Hill, Helen Topping Miller, Ella
Wheeler Wilcox, et al.) and feel much more comfortable
with just plain Mary McCarthy.   After reading about a
hundred pages I realized my mistake, but it was then too
late to turn back.   As a result, I now formally submit
Night and Silence Who Is Here?   as my candidate for the
most boring novel of the year.

         It is always dangerous for an outsider--Pamela Hans-
ford Johnson, the wife of C. P. Snow of "Two Cultures"
fame, is English -- to presume to write what the author
calls "An American Comedy."   It is true that one can sometimes say perceptive things about a foreign land in a diary
or journal, but fiction requires an unquestioned knowledge
and verisimilitude if it is not to play havoc with the author's
intentions.   Unfortunately, Pamela Hansford Johnson has
more confidence in her writing ability than knowledge and
understanding of the American scene.

         What is this so-called American comedy?   It is still
another satire of academic life and part of Pamela Hansford
Johnson's difficulty is that others more gifted than she have
done the same thing better in recent years, including of
course the previously mentioned Miss McCarthy (The Groves
of Academe), Kingsley Amis (Lucky Jim), Randall Jarrell
(Pictures from an Institution) and my own favorite, Bernard
Malamud (A New Life).

         Night and Silence Who Is Here?   (the title is bor-
rowed from Shakespeare) is about a kind of Lucky Jim
character named Matthew Pryar, who comes to a small,
richly-endowed college in New Hampshire as a Visiting
Fellow, where he is to complete his book on Dorothy Mer-
lin, the obscure author of "twenty shortish poems and four
slim verse-dramas."   As it turns out, he has no talent
for scholarship at all, but is really interested in "adminis-

tration. " The plot -- such as it is -- concerns the Visiting Fellow's machinations to become Head of the Center (or Centre?) for Advanced Studies at the college. (The author and publisher's blurb writer really should have gotten together on the American or English spelling of the word, but this little oversight is no doubt symptomatic of what ails the book.)

Of course the farcical plot is only an excuse to enable Pamela Hansford Johnson to observe the American academic community and pass bland comment on it. Despite all the high jinks, the author's observations are commonplace and uninteresting. Her main target seems to be American eating habits and she also makes snide references to anything the least bit off-beat, whether it be Samuel Beckett's Waiting for Godot or the expressionistic drama of the 1920's, which for some private reason she finds excruciatingly funny. And as already suggested, she is not even able to make her small New England college recognizable as an American institution.

To paraphrase Gertrude Stein, a farce is a farce is a farce... but it should also be something more. It is this "something more" that eludes Pamela Hansford Johnson.

THE TENANTS OF MOONBLOOM

By Edward Lewis Wallant (Harcourt, Brace and World, 1963).

The immensely gifted author of The Tenants of Moonbloom died last year at the age of thirty-six. Presumably
this reviewer knows something about books and yet he must
humbly confess that, until last week, he can scarcely remember having heard of Edward Lewis Wallant. There is
something sad and frightening in the realization that a remarkable artist can be gone even before we know he exists.
The only consolation, of course, is his work.

Norman Moonbloom is a humble, mild-mannered
rental agent who works for his brother Irving, the owner
of four dilapidated tenement houses in New York City. Norman, who wryly calls himself New York's most educated
rent collector, is a man without purpose or illusions.
"Don't you have any initiative?" Irving exclaims sarcast-
ically over the phone. "I'm a small man of definite limitations," Norman has to admit, relaxing in the admission.

But the tenants make demands on him, impossible
demands. The toilet gets clogged. An army of cockroaches
troops across the peeling walls. The roof leaks. "I don't
ask for these intimacies," Norman says bitterly. "I'm
the agent, I collect the rents. This whole setup is a mad-
house."

Despite his good intentions, however, Norman Moonbloom finds himself becoming involved with his tenants and
their problems. They may be psychological cripples, but
their humanity can no longer be denied. Overcome with
guilt and a terrible despair, an outrageous idea occurs to
him. He will take care of all the complaints! It will cost
over five thousand dollars, but he will do it! Suddenly
Norman begins to laugh ... And was he including what needed to be repaired in the tenants? Suppose he made a list
of those things too, tried to find the cost of those breaks
and chippings? Three hundred dollars for the Hausers for
new hearts; six hundred and fifty for Kram's new body ...

It is like something out of Dante's Inferno, these
people squeezed of all their youthful dreams of dignity and

joy.   Hell is the subway into which they stream or the cheap lunch counter where they cram tasteless food into their ruined stomachs.   Heaven may be a penthouse on Park Avenue (not to be found in these pages), but Purgatory is most assuredly the tenement house in which Bodien, the plumber, examines a leaking pipe with "the gravity of a doctor examining a biopsy."

And tying it all together there is Sugarman, the candy butcher with the poet's soul, hawking his wares out of Grand Central Station: "Awright drinks, cheese sandwiches, peanut butter Nabs."

The Tenants of Moonbloom is surely one of the most powerful and disturbing novels to come along in many years.   It is bitter and yet compassionate, hauntingly sad and yet somehow extravagantly funny.   It is filled with a lyrical intensity.   Its author, Edward Lewis Wallant, is dead at the age of thirty-six, but we can say with old Hirsch, one of Norman Moonbloom's tenants, "Thank you Moonbloom nice meeting you."

CAT AND MOUSE

By Günter Grass (Harcourt, Brace and World, 1963).

        Translated from the German by Ralph Manheim, Cat
and Mouse is by the author of the sensational first novel,
The Tin Drum, already reviewed in this collection.   This
reviewer used the term "genius" to describe Günter Grass,
a verdict that seems to have been substantiated by the fact
that The Tin Drum has been translated into every major
European language and has already made the author a world-
renowned literary figure.

        Like many works of genius, The Tin Drum has been
violently denounced as well as highly praised.   "Here is
one long, crazy, unalleviated nightmare," one reviewer
wrote, "void of any beauty or sanity. " And yet even he had
to admit that "If you can stick with it and stomach it, you
will, perhaps, find a brilliant artistic experience. "

        Cat and Mouse is likely to offend the same delicate
sensibilities that were offended by The Tin Drum, yet it, too,
will be hailed far and wide by discriminating readers as a
work of genius.   Although shorter and much less forbid-
ding than the sprawling autobiography of Oskar Matzerath,
the eternal three-year-old drummer, its Kafka-like symbolism (it should be noted that Günter Grass is a sculptor
and draftsman as well as writer) still makes it a much more
profound and difficult book than we are perhaps used to
reading.   And yet ironically it is the very simplicity of the
imagery that creates this profound effect.   Perhaps genius
is after all nothing more than the conjunction of the very
simple and the very complex.

        The two principal symbols are given in the title.
The hero of the book is a fourteen-year-old schoolboy,
Joachim Mahlke, who possesses an extraordinarily large
Adam's apple.   When a classmate sicks a cat on Mahlke's
"mouse" or Adam's apple he instigates a tragicomic game
of "cat and mouse" that does not come to an end until
Joachim, erstwhile ace diver, disappears while diving from
a half-submerged Polish mine sweeper sunk in the Gulf of
Danzig.

Now these symbols can undoubtedly be interpreted in more than one way, but it seems fairly clear that the cat poised to pounce on Joachim's "mouse" is society in general which refuses to tolerate the exceptional individual in its midst, the artist, say, or man of genius.   For there is no denying that Joachim Mahlke is an exceptional individual who is successful in everything he attempts.   His youthful companions regard him with awe and even call him "The Great Mahlke."

On another level Cat and Mouse is a poignant reminiscence of what it was like to grow to manhood in Danzig during the Second World War.   For three summers Joachim and his friends cavort on the hulk of a half-submerged mine sweeper, where Joachim amazes everyone with his diving ability.   He brings up all kinds of loot from the submerged half of the ship and strings it around his neck, concealing his Adam's apple.

Obviously these activities are designed to stave off the greedy, omnipresent cat.   After leaving school, Joachim goes to war and wins the country's highest decoration, the Order of Merit.   But even this is not enough.   Mahlke is different.   Mahlke is doomed.

THE LAND OF RUMBELOW

By Carlos Baker (Scribner, 1963).

The Land of Rumbelow by the well-known scholar and
critic, Carlos Baker, is subtitled "A Fable in the Form of
a Novel. " It is not difficult to see why the author decided
to call the book a fable. It is so improbable as realistic
fiction, so full of extraordinary coincidences, that no one
could possibly take it seriously as anything more than a
kind of fable or legend that tries to enforce some useful
moral.

Dan Sherwood, the central figure in what is an extremely complicated narrative, is a young scholar who is
doing research on Nicholas Kemp, a famous novelist, now
in his fifties, who is known as "the Döstoyevsky of the
1920's. " Kemp is almost as elusive a character as J. D.
Salinger and lives far from civilization in the northern
Cascade Mountains of Washington. Dan writes to Kemp,
but gets a nasty letter in reply. "My life is my own to
live as I see fit," he writes. "I do not propose to have
it guessed at, lied about, cheapened, sentimentalized, or
otherwise degraded or misrepresented."

A conscientious scholar, Dan still persists in fer-
reting out elusive biographical facts which will help to solve
the mystery of Nicholas Kemp, even though he is somewhat reluctant to do so. Why is he reluctant? Could it
be, he wonders, a simple act of self-defense? Am I not
projecting myself into Kemp's position? Are there not facts,
whole sequences of action--in my life as in his--that I do
not want to reveal or to have revealed by someone else?

Ah, there's the rub! Poor Dan Sherwood, New
England Puritan that he is, has a guilty conscience. He
once betrayed his best friend and has never managed to get
over it. Furthermore, he is obsessed with an overpowering
vision of evil and this obsession is confirmed in the novels
of Nicholas Kemp. Rumbelow, according to an ancient morality play, is a region three miles out of Hell. And most
of the action in this fable in the form of a novel takes place
in Arizona, a region that bears a striking resemblance to
the land of Rumbelow. In the very first chapter our poor

hero is knocked unconscious by a hitchhiker whom he has picked up "three miles west of Show Low," thus deepening his already pronounced propensity for pessimism.

In the end Dan Sherwood emerges from the shadow of the land of Rumbelow. He falls in love with beautiful Connie Haybright and, lo and behold, she turns out to be none other than the daughter of Faith Collins who had a child by Nicholas Kemp way back in 1918 in France during the First World War! Although this comes as a shocking revelation at first (and quite a coincidence, too) there are several consoling features. Now there is no question of publicizing Kemp's biography and revealing to Connie Haybright what she is better off not knowing. Later Dan has a nice chat with Connie's mother who tells him the whole story from the beginning. Far from being the American Döstoyevsky, it seems that Nicholas Kemp could almost qualify for membership in Rotary or the P. T. A. The world isn't such a bad place, after all.

And as in most fables, the hero and heroine live happily ever after far from the land of Rumbelow.

FAIL-SAFE

By Eugene Burdick and Harvey Wheeler (McGraw-Hill, 1963).

Fail-Safe, last year's best-selling novel by Eugene
Burdick and Harvey Wheeler, has now been published in a
paperback edition by Dell and is no doubt selling thousands
of copies a day.   There is nothing surprising in this.
People everywhere are naturally concerned about the possibility of accidental nuclear war and Messrs. Burdick and
Wheeler must have known they had a sure-fire best seller.
What is surprising is the fact that supposedly intelligent
critics such as Norman Cousins and Clifton Fadiman
should have been swept along in the general conflagration.

"Fail-Safe is the most exciting novel I have read
in at least ten years," exclaims Mr. Fadiman in the Book
of the Month Club News.   "The book leaves the reader
defenseless," says Mr. Cousins.   "He is quickly subdued
into staying with it until he finishes it because of its narrative pull and because it is his life that is directly involved in the outcome. "

Now there are some of us who happen to think that
Fail-Safe is a shoddy book, neither exciting or dramatic as
literature nor credible as an account of how accidental war
could occur between the two great atomic powers.   Indeed,
so badly have the authors bungled the job that the effect
on many readers is more reassuring than frightening.

If I understand them correctly, this is what Burdick
and Wheeler ask us to believe.   Because of mechanical
failure, a group of atomic bombers fly through their Fail-
Safe position and proceed toward Russia at fifteen hundred
miles per hour, prepared to drop a load of twenty-megaton
bombs on Moscow.   The Fail-Safe point is a fixed point
where the planes will orbit while awaiting a positive order
to attack.   Without this order they must return to the
United States.   Ordinarily the bombers could be recalled by
radio but the Russians have chosen just this moment to jam
our radio communications.   Ironically, they do this on the
assumption (and why they should make this ominous assumption in the first place is glossed over in very vague terms)
that our bombers have been sent to their Fail-Safe position

not as an ordinary precautionary measure (this happens frequently), but as the prelude to an actual attack. They hope to prevent the final order to attack from going through. Instead they prevent any chance of recalling the planes.

There is still the possibility that the errant bombers can be shot down either by us or the Russians. When it appears certain that two of the bombers will get through, however, the President uses the "hot line" to the Kremlin for the first time and tries to convince Khrushchev that the whole thing is a ghastly mistake.

Finally Krushchev agrees not to retaliate provided the U. S. drops four bombs on New York to make up for the four bombs about to be dropped on Moscow. At this extraordinary juncture, Congressman Raskob of New York City, who has been standing by in the War Room of the Strategic Air Command at Omaha, utters the only convincing words in the entire novel. "He can't do it," Congressman Raskob says. And then realizing the enormity of what is about to happen, he says incredulously: "Emma, the kids, the house, all gone. The whole 46th Congressional District. All gone." Spoken like a true politician!

THE GROUP

By Mary McCarthy (Harcourt, Brace and World, 1963).

      Is it possible that a book by Mary McCarthy, whom
Time called "quite possibly the cleverest writer the U. S.
has ever produced," could be dull? After making his way
slowly through The Group, Miss McCarthy's long-awaited
novel about eight Vassar girls of the Class of '33 and what
happens to them after graduation, this reviewer has reluctantly come to the conclusion that she not only can write a
dull book but has.

      The Group is one of those ambitious John Dos Passos-
like chronicle novels that attempts to sum up an entire generation between the covers of a book. The trouble is the
generation refuses to be summed up so succinctly and what
we are left with are eight characters in search of a theme.
Individual chapters are often well done (some of them originally appeared as stories in the New Yorker and other magazines), but they do not seem to gain much by being placed
together in a book.

      When I noted that what we were left with were eight
characters in search of a theme, I may have inadvertently
stumbled upon the author's precise intention in this novel.
For these eight Vassar graduates, who have read Franz
Kafka and James Joyce, Sigmund Freud and Margaret Mead,
consider themselves superbly equipped to live (as the saying goes) to the limit of their capabilities. As they are all
quick to agree, this is a fresh new generation, not stuffy and
conservative like their elders.

      But the point Miss McCarthy apparently intends to
make is that this is a delusion. The novel opens on a
starry-eyed and optimistic note with the rather unconventional New York wedding of Kay Strong and Harald Petersen
(Reed '27). But in the end it is Kay's funeral that brings
the group together for the last time. Kay's marriage has
not lasted and it is unclear whether she has jumped or fallen
accidently from the twentieth floor window of the Vassar
Club. Seven years have passed (it is now the summer of
1940) and with them the hopes and aspirations of a whole
generation.

Between the wedding and funeral there is a great deal of feminine gossip and tittle-tattle that is evidently supposed to represent the intellectual ferment of the period. There are long disquisitions on child-rearing, interior decoration, psychoanalysis, sex and the relative merits of Boston and iceberg lettuce. This hardly adds up to intellectual ferment, but it is social reporting of a sort.

One searches almost in vain for the author's celebrated wit. The pages follow one another in dreary, solemn succession. Not until page 351 is there a real laugh in the book. But this book will be followed by other books and Mary McCarthy, so gifted and irreverent, will no doubt have the last laugh. It will probably be on us.

THE BATTLE OF THE VILLA FIORITA

By Rumer Godden (Viking Press, 1963).

Rumer Godden's The Battle of the Villa Fiorita is a fairy tale in modern dress, albeit a very well-written fairy tale. It is also a book that addresses itself primarily to women. Such a sure-fire combination almost inevitably catapults it to the top of the best-seller list. I say this not condescendingly but in deep humility and awe. The Battle of the Villa Fiorita is not so much a book as a mystique.

The battle begins when forty-three-year-old Fanny Clavering, the mother of three, falls passionately (and somewhat implausibly) in love with an Italian film director, Rob Quillet, and runs off with him. Colonel Clavering obtains a divorce and is awarded custody of the two younger children.

It is at this point that the children, twelve-year-old Caddie and fourteen-year-old Hugh, decide to take things into their own hands. Signor Quillet and Fanny have secreted themselves at an old Italian villa on Lake Garda, where they proceed with their wedding plans. Caddie and Hugh arrive unannounced and uninvited, having made the long journey from their London flat to this exotic place deep in the lake country of northern Italy. They are determined to break up this relationship which has already broken up their home. They are joined in this endeavor by Pia, Signor Quillet's teen-age daughter by his first marriage.

The battle is evenly fought as skirmish follows skirmish. Fanny and Rob try desperately to return Caddie and Hugh to their father, but this is not so easily done. Hugh becomes violently ill. No sooner is he better than the two girls -- sisters-in-arms -- go on a hunger strike. The climax is reached when Hugh and an Italian friend venture out on treacherous Lake Garda during a bad storm.

I said that this was a fairy tale and this is what I mean: Fanny Clavering is Little Red Riding Hood, a proper English girl. Little Red Riding Hood is lost in the wicked forest of northern Italy, so different from the genteel landscape of her native land. Signor Quillet, brilliant but unstable film director ("They say he will be either a de Sica or a Renoir"), tempts her and she is temporarily beguiled by his blandishments. But suddenly, being a proper English girl, Little Red Riding Hood comes to her senses. She will leave the wicked forest and, with her proper English children, return to her proper English husband.

And, of course, they will live happily ever after. There are no tragedies in a proper English novel.

THE ROCK GARDEN

By Nikos Kazantzakis (Simon and Schuster, 1963).

The Rock Garden by the great Greek novelist, poet
and philosopher, Nikos Kazantzakis, was first written in
French in 1936 on the author's return from his first trip
to the Orient.   Into this intense and passionate novel he
poured all that he saw and felt while visiting China and
Japan.

It was a time of great upheaval, of course, when the
Japanese were trying to conquer the "thick, elastic and
fecund rind of China" and the Chinese in turn were trying
to drive both the Japanese and the white man back into the
sea.   Kazantzakis admits that his own personal anguish had
driven him to these distant lands to find an outlet for his
own conflicts and desires.

The story exists on two levels of experience.   It is
first of all a tender love story about a European traveler
who courts the beautiful daughter of a Chinese mandarin.
On this level The Rock Garden is a novel of romantic intrigue which expresses not only the heroic struggle between
China and Japan, but also the struggle to merge the races
-- white, yellow and black -- into one triumphant race of
man, to breathe in "the transoceanic song."

This last phrase is very reminiscent of our own
Walt Whitman and indeed it is Nikos Kazantzakis, the philosopher and mystic, who predominates in The Rock Garden
and raises it from a tender love story to a philosophic
quest.   "To vanquish hope," he exclaims, "to realize that
there is no escape, to draw from this revelation an invin-
cible joy -- that is the highest peak to which man may as-
pire."   "Yes," he continues, "delight in beauty is a mortal
sin today.   Kindness, sensitivity, patience are not the virtues of our time, but violence, impatience, the heroic and
austere conception of life."

As we read these passionate words, we cannot help
but wonder if history has not discredited this austere philosophy not only in China and Japan but in Hitler's Germany
and lately on a street in Dallas.   This is not 1936 but

1963 and we may be forgiven if we have had enough of violence and prefer the homelier virtues.

But of course the danger here is in taking the author's meaning too literally, for in The Rock Garden, as in all his works, Nikos Kazantzakis is really not writing a novel in the usual sense but posing questions about the ultimate nature of the universe.   Ostensibly he has come to the Far East to seek answers to these questions and has been richly rewarded.   Here in these ancient lands where the dead dominate the living, utilitarian morality (Confucius) and divine madness (Lao-tse), the eternal pillars of the world, coalesce to create the rich civilization of China.

Actually Nikos Kazantzakis has come to the Orient not so much to seek answers as to confirm what he already knows.   At one point he pays tribute to the "voluptuous and balanced genius of my race, which first succeeded in combining logic and intoxication into one tragic vision. "   It would be hard to find words that better describe the genius of Nikos Kazantzakis, true descendant of the immortal Homer.

THE DARK TRAVELER

By Josephine Johnson (Simon and Schuster, 1963).

In 1934 Josephine Johnson won the Pulitzer Prize for her first novel, Now in November. "Told in a prose so subtly cadenced," wrote Burton Rascoe, "with overtones of aspiration and undertones of tragic feeling that it is like profoundly moving music; and one is almost incredulous upon hearing that this mature style and this mature point of view are those of a young woman in her twenties." Coming from Burton Rascoe this is high praise indeed, and it is no wonder that Now in November was compared favorably with such classic American novels as Ethan Frome and My Antonia.

Now some two novels and thirty years later (and after a silence of over fifteen years), Josephine Johnson has written The Dark Traveler, a novel that is already being compared with her own best work. And all one can say is that fifteen years is not too long to wait for a work of such consummate artistry.

The dark traveler is Paul Moore, an emotionally disturbed youth of twenty-eight. Unlike his brother, Andrew, killed in the war, Paul had always been an odd, quick child, who baffled and angered his father. Now under the incessant battering of Angus (Bus) Moore, the Friendly Used Car Dealer, he has retreated further and further into the fantasy world of his own desperate conjuring.

When Paul's mother dies, Angus is finally prevailed upon to let his brother's family care for the boy, as an alternative to having him committed to an institution. For the first time Paul begins to receive love and understanding and he responds to it as naturally as a delicate plant responds to light and air. Douglass Moore is as different from Angus as Paul is (or was) from Andrew, and there can be no doubt that Miss Johnson's book is in part a profound cry of indignation and pain hurled at a world that can produce such monsters as Angus Moore. "After such knowledge," she asks wearily, "what forgiveness?"

But this is a deeply religious book and no matter what

bitterness and self-doubt may have momentarily come to the surface, it is all swept away through the redemptive power of love. In the house of Paul's uncle hangs a small framed verse from the Bible, the words of St. Paul in the fourth chapter of the Philippians: "Whatsoever things are true ... Whatsoever things are honest ... Whatsoever things are just ... Whatsoever things are pure ... Whatsoever things are lovely ... Whatsoever things are of good report ... If there be any virtue, and if there be any praise ... Think on these things ... "

But these are not just words. Whether creating in Christopher, Paul's small companion, "a talisman, a protection against the unforeseen evils of the adult world, " or slyly drawing a parallel between Paul's excited swatting at cobwebs with a broom and Don Quixote's tilting at windmills, Josephine Johnson turns everything she touches (including the dross of our common life) to artistic gold.

A FAVOURITE OF THE GODS

By Sybille Bedford (Simon and Schuster, 1963).

A Favourite of the Gods is by the English author of
The Legacy, a first novel that was very highly praised on
its publication in 1957.   There was at least one dissenting
opinion, however.   "If there existed an annual award for
snobbery," wrote Richard Plant in the New York Times,
"this year's prize ... should go to Sybille Bedford ...
Once in a while the author lets down her defenses, takes
off the mask of blinding brightness and creates a scene
with real human beings who touch our emotions.   Unfortunately, these moments are rare and on the next page Miss
Bedford is again back to being pitilessly sophisticated."
Now I must admit that I have not read The Legacy and only
quote Mr. Plant because he expresses so well my own feeling about A Favourite of the Gods.   Not since Catch-22
have I been so disappointed in a book that almost everyone
else appears to have admired without reservation.

A Favourite of the Gods is a very ambitious narrative that encompasses three generations, beginning with the
closing decades of the nineteenth century.   Anna Howlands,
an American heiress, marries an Italian prince and comes
to the eternal city of Rome to live.   When she discovers
that her husband has been keeping a mistress (as Italian
princes are wont to do) almost from the moment of their
marriage, she is morally outraged and flees to England.

"Oh, shall we never escape the muddling consequences
of our family history?" asks Constanza, Anna's first-born.
She can no more escape the consequences of her parents'
marriage than can her brother, Giorgio, whose ambition
is to "marry a rich woman and race cars," or her own
daughter, Flavia.   The American Anna, it seems, is a
puritan, the Italian Constanza is a pagan and the English
Flavia is a realist.

Which is fine as far as it goes, but does anyone
really care?   Set in the worldly and intellectual centers
of Europe (to borrow a snobbish phrase from the dust
jacket) -- Italy, France and England -- and describing
a way of life that perhaps no longer exists, this novel is

an exquisite and irrelevant anachronism. Dame Sybille obviously knows her milieu (as in Mary McCarthy's The Group there is a surface glitter that is deceptive), but she has not been able to make it meaningful to anyone outside her immediate circle. And there is in particular a lack of human sympathy that is positively fatal.

The book might have been called "How to Live in a Villa on 100,000 Pounds a Year." For all their supposed intelligence, their wide-eyed interest in literature and liberal causes, Miss Bedford's characters are really only interested in their trust funds, their villas and what wine to serve for dinner.

The climax comes when Constanza's mother threatens to cut her off without a cent. "When women of my age lose their money they try to become secretaries," Constanza says to Flavia, "Or do translations. I can't even spell in Italian. And farm labour isn't very adequately paid."

But Constanza needn't have worried. It seems that she will inherit her mother's money after all and won't have to become a secretary or do translations.

Flavia is happy, too. "We can forget all about it, mummy," she says brightly. "You need never milk goats."

THE BENEFACTOR

By Susan Sontag (Farrar, Straus, 1963).

The Benefactor is a remarkable first novel by Susan
Sontag that practically invites comparison with such literary
masterpieces as Vladimir Nabokov's Lolita, Albert Camus'
The Fall and Günter Grass' The Tin Drum. Of course it is
always possible that the reviewer is imagining things, but
in this case I doubt it.

Put in the simplest terms, The Benefactor is about
a man who literally falls in love with his dreams. It is
presented in the form of a journal written by a sixty-one-
year-old man, a resident of Paris, whose dreams have at
last deserted him and left him beached upon the shore of
a solitary old age. "You may imagine me in a bare room,"
he writes, "my feet near the stove, bundled up in many
sweaters, my black hair turned grey, enjoying the waning
tribulations of subjectivity and the repose of a privacy that
is genuine."

It all started some thirty years before with the
"dream of the two rooms." Hippolyte, a young man of independent means, has always had a passion for speculation
and investigation. (He admits that he is inclined to take
himself rather seriously and lacks a sense of humor.) Having never dreamt before, Hippolyte becomes obsessed with
the task of interpreting the "dream of the two rooms."
"This dream was my first immoderate act," he acknowledges.
"Since the dream haunted me, I would now haunt the dream."

Other dreams follow: The "dream of an elderly
patron," the "dream of the piano lesson" and the "dream
of the mirror." Although his thoughts turn more and more
inward, he continues to live in the outside world as the
lover and benefactor of Frau Anders, who figures prominently in his dreams, as the friend and patron of a former
prize fighter turned writer who composes his novels while
dressed in boxing trunks, Jean-Jacques, as a dabbler in
occultism, as a frequenter of cafés and spectator of the
Parisian underworld, as a white slaver in North Africa and
would-be murderer.

Actually the main difference between Hippolyte and the rest of us is that we interpret our life through our dreams whereas he interprets his dreams through his life. As has already been indicated, this leads to excesses. Inevitably Hippolyte's dream-life becomes more real than his waking life. Toward the end, he is no longer able to distinguish one from the other.

And so we are left with a solitary old man, cleansed and purged of his dreams. "Far be it from me, however, to decide that the active part of my life is really over," Hippolyte concludes. "Who knows if a new series of dreams may not someday be forthcoming, which will launch me on a series of speculations far different from those which I have experienced?"

Who knows? Perhaps only Susan Sontag, the brilliant young author of this bizarre, philosophical, comic, terrifying and imaginative novel, truly knows.

THE PALACE

By Claude Simon (Braziller, 1963).

The Palace is by Claude Simon, the brilliant French
author whose powerful stream-of-consciousness novels
recall Proust and Faulkner.

A Frenchman, who had fought in the Spanish Civil
War on the Loyalist side, returns to Barcelona after an
absence of fifteen years. Everything is the same (the
smells, the fog, the pigeons, the esplanade around which
revolve the "eternal round of little streetcars"), and yet
everything is different. People and things and ideals, alas,
grow old, wither and die. And the Palace, the huge mansion which during the war served as headquarters for the
Republican forces, is now a bank.

Although Claude Simon has been rightly compared to
Proust and Faulkner, he seems to combine two very different techniques. He has obviously been influenced by the
"New Realist" group in his own country (Butor, Alain
Robbe-Grillet, et al.) and will devote pages to the meticu-
lous description of each piece of furniture in a room. It
is almost as though the furniture had a life of its own (as
it may well have) and must not be taken for granted. There
is a one-sentence description of an empty cigar box, for
example, that begins on page 179 and doesn't end until page
184. Now this is an interesting experiment, but the ordinary reader is apt to grow restless and wonder what significance this minute and painstaking description of an empty
cigar box can possibly have in terms of the narrative he
is attempting to follow.

No particular significance, one can imagine the author
saying, except that while the narrator is examining the
cigar box he is not doing something else. Who can say that
this is not important? The traditional novelist, we reply,
but then Claude Simon is not a traditional novelist. He
has no intention of delivering a moral lecture or plotting
a story that begins, "Once upon a time. "

As I have said, Claude Simon combines this "New
Realist" technique (which does seem somewhat forced and

derivative, an "experiment") with an intensely passionate lyrical quality that is uniquely his own and bears the authentic stamp of his genius.   If The Palace is not as good a novel as The Wind (published in this country in 1959), it may be due to the fact that he has sacrificed some of this lyrical quality in order to experiment after the manner of the "New Realists."

And what is Claude Simon passionate about?   He is passionate about that "invisible sliver of time," that enormous "maelstrom of sensations, sights, noises, feelings and contrary impulses rushing together, mingling, superimposing, impossible to control and to define ..."

"No doubt there was something he hadn't been able to see," muses the hero of this unusual novel who remembers forty-eight hours during the early weeks of the Spanish Civil War, "something that escaped him, so perhaps he too could gain a footing, get inside, gate-crash this tangential, comestible and optimistic derivative of metaphysics baptized carp or History ..." This is the artist's role Claude Simon has envisioned for himself, not footman but eternal gate-crasher and scorner of tradition.

THREE BEDS IN MANHATTAN

By Georges Simenon (Doubleday, 1964).

        Three Beds in Manhattan by Georges Simenon, the
creator of Inspector Maigret, was first published in France
in 1946 under the title Trois Chambres à Manhattan. It is
every bit as banal as the title would suggest. This reviewer's mistake was in thinking that Simenon, the writer whom
André Gide admired, would be able to salvage a good book
out of so unpromising a title.

        The story is negligible. Francois Combe, a well-
known French actor in his late forties, finds himself sitting next to an unattached young lady at an all-night lunch
counter in Greenwich Village. They are both lonely.
What could be more natural, then, that they should become
attached to each other. As Simenon puts it, "...they were
little more than strangers who had met by some selective
miracle in the world's biggest city and now clung to one
another as if the cold of loneliness was about to close in
on them again."

        So far, so good. Simenon is a kind of poet of the
lonely and the disaffiliated. Compassion is his stock in
trade. He is especially good at depicting the anonymous
nighttime world of the city. In this world a night club
closes, spewing its "last-gasp customers" out to the curb.
Trash cans line the curb in "homely expectancy." Street
lamps festoon the "almost deserted avenues with their garlands of softly glowing globes."

        But when it comes to depicting his characters in
depth rather than as mere shadows flitting among shadows,
it is another matter. Why is Francois Combe, the well-
known French actor, sitting at an all-night lunch counter
at three o'clock in the morning? Because six months ago,
in Paris, his wife left him for a much younger man. And
what is Catherine, the daughter of a famous concert pianist,
doing there? She has run away from her husband, Count
Larski, the distinguished Hungarian ambassador. It is
all very crude and amateurish, to say the least. Harold
Robbins couldn't be more banal.

But to return to the luncheonette, Francois and Catherine meet over grilled sausages (him) and a platter of bacon and eggs, (her), and then commence to walk all over Manhattan, from a garish Times Square hotel to his shabby apartment in the Village, to her equally unprepossessing domicile. The more he learns about Catherine's past, the more jealous he becomes. Only when she is suddenly called away to Mexico City (her daughter is very ill) does he finally become purged of his jealous foreboding and learn that, however so humble, three beds in Manhattan equal, if not love, good sales on both sides of the Atlantic.

A FINE MADNESS

By Elliott Baker (Putnam, 1963).

With his first published work, A Fine Madness,
Elliott Baker has not only won the $10,000 Putnam Award
for fiction but the respect and admiration of the critics as
well. "Very good fun throughout," Richard Wilbur is
quoted as saying on the dust jacket. I wonder if this is
not a considerable understatement.

Certainly in Samson Shillitoe, the exuberant poet who
dances nimbly and outrageously through these pages, Mr.
Baker has created a character to be reckoned with for years
to come. He is a kind of American version of Oskar Matzerath, the "eternal three-year-old drummer" of Günter
Grass' widely acclaimed novel, The Tin Drum. They are
both poets who refuse to become ensnared in a world of
"orators, thieves and traitors" that would reduce them to
its own lackluster level. Or to put it in more vivid terms,
Samson resolutely refuses to accept what he calls "the Fox
Movietone News version of existence."

All that matters to Samson Shillitoe is completing his
epochal four-part poem which will be his masterpiece. His
only previously published work, Hellebore, sold only 138
copies. Samson acknowledges that at this rate he will never
make the Oxford Book of American Verse. But even this
has its bright side, for it means not having to worry about
autograph sessions at Brentano's or droning into a micro-
phone until out comes a longplaying record!

Events conspire to defeat him. As Daniel K. Papp
never lets him forget, he is behind in his alimony payments
to his first wife. His present helpmate, a waitress named
Rhoda (Shillitoe irreverently describes their union as the
result of the accidental collision of a tired genius and a ripe
vegetable) unwittingly gets him involved with a group of
psychiatrists. In one of his mad flights to freedom he is
intercepted by a traffic cop in the Holland Tunnel where a
bizarre scuffle ensues. An indulgent mother and a small-
town sheriff add insult to injury.

It is all narrated dead-pan in a style which, unlike

Catch-22, never descends into caricature.   Despite the emphasis of some of the reviews I have seen, it isn't the farcical element that makes A Fine Madness such an outstanding novel, but rather the author's marvelous, pinpoint control which keeps it just within the bounds of credulity.
Elliott Baker has infused it with the glow of artlessness
which the author of Catch-22 might well emulate.

Thanks to this amazing control, the novel gathers mo-
mentum as it goes along.   The denouement is as chilling
as anything this reviewer has ever read, not excepting
George Orwell's 1964 (excuse me, 1984).   Samson Shillitoe
falls into the hands of the psychiatrists, who either do not
think he is a genuine poet (their diagnosis is "excessive
psychomotor activity") or prefer not to believe it.   Now it
is just a matter of performing a little operation.

But the orators, thieves and traitors cannot so easily
dispose of Samson Shillitoe.   He is a poet and he is impenetrable.   Ditto, Elliott Baker!

LOOKING FOR THE GENERAL

By Warren Miller (McGraw-Hill, 1964).

        At its best Warren Miller's <u>Looking for the General</u>
is first-rate satire of an almost Swiftian savagery and intensity.   At its worst it comes uncomfortably close to the
banal with a Peter De Vries kind of cleverness that is merely
amusing.   As an example of the former, there is a merciless dissection of those new scientific research foundations
á la Herman Kahn which seem to be sprouting up everywhere
under the protective shadow of the hydrogen bomb: "Drive
into the countryside; you will see them.   Under widespread-
ing ancient oaks in Platonic seminar circle, Discussion
Leader summing up in the birdless silence, 'Then I take it
we are all agreed: we are prepared to lose 20,000,000 on
the first day."   So much for Mr. Kahn!

        In a single paragraph TV commercials for soap are
combined with learned allusions to <u>Moby Dick</u>.   And yet
somehow it all makes sense.   I should like to quote this
paragraph in full because it brilliantly reveals the author's
unconventional method: "Yes, nowadays we package even
that.   The music of time; just heat and serve.   They'll
learn.   Or maybe not.   Perhaps they'll go on to the very
end, tinkering, tampering, packaging and, at the end of the
precipice itself, continue their surveys.   Madame, before
you leap, please tell us, which pile of laundry is whiter?
-- Why, this one, of course. -- Then over the edge, voom,
whiter than white, falling softer and sudsier than her favorite detergent, from her bowels unwinding sheets and
pillow-cases, absolute miracles of whiteness; dying, uttering her final words: 'It's Spic 'n Span for me, for clothes
and dishes too.   Was Duz good to me?   Was Duz ever!'
Ah once, once we looked white, white terror straight in its
razored half-moon mouth; in the longboats, harpoon in hand,
faced its whiteness; once; committed ourselves to the living
element where it has its living and its breath, before money
was ever invented.   Not now.   Not any more.   Not at all."

        If you haven't already guessed, <u>Looking for the Gen-
eral</u> is an impassioned plea for reason in a world poised
on the edge of nuclear annihilation.   It is a fierce, angry,
bitter, outspoken book that cries out against "the criminal

act, the frightful crime, man's inhuman intercession, the
poisoning of the central well, the murder of the world."

Bill Brown is a physicist working on the problem of
"the thermal thicket" at a huge research laboratory under
contract to the Air Force.   The head of the lab, a retired
general who is dying of cancer, disappears with his aide,
Greystone.   Convinced that there are beings in outer space
who disapprove of our nuclear buildup on earth, they have
gone to join them.   Suspecting as much, Bill quits his job
at the lab and strikes out after the General in his old Ply-
mouth, an odyssey that takes him from one zany adventure
to another across the heart of America to Twelvepalms
Arizona.   It is here in the desert that the final bizarre
rendezvous takes place featuring the General, Ironsides (a
retired admiral), Greystone, Billy and a tribe of painted
Indians.

Is Warren Miller a novelist of the first rank or a
superior kind of pop artist, a Jasper Johns or Roy Lich-
tenstein of the written word?   On the basis of this one book
(alas, I have not yet read <u>The Cool World</u>, <u>Flush Times</u>
or <u>The Sleep of Reason</u>) it would be presumptuous of this
reviewer to say.   But of one thing there can be no doubt:
he certainly gives one pause to think.

QUICK BEFORE IT MELTS

By Philip Benjamin (Random House, 1964).

      Quick Before It Melts is blatantly advertised on the
front cover as "a very funny novel by Philip Benjamin."
Such a legend is enough to make the most tenderminded
critic suddenly become suspicious.   Is the book really as
funny as all that?   I am afraid I cannot agree with either
the publisher or some of my fellow reviewers who, to
judge from their ecstatic comments, have been in stiches
ever since the darn thing came out.

      Furthermore it isn't even a novel.   This reviewer
is an avid reader of novels and knows when a novel is a
novel and when it is a travel book disguised as a novel.
Philip Benjamin has made two trips to the Antarctic as a
reporter for the New York Times.   And to dispel any further doubts as to his qualifications as a bona fide visitor to
the South Pole, they have taken the precaution of photo-
graphing the intrepid author in beard and fur-lined parka
on a leisurely stroll in the neighborhood of eighty-six degrees south latitude.

      But just to be obliging let's pretend that this is a
kind of novel.   Oliver Wendell Holmes Cannon, a writer
for Sage, The Magazine That Thinks For You, is sent to
the Antarctic during the International Geophysical Year to
cover Operation Deep Freeze.   En route he makes friends
with Peter Santelli, a happy-go-lucky photographer,
whose preoccupation with women doesn't interfere with his
work more than ninety percent of the time.   Others who
figure prominently in the zany goings-on are a Russian
weather observer, Mikhail Drozhensky, a beautiful air line
stewardess of Maori descent, Tiare Marshall, a wacky
Congressman, Waldo Wilkes, and a penguin named Milton
Fox.

      The author devises a perfunctory plot to satisfy the
requirements of fiction.   Since it is a farce he is spared
the necessity of taking pains with it.   Any old plot will do,
the sillier the better.   Suffice it to say that Oliver manages
to discover gold, fall in a crevasse, steal the South Pole
and take the rectal temperature of a seal in the wild state.

Santelli's main achievement is to succeed in making love to a woman at eighty degrees south latitude. Among their more mundane pursuits are dancing in the enlisted men's recreation hut, participating in a beard-growing contest and talking to relatives in the States via shortwave radio.

The humor is of the coarse masculine variety which automatically produces the loud guffaw. It is rampant with parodies, puns and bad poetry. Some of it is even funny.

The question remains. If truth is stranger than fiction (and I am sure it is), why go all the way to the South Pole to find the inspiration for writing a farcical novel? Well, the answer is probably simple. Philip Benjamin did it because he wanted to. He enjoyed doing it even if some of us did not. Could there be a better reason?

ONE FAT ENGLISHMAN

By Kingsley Amis (Harcourt, Brace and World, 1964).

Kingsley Amis is the English writer whose second novel, Lucky Jim, became almost the prototype for a certain kind of outrageously farcical novel. In it the protagonist is the model par excellence of the anti-hero. While the heroes and heroines of American fiction were still inclined to be larger than life, Lucky Jim surreptitiously removed his thumb from the crumbling dike of tradition and irreverently placed it in the vicinity of his nose. It was quite a spectacle.

Now ten years later, whatever happened to Lucky Jim? Well briefly, he reappeared as the small-town librarian of That Uncertain Feeling, as the provincial author abroad of I Like It Here and now as the fat, middle--aged English publisher on a visit to the U. S. of One Fat Englishman.

How Lucky Jim has changed! How Kingsley Amis has changed! How we all have changed!

Not only is this latest version of Lucky Jim fat and middle-aged, he is just plain awful to boot. He is a walking, living, breathing advertisement for the seven deadly sins with special proficiency in (1) gluttony, (2) sloth and (3) lust. He is also a drunkard, thief and snob who incidentally uses snuff, despises Americans and insults everyone in sight.

His name is Roger Micheldene and he spends several weeks shuttling back and forth between Budweiser College in Pennsylvania and New York City, usually in pursuit of women. Several others whom he comes into contact with are a visiting philology professor and his wife, their "terrifyingly bright" seven-year-old son, an undergraduate author of an avant-garde novel and a literary agent and his nymphomaniacal wife.

Granted that the original Lucky Jim wasn't exactly a model of good behavior, he did at least have youth, charm and a general insouciance on his side. Roger Micheldene

has no such attributes.   How to make this altogether repug-
nant character merit our interest and attention?   This is
the problem the author had to solve and, as much as I admire the attempt, I do not think he has quite succeeded.
Kingsley Amis' dilemma is reflected in the flat, uninspiring
choice of title, <u>One Fat Englishman</u>.   Can this really be the
name of a book?

     One also senses beneath the surface a confusion of
purpose.   It is neither fish nor fowl.   One suspects that the
author started out to write a funny novel but got bogged
down in a general misanthropic view of the world.   (Does
Kingsley Amis despise the opposite sex as much as this
book would seem to indicate?)   It is equally possible that he
started out to write a mordantly serious novel but couldn't
help indulging a somewhat incongruous flair for comedy.
Either way it amounts to the same thing.

     In any case, Lucky Jim has grown fat, middle-aged
and something of a scold in the manner of Evelyn Waugh
(this book bears a remarkable resemblance to <u>The Ordeal</u>
<u>of Gilbert Pinfoil</u>).   In a sense this is our common fate.
As much as we would like to, that is why we cannot completely ignore this fat, contemptible Englishman.

THE WAPSHOT SCANDAL

By John Cheever (Harper and Row, 1964).

Probably the most overrated novel this reviewer
read last year was The Group by Mary McCarthy.   So far
this year that dubious honor would have to be accorded to
The Wapshot Scandal by John Cheever.   Frankly, The
Wapshot Scandal is a scandal in more ways than one.

It is perhaps no coincidence that both The Group and
The Wapshot Scandal are extremely pretentious works that
attempt to document the fall from grace of an entire generation.   Mary McCarthy's failure is a rather complicated one,
but in John Cheever's case it is simply that he doesn't
possess the intellectual and artistic resources to breathe
life into his ambitious scheme.   Actually he is a short
story writer who reached his zenith some years ago writing
slight, sardonic stories for the New Yorker.   Although he
somehow managed to win the National Book Award for his
first novel, The Wapshot Chronicle (1957), he never really
had any place to go after writing "The Enormous Radio"
and similar stories.

The Wapshot Scandal follows the fortunes of Moses
and Coverly Wapshot, the well-bred heirs of a distinguished
old New England family whom we met in the earlier book,
into the second half of the twentieth century.   Coverly is
in the public relations department of a huge missile site
out west.   Moses has thrown up his job as a banking apprentice to work for Leopold and Company, a shady broker-
age house.   Coverly has married Betsey Marcus, a counter
girl in a Forty-Second Street milk bar.   Moses has married Melissa Scaddon.   They live in the tree-lined suburb
of Proxmire Manor.

It is already possible to discern here those intimations of class prejudice and provincial snobbery ("John
Cheever was born on the south shore of Boston in 1912,
the son of a Massachusetts Yankee and an English em-
igrant...") which become the philosophical rock on which
this saga of the Wapshots is built.   Twentieth century America must be a vulgar place indeed if it can pluck the Wapshots out of their snug little nest at St. Botolphs and put

them rudely down at a missile site out west or some ugly
split-level in the suburbs.

Certainly there is a case to be made for the vulgar-
ization of American life, but Mr. Cheever stacks the deck
in such an obvious way that it is almost impossible to take
him seriously.   The scenes which depict a brilliant atomic
scientist's interrogation before a Congressional investiga-
ting committee ("Oh, please, please don't destroy the
earth...") and Melissa Wapshot's affair with a callow youth
who works in a grocery store and is always hungry, break
down into sheer maudlin inanity.

And it is all put down in such a tired, finicky style
(who else would write, "It was a harsh and an ugly light
...") that it almost lulls one to sleep.

It's a scandal.

LINDMANN

By Frederic Raphael (Holt, Rinehart and Winston, 1964).

According to <u>Webster's Third New International Dictionary</u> the term 'tour de force' has two different meanings: (1) a feat of strength, skill, or artistic merit, and (2) a merely adroit or ingenious accomplishment or production. Frederic Raphael's <u>Lindmann</u> is a tour de force according to the first meaning of the term.

Perhaps the quality that most distinguishes a literary tour de force is passion.   The writer must have something to say and want to say it so badly that he literally makes us sit up and take notice.   The words must spill out and not be squeezed out.   There must be inspiration behind them.   The language must determine the form and not the other way around.   There must be an inevitability and rightness about the narrative that is absolutely beyond question.

These thoughts are prompted not only by <u>Lindmann,</u> but also by John Cheever's <u>The Wapshot Scandal</u>.   Despite all the publicity (and did you know that Mr. Cheever is now featured on the cover of <u>Time</u>?), <u>The Wapshot Scandal</u> is a very bad novel.   It is neither a good bad novel nor a bad good novel, but simply a bad bad novel.   It is bad precisely because it lacks passion, inevitability, force, rightness -- all the qualities, in short, that <u>Lindmann</u> possesses to such an extraordinary degree.   It is an altogether contrived piece of work.   It is a tour de force all right, but according to <u>Webster's</u> second definition rather than the first.

So now having gotten this off my chest, who is Lindmann?   In 1942 the S. S. Broda, packed with Jewish refugees fleeing from Hitler's concentration camps and bound for Palestine, sank off the Turkish coast.   Of the 683 people abroad only two survived.   One of the survivors bears the name of Jacob Lindmann.

Twenty years have passed and Jacob Lindmann is living in a ramshackle boarding house in London.   Although he lives among the ordinary denizens of a teeming metropolis -- artists, teachers, club members, husbands and

wives -- the true companions of his life are the 681 refugees
who went down with the Broda.   Twenty years after the
event he is still methodically seeking answers to the age-old
question of human guilt and responsibility.   "You are a
killjoy, Lindmann," old Gerstenberg says.   "We must live.
That is the lesson of the dead, that is all they can teach
us."   "You make all suffering ridiculous," Lindmann replies.   "You are an insult to the dead."

The sinking of the S. S. Broda is an actual occurrence which Frederic Raphael has used as the basis for
this striking novel.   No one can deny that the S. S. Broda,
packed with humanity, sank off the Turkish coast with great
loss of life.   No one can deny that the Broda was unseawor-
thy.   No one can deny that British and Turkish officialdom
were partly responsible for the disaster because they refused to accept any responsibility.   (It is perhaps ironic
that one can only be held responsible if one has shunned
responsibility.)

Frederic Raphael has not forgotten what happened to
the S. S. Broda.   Neither has Jacob Lindmann.   And as
long as one person remembers there is hope for the rest
of us.

PILGRIM AT SEA

By Par Lagerkvist (Random House, 1964).

In Frederick Raphael's powerful novel, Lindmann,
just reviewed in these pages, a refugee ship bound for
Palestine sinks off the Turkish coast with great loss of
life. Coincidentally, Par Lagerkvist's Pilgrim at Sea is
also about a journey to the Holy Land in which the passengers are destined never to reach their goal.

Pilgrim at Sea completes the tetrology begun in Barab-
bas (1951) and continued in The Death of Ahasuerus (1962).
The theme of the tetrology (as in practically everything else
the great Swedish playwright, novelist and poet wrote) is
the search for God. Like the ill-fated passengers on the
S. S. Broda in Frederick Raphael's novel, we set out on a
journey to the Holy Land, but never arrive. We are pil-
grims at sea.

As readers of The Death of Ahasuerus will remember,
Tobias, the unbeliever, is about to embark on a pilgrimage
to Jerusalem in behalf of an unknown woman whom he found
dead with the stigmata or marks of the Crucifixion. Tobias
has missed the regular pilgrim ship and boards a miser-
able old hulk of a vessel with a crew of cutthroats and
thieves under the command of a pirate captain. Tobias
immediately strikes up an acquaintance with a defrocked
priest named Giovanni.

Although they set sail in a raging gale, Tobias is at
peace. "One learns a great deal from the sea," Giovanni
tells him. "... You may walk through country after country,
through lands and through huge cities you've never seen before, and over the whole wide earth, and never learn as
much as you will from the sea. The sea knows more than
anything else on earth if you can get it to teach you. It
knows all the ancient secrets, because it's so old itself
-- older than all things. It knows your own secrets too,
make no mistake. If you give yourself to it entirely and
let it take charge -- not jib or dig your toes in about trifles,
not expect it to hear your petty murmurings while it is
speaking, while it's hurling itself over the ship -- then it
can bring peace to your soul. If you have one. "

Admittedly this is a beautiful passage, though it is beautiful in a rather special way. Par Lagerkvist is really a kind of mystic who is concerned not so much with telling a story as with earnestly pursuing certain moral and spiritual insights. It is true that there is a "story within a story" in <u>Pilgrim at Sea</u>, for at least half of the brief narrative is taken up with Giovanni's story of how he came to be excommunicated from the Church. It is a story of adultery between confessor and penitent who commit a mortal sin against God and man. But somehow this "story within a story" is only one more didactic sermon adumbrating Par Lagerkvist's eternal quest to come to terms with "the inscrutable grace of God."

It is paradoxical in a way that parables, even when expressed with the classic rigor and simplicity of a Par Lagerkvist, are inclined to be somewhat pretentious and murky (William Golding, please note). Nonetheless there are passages of great beauty in this book and a grappling with the mystery of existence which compels our admiration and respect.

THE NIGHT IN LISBON

By Erich Maria Remarque (Harcourt, Brace and World,
                    1964).

    The two books that made the greatest impression on
this reviewer during his adolescence were The Constant
Nymph by Margaret Kennedy and Three Comrades by the
famous author of All Quiet on the Western Front, Erich
Maria Remarque. Now a quarter of a century later, I have
just read Remarque's latest novel, The Night In Lisbon,
translated by Ralph Manheim.   The innocent youth who
thrilled to the roar of engines and shared the bold fraternity
of the race track with the three comrades, is no more.
The romantic egoist who was so deeply moved at the death
of the heroine (if I remember correctly her name was Margaret and she developed a high fever and died of pneumonia),
is no more. This writer has changed, the world has changed, perhaps even the author of The Constant Nymph has
changed.   Only Erich Maria Remarque has not changed and
continues to write the same book over and over again as
though nothing has happened for twenty-five years.

    Please don't misunderstand me.   The author of The
Night in Lisbon is a real professional who knows how to tell
a story. We Americans are proud of professionals and re-
ward them well.   If this novel isn't a Book-of-the-Month
Club selection, it will be condensed in the Reader's Digest.
If it isn't condensed in the Reader's Digest, it will be sold
to the movies for five million dollars.   The Night in Lisbon is about refugees who dream of leaving the Old World
behind and entering the golden portals of the New World.
Erich Maria Remarque is one of the most fortunate refugees
who ever passed through the golden door.

    And so The Night in Lisbon is the Three Comrades
all over again, a romantic fairy tale, told against a background of suffering and misery that was Europe in the
1930's and 40's.   There is something faintly indecent about
it.   It almost seems as if the suffering and misery, that
terrible backdrop of history, were being used as a colorful
prop to enable the author to write yet another best-seller.
Perhaps this is too uncharitable a view.   I hope so.

In his novel Remarque uses one of the oldest and simplest narrative devices to tell his story. The scene is Lisbon, Portugal, in 1942. A ship about to sail for America lies at anchor in the Tagus. A refugee and his wife desperately wish to board the ship, but they are three hundred dollars short of the fare and have no American visas. An angel in the form of a refugee named Josef Schwarz appears out of nowhere and offers the younger man money and two American Visas for which he no longer has any use. All he asks in return is the opportunity to tell his story.

It is a love story about a man who has escaped from Nazi Germany only to return after an absence of five years to see his wife. Their love blazes anew and together they escape to France. When France falls to the Nazis, they are not even safe there. Europe is in chains, people are dying by the thousands, but they find moments of happiness together as the world lies in ruins about their feet. "One day we'll be able to forget all this," Josef whispers reassuringly. Alas, he does not know that she is dying of an incurable disease. Although they manage to escape to Lisbon, she dies just as they are about to embark for America.

The one concession to time that the author makes in this book is that his heroine doesn't develop a high fever and die of pneumonia. However, Josef Schwarz, romantic to the bitter end, goes off to join the French Foreign Legion.

C'est la guerre!

THE BELLS OF BICETRE

By Georges Simenon (Harcourt, Brace and World, 1964).

If Georges Simenon, the famous creator of Inspector Maigret, has always been more than a writer of detective stories, he has probably never been as good a novelist as his most fervent admirers have claimed. Three Beds in Manhattan, published last year (and reviewed in this book), is not a good measure of his talent. It is generally agreed that it is a poor novel. And besides being inferior Simenon, it is old Simenon, as it was first published in France in 1946 under the title Trois Chambres à Manhattan.

The Bells of Bicêtre, translated by Jean Stewart, is Simenon at his most recent and at his best. The big question is how good is Simenon's best?

The novel is about a man who suffers a stroke and, while convalescing, is able to reevaluate his life with extraordinary detachment. As the novel begins, Rene Maugras, the influential editor of a large Paris newspaper, is lying in a private room in the Bicêtre Hospital where he has just emerged from a coma. He has crossed an invisible barrier and now finds himself in the strange world of the hemiplegic. The mysterious thing is that he is now able to see himself from the outside, just as others might see him.

He is not exactly pleased with what he sees. Using the flashback technique with his usual skill, Simenon reconstructs Rene Maugras' life. It seems he is not a model character. Although he has risen to the top of his profession, he lacks talent and is not even capable of writing a good article. He is a man without principles or convictions who always does the politic thing. His private life is a complete failure. He has a thirty-one-year-old daughter by his first marriage whose existence he scarcely acknowledges. His second wife, a pathetic alcoholic, desperately needs help, but he regards her with ill-concealed loathing and contempt.

Furthermore, he is a man of humble origins who has cut himself off from his own roots. This is the worst thing that can happen to a man, Simenon seems to be saying.

Ironically, Bicêtre is primarily an institution for the old
and indigent, and Rene Maugras derives solace from simply
watching the old men sitting quietly on their benches in the
courtyard, their eyes lost to the immensity of nothingness.
Instinctively he feels that he belongs among these people.
He marvels at their apparent will to live. He is reminded
of his own father, now in his eighties, who goes on living,
though he would be hard put to say for what. "Was it
possible that all this signified nothing?" he wonders.

Gradually Rene Maugras regains his health. The
invisible barrier of his illness is rapidly dissolving. He
no longer dreams guiltily of the past. He is impatient to
leave the hospital and resume his important duties as the
editor of the largest newspaper in Paris.

According to the dust jacket, Rene is no longer the
man he was before the stroke and has learned compassion.
I think this interpretation is open to question and perhaps
misses the irony implicit in the last couple of pages.
Whether he has learned compassion or not, however, it is
difficult to take him very seriously. For all his deep introspection, he thinks primarily in terms of clichés. It is
a cliché to say that man has lost contact with the natural
world. The point is what is he supposed to do about it?
Simenon is an extremely gifted observer, a kind of poet of
the lonely and the disaffiliated, but he is not a very profound thinker. He can imbue a garbage can on a city
street at four a. m. with all the romance of the ages, but
he cannot depict character in depth or elucidate man's
plight with boldness and originality.

THE NATURE OF WITCHES

By Joan Sanders (Houghton Mifflin, 1964).

Joan Sanders, whose The Marquis, an historical novel set in the France of Louis XIV, recently drew praise in the New Yorker and the New York Times Book Review, has now written a conventional novel, a love story, set in the Sweden of today. The Nature of Witches is a unique book in this reviewer's experience. Has there ever been a novel which exhibited so many good qualities and yet failed so dismally, even ludicrously?

Gil Barham, a young American scientist, is doing research at the university in Uppsala on a fellowship. At the last moment his wife Lynne refused to go with him and announced her intention of obtaining a divorce. Gil is grief-stricken at this sudden rejection. However, he bravely attempts to lose himself in his work. To further assuage his grief, he drifts into a love affair with the wife of an elderly professor. Maj Tryselius is a placid Nordic "snow queen" type, completely different from gay, impulsive Lynne with whom he cannot help comparing her. Gil has also made the acquaintance of a young American girl, Polly. Polly is in love with Gil, but knows that she will never have a chance in his affections until he breaks the spell cast by the omnipresent Lynne. She fears that Lynne, as befits the nature of witches, will never let him go.

As may be gathered from this brief synopsis, the plot is pure drivel. The extraordinary thing is that the author of this banal story is the possessor of a beautiful prose style. And the way she employs this poetic style to evoke a particular place, whether it be San Francisco or Uppsala, is perhaps her chief virtue as a writer. This is how she describes (or rather how Gil Barham remembers) San Francisco: "A very murky interlude of blues came on, and for a minute I was in San Francisco on a November night, the way it used to be, long ago before the Beats came or any of the urban renovators ... this music was all about streets in North Beach with a cold wet fog moving off the Bay, and opening doors letting out gusts of cheesy pizza aroma, the diminishing fuzz of lights up hills almost ladder-steep; pseudo-aesthetes in sandals browsing

through books in front of the City Lights Bookstore; Chinese
businessmen clean as ivory ... Bright windows full of
ethnic bead and copper earrings; dim windows with BEER
lettered in tarnished paint like stained glass ... and down
the street where the Italian men play bocci ball, a staccato
noise of sport and acclaim. " Has San Francisco ever been
more bewitchingly described?

Alas, the novelist's stock in trade is characterization
and the characters in this novel -- especially Gil -- are
ciphers.   They perform like sleepwalkers, while all around
them the landscape shimmers with life.   These dull characters are wasted in Uppsala and San Francisco.   And as
if realizing this, the author finally has Gil accept a teaching position in Ohio.   Having escaped the spell cast by the
omnipresent witch, Polly and Gil will set up housekeeping
there.   Polly (Polly!) envisions an old house with a big
front porch and walnut trees in the yard.   There will be
a grape arbor out back.   Maybe a rose arbor too, for
sewing doll clothes in.

Ohio is where Gil and Polly have been heading all
their lives.   It is where the landscape is finally reduced
to the banal level of Pollyanna.

THE SPIRE

By William Golding (Harcourt, Brace and World, 1964).

The Spire is the new novel by the celebrated author
of Lord of the Flies, William Golding.

Like the earlier book, The Spire is full of portentous
symbolism.   The dean of a church in the Middle Ages is
obsessed with the idea of building a spire which will soar
four hundred feet above the Cathedral Church of the Virgin
Mary.   This ambitious work, which soon becomes known
as Jocelin's Folly, has been revealed to him in a vision.

The Master Builder, Roger Mason, a practical,
down-to-earth man who stands sturdily in leather hose,
brown tunic and blue hood, tells Jocelin that the spire is
an impossibility in stone.   To build such a spire there must
be a strong foundation, but in fact there is only mud.   Dean
Jocelin tells the Master Builder that he lacks faith.   "You
and I were chosen to do this thing together," he says.   "It's
a great glory... The thing can be built and will be built in
the very teeth of satan.   You'll build it because nobody else
can.   They laugh at me, I think; and they'll probably laugh
at you.   Let them laugh.   It's for them, and their children.
But only you and I, my son, my friend, when we've done
tormenting ourselves and each other, will know what stones
and beams and lead and mortar went into it. "

Octagon by octagon, pinnacle by pinnacle, the spire
soars skyward, but it does not bring peace to men's souls.
Jocelin sacrifices everything to the dream.   He neglects his
duties as spiritual shepherd for the "impossibility of the
spire. "   As a result, the spire casts its lengthening shadow
upon a countryside increasingly dominated by human discord,
lechery and greed.   "Imagine it," Jocelin confesses bitterly
at the end, "I thought I was doing a good work; and all I
was doing was bringing ruin and breeding hate."

The symbolism speaks for itself; it hardly seems
necessary to belabor the obvious.   The spire is a monument to man's faith as well as to his pride.   It is also a
phallic symbol.   It is also a tribute to the artist himself,

laboriously constructing his work of art. Many readers
(and I must number myself among them) will find this kind
of overt symbolism unpalatable, rather like having a strong
dose of castor oil forced down one's throat. But this much
is certain. William Golding is himself a Master Builder of
unusual skill, and once having entered his building we cannot help but marvel at the stones and beams and lead and
mortar which have gone into it. There is not a stone out
of place. There are no rough edges or unseemly dust.
(There are a few platitudes, however.)

But perhaps this partly explains why the book, despite the brilliance of its construction, seems dull. And
somewhere the author uses the phrase, "a purely human
prerogative." It is precisely this "purely human prerogative" that is so conspicuously absent from William
Golding's fiction. There are no real human beings in The
Spire, only human attributes. There are no individuals,
only vast impersonal armies swept with confused alarms of
struggle and flight.

Moby Dick is a symbolic novel too, but for over a
hundred years it has also been revered simply as a story
of adventure that begins with profound human relevance and
excitement, "Call me Ishmael." William Golding forces
us to climb, octagon by octagon, pinnacle by pinnacle, to
the top of the spire, whether we like it or not. And from
this dizzy height humanity -- mere insects scurrying below -- looks very small indeed.

I WAS DANCING

By Edwin O'Connor (Little, Brown, 1964).

        Edwin O'Connor has said that his strength as a
writer lies not in any autobiographical element in his work,
but in his ability to create interesting characters. Apparently he is not alone in this belief, for his novels consist-
ently rate high on the best-seller list.   They have also been
well received by the critics.   The Last Hurrah, published
in 1956, won the Atlantic Prize and in 1961 his third novel,
The Edge of Sadness, received the Pulitzer Prize for fiction.

        Despite these impressive accomplishments, this re-
viewer would suggest that Edwin O'Connor falls short of being a novelist of the first rank precisely because his characters are not interesting enough.   This is particularly true
of his latest novel, I Was Dancing.

        Let's face it.   I Was Dancing is a very slight book
and Mr. O'Connor desperately needed an interesting character or two to sustain interest and create something more
than the tedious monologue it unfortunately is.   So what do
we have? A garrulous old ex-vaudevillian (or more precisely, vaudevillain), full of blarney and not much else,
known as Waltzing Daniel Considine, his colorless son, Tom,
a dismal chorus made up of several of Daniel's old cronies
whose sole function is to advance the plot and keep Daniel
(and the author) from talking to the four walls.

        But the success of this slight book utterly depends on
Waltzing Daniel Considine being an interesting, sympathetic
character and he is not.   He is a bore.   What Daniel evidently did not take into consideration when he turned up
after an absence of twenty years (and he had seldom been
home before that) was that he was a virtual stranger to his
son.   It is difficult to become emotionally involved in the
affairs of a complete stranger, even if the stranger is one's
own father.

        Edwin O'Connor has made the same miscalculation
that old Waltzing Daniel made.   The ex-vaudevillian is as
much a stranger to us as he is to his son.   We know that

we should be moved by his shenanigans, but we are not.   He
has been away too long.   It is almost impossible to sympa-
thize with him.   He remains a vain, selfish, posturing old
man for whom we feel nothing -- well almost nothing --
but contempt.

Waltzing Dan has come home to his son after an
absence of twenty years.   What started out as a brief visit
has now turned into a prolonged stay of over a year.   It
has become apparent that the self-centered, determined old
man intends to live out his life with his son and daughter-
in-law, Ellen.   But the "continuing, cumulative, ever-present
fact of Daniel" is more than Ellen can bear.   "It's just
not my house any more," she sobs.   "It just isn't.... every
day, day after day... he's everywhere... he's got that soft
walk, I can't even hear him coming... that awful old man.
I'm sorry, I know he's your father and all that, but that's
what he is... and all those friends I don't know and don't
ever want to know... in my house... he's just eating us
up.... "

The only solution seems to be to move Daniel to a
nearby rest home where he will be well cared for called
St. Vincent's Smiling Valley for Senior Citizens.   I Was
Dancing is a contest of wills between Daniel Considine and
his son and daughter-in-law.   As Tom is well aware, it is
not a fair contest, since he holds the upper hand.   As the
novel comes to an end, the old man realizes that he has
come to the end of his resources and has no more tricks
left to play.   To his eternal credit, he goes out dancing.

THE GRANDFATHERS

By Conrad Richter (Knopf, 1964).

        Conrad Richter's The Grandfathers is very reminis-
cent of William Faulkner's comic novel of several years
ago, The Reivers. Both novels deal with rural America.
They are written by extremely gifted writers (perhaps the
most gifted we have) who are or were intimately connected
with the people and milieu about which they write. Faulkner
staked out a whole mythical county in Mississippi to express
his love and loathing, the fruit of his tortured imagination.
Conrad Richter, a milder and possibly subtler man, has
chosen as the locale of his latest novel a mountain valley
community in western Maryland. The result is a book that
may well become the classic novel of Appalachia. The
Grandfathers, written with seemingly inexhaustible reserves
of love, humor and understanding, is Conrad Richter's
answer to the shrill libels of Mr. Erskine Caldwell and
his demented hillbillies.

        One important difference between Conrad Richter and
Erskine Caldwell is that the former takes his rural folk
seriously and does not caricature them. He laughs with
them (The Grandfathers is a very funny book), but never at
them. There is nothing ambivalent about his feelings toward
them. He is on their side from beginning to end and doesn't
find it necessary to apologize for it.

        He is certainly on Chariter Murdoch's side. Sixteen
years of age, Chariter is the eldest of a brood of father-
less children growing up in the shadow of Kettle Mountain.
Apparently it isn't at all unusual not to know who your father
is in the mountains of western Maryland. It is something
you soon learn to accept. Chariter wasn't born yesterday.
It didn't take her mam to tell her that life wasn't all it
was cracked up to be. No, she reckoned, that's the way
life ran and that's the way it would stay.

        Still a body couldn't blame her for being just a mite
curious to know who her real pappy is. If adolescence in
Suburbia, U.S.A., means boy friends, rock 'n' roll and
curling up with a pastel blue princess telephone, on Kettle
Mountain it means searching for one's father. Sometimes

the best clues (mothers are apt to be close-mouthed and uncooperative) are furnished by the old folks.   In The Grandfathers there is one real grandfather, a crotchety old man who carries a map of Washington County in coffee stains on his white shirt front named Hercules (Culy) Murdoch, and three potential grandfathers, a farmer, a blacksmith, and a local judge.   When Chariter Murdoch offers to keep house for Squire Goddem after the passing of Miss Belle, she appears to be getting very close to the secret of her paternity.

But the future is more important than the past, especially for the young and the young-in-heart.   Chariter may not know who her father is, but she has a pretty good idea who her husband is going to be.   It is none other than Fulliam Jones, an up-and-coming undertaker's apprentice from Earleville.   When he shows up for the wedding in a brand new hearse to advertise his business in the valley, it looks as if their future were secure.

"You're good for the soul, Charity," Miss Belle remarks at one point in this superb novel.   Yes -- and so is Conrad Richter!

THE KEEPERS OF THE HOUSE

By Shirley Ann Grau (Knopf, 1964).

        With the death of William Faulkner, it may well be
that the foremost living southern writer is New Orleans-
born Shirley Ann Grau, author of The Black Prince, a
collection of short stories, and two novels, The Hard Blue
Sky and The House on Coliseum Street.

        The Keepers of the House is probably her most am-
bitious novel to date.   The author has been called a "master of the Soft-Focus School of fiction," but if this is supposed to mean that her prose is not sharp-edged, hard and
masculine there is little evidence of it in this particular
novel.   Shirley Ann Grau seems much closer in style and
temperament to Faulkner than to Eudora Welty.   Her description of William Howland's excursion into Honey Island
Swamp is as vivid a piece of writing as Faulkner's famous
short story, "The Bear." Obviously Miss Grau's prose style
wasn't formed at Sweet Briar or Goucher.   It was formed
in the sultry, brooding streets of nameless southern towns,
the scene of bloodshed and violence for more than a hundred years.

        The keepers of the house are the Howlands, the
original settlers of the Providence Valley, the rich cotton
land near the Gulf Coast.   Although there has been a William Howland in each generation since William Marshall Howland straggled north from New Orleans in 1815 with Andrew
Jackson's army, this is the story of the William Howland
who married Lorena Hale Adams prior to the First World
War, and of his granddaughter, Abigail, and his housekeeper and mistress, Margaret Carmichael.   In essence it
is the story of one piece of blood-stained earth -- the
American South -- fought over by Indians and outlaws, Civil
War raiders and modern raiders who come in cars instead
of on horses to raze barns and churches and kill dumb
animals and, sometimes, innocent children.

        William Howland's wife, Lorena, dies not long after
their marriage and for fifteen or more years he remains
a widower.   He sees his daughter through college and gives

her away in marriage.   Then he puts his blanket in the
bow of his skiff and disappears into the great Honey Island
Swamp in search of a contraband still.   Several days later
he emerges from the swamp near New Church and comes
across a tall young woman kneeling by the side of a creek,
washing clothes.   That is the way it began.   That is how
he found Margaret Carmichael, washing clothes by a creek
that didn't have a name.

Housekeeper and mistress, she lives with him for
the next thirty years, all the rest of his life.   She lives
with him and bears his children.   They do not take his
name, however, but Margaret's.   They are Carmichaels,
not Howlands.   And one by one they are sent away to the
anonymous North, never to return.

"Living with him," William Howland's only living
white granddaughter recalls, "she lived with us all, all
the Howlands, and her life got mixed up with ours.   Her
face was black and ours was white, but we were together
anyhow.   Her life and his.   And ours."   Years later
Abigail marries a segregationist politician and the Howland
past is exposed.

That is the way it has always been.   This one piece
of ground now, fought over, blood-spilled, outlaws and
Civil War raiders, and before all of them, the Indians.
And modern raiders now, who come in cars instead of on
horses ...

BELMARCH

By Christopher Davis (Viking Press, 1964).

With his fourth novel Christopher Davis turns from the contemporary scene of <u>Lost Summer</u> (1958) and <u>First Family</u> (1961) to write what he calls <u>A Legend of the First Crusade.</u> This reviewer could not help comparing <u>Belmarch</u> with William Golding's recent <u>The Spire</u>, also set in the Middle Ages. They are both allegories, but whereas Golding's seemed somewhat contrived and superficial, Christopher Davis' reverberates and echoes in the mind long after the novel has been read.

The focal point of the novel is the massacre of some seven hundred Jews in the palace of the Archbishop of Mainz in 1096 by the Crusaders while on their way to the Holy Land. Belmarch, a simple foot-soldier in the army of William Carpenter and the fanatical Count Emico, has taken part in the slaughter of defenseless women and children. Overcome by guilt, he wanders off from the scene of the massacre, intending to kill himself. He cannot recall clearly his role in the killings and even wonders if it has all been a terrible nightmare from which he has just awakened.

Annas, a Jew who has somehow survived the massacre, overtakes Belmarch and alternately threatens the soldier's life and protects him from taking his own life. For a week Belmarch wanders in a daze across the lunatic landscape of the times (so vivid is the author's writing that one is reminded of an Ingmar Bergman movie), sometimes following Annas and sometimes being followed. Actually he is being led on a circuitous route that leads back to Mainz where he will relive the bloody carnage at the Archbishop's palace in all its sickening horror and despair.

At the outset of this review I said that the author of <u>Belmarch</u> had turned away from the contemporary scene so ably depicted in his previous novels. This is not exactly the case, since there can be no doubt that Christopher Davis is deliberately drawing a parallel between the massacre of the Jews of Mainz in 1096 and the massacre of the

Jews by the Nazis of recent infamous memory.

"Things are the same, yet different," the author
writes. "Recollection starts and stops and in the end is
imperfect." Do we choose our role or does our role
choose us? Does history merely repeat itself or does it
repeat itself with a difference? Is it impossible to forgive
our enemies, no matter what unspeakable crimes they may
have committed against us? ("Don't you see that that's
the point -- to master the thing?" Annas says to Belmarch.
"I've mastered this entirely, so don't you think about it.
All right? The part of my mind in which I'd think about
my children is closed up. It's the left side.... They're in
there. I have them locked up in there. I've mastered the
thing you see.")

These are some of the philosophical questions that
Christopher Davis raises in this absorbing legend of the
First Crusade.

THE SCARPERER

By Brendan Behan (Doubleday, 1964).

On October 19, 1953, the <u>Irish Times</u> announced the publication of the first installment of a serial about Dublin's underworld, <u>The Scarperer</u>, by Emmet Street. It ran for thirty days and nothing further was heard of the author. Nothing, that is, until Rae Jeffs, in a conversation with Brendan Behan in 1962, discovered that Emmet Street was none other than the boisterous Borstal Boy himself. "It is a part of the tragedy," Mr. Jeffs writes in a brief post-script to the book, "that Brendan Behan did not live to see the publication of the book for the first time under its right-ful author's name. He knew, of course, that it was to appear. It is a story which he was particularly fond of and one which he thoroughly enjoyed writing ... I believe it to be one of the best stories he ever wrote; true vintage Behan."

<u>The Scarperer</u> is one of the quaintest, most unusual detective stories this reviewer has ever read. Like the name Emmet Street, it is something of a hoax. Is it really to be taken seriously as a detective story or is it simply a tongue-in-cheek spoof of the genre? The author teases us with this question and never quite gives himself away. If we are inclined to the view that it is all in jest, how are we to account for the extraordinary realism of the characters and setting? And if we are inclined to the view that this is a detective story pure and simple, how are we to account for the aura of conviviality and joy that bathes all the characters -- from the mysterious eminence known as The Scarperer to the ludicrous thug called Lugs -- in the warm Irish whiskey glow of Brendan Behan's tal-ent?

But of course Brendan Behan being Brendan Behan, a Brendan Behan detective story is sure to be distinctive and like no one else's. It would be a mistake not to take it seriously enough.

Three toughs break out of Dublin's Mountjoy Peni-tentiary. They take with them a fellow prisoner called

The Limey.   The Limey is under the impression he has
been taken along out of the kindness of their hearts and the
munificent sum of five thousand francs.   The Scarperer has
other ideas.   He plans to take The Limey for a boat ride
off the coast of France and dump him neatly overboard.
The current will do the rest.   It will wash the body onto
the beach where it will be identified as the notorious Pierre
le Fou or Peter the Mad One.   Pierre will thus escape the
clutches of the law and The Scarperer will be fifty million
francs richer.

        So much for the plot which is the least important
part of the book.   Where Brendan Behan excels is in
characterization and dialogue.   It really doesn't matter who
murders whom, but where else can one find such delightful,
witty (Irish wit observes no class distinctions!), outsize
characters as Tralee Trembles (alias James Guiney), Pig's
Eye O'Donnell, Glimmers Gleeson and Msieu le Tramtrack
who, on advice of counsel, remained in bed for thirty years
to collect damages from a trolley company?

SECOND SKIN

By John Hawkes (New Directions, 1964).

        John Hawkes has achieved an enormous reputation
on the basis of a very few books without making much of
an impression on the general public.   "I think Hawkes is our
most interesting writer," Flannery O'Connor has written.
"He is the only one I know of who isn't doing what is done
every day of the week."   And says Saul Bellow (who isn't
doing what is done every day of the week, either):   "John
Hawkes is an extraordinary writer.   I have always admired
his books.   They should be more widely read."

        Actually John Hawkes has so much talent that we
stand a little in awe of him.   He frightens us.   He frightens
us because he takes common everyday events -- a kids'
snowball fight or a dance in the high school gymnasium --
and invests them with an extraordinary clarity and horror.
Even Shirley Temple does not come out unscathed.   In one
episode she appears as the narrator's daughter, Cassandra,
at the helm of the fishing boat "Peter Poor" in a heavy
sea.   Dressed in a man's yellow oilskins and sou'wester,
she looks like a "child, a smiling child, in a captain's rig.
She had a little face that should have been on a box of
pilot biscuits."   And from what dim mythic past, through
how many late, late movies on television, does our long
lost innocence come back to haunt us in the pages of this
book?

        The narrator and central figure of the novel is a
"heavy baldheaded once-handsome man," a former naval
officer (old Ariel in sneakers) known variously as Papa
Cue Ball and Skipper.   Skipper is, figuratively and sometimes literally, at sea in a destructive world.   "It was a
malevolent unpromising scene," he acknowledges at one
point in his nightmarish, phantasmagoric odyssey.   Second
Skin is made up of such scenes, including a wartime mutiny
in the South Pacific, an abandoned lighthouse off the Maine
coast where Cassandra plummets to her death, and the
sleazy hotel on Second Avenue in New York City where, on
his final shore patrol, Skipper discovers the body of his
murdered son-in-law Fernandez.   And it also includes the
tropical island where Skipper records this "naked history"

of his life.   "From the frozen and crunchy cow paths of the
Atlantic island," he writes, "my mythic rock in a cold
sea -- to this soft pageant through leaf, tendril, sun, wind,
how far I had come."   Fifty-nine years of age in his "old
time out of time," he has somehow survived mutiny, the
death of three members of his immediate family by their
own hand and the murder of his brother-in-law to find a
degree of peace and contentment with Catalina Kate on a
bucolic tropic island.

Although Second Skin is supposed to be a comic novel
and ends on a note of triumph with the birth of a child, the
predominant note is one of loathing and self-disgust.   In this
respect it is like J. D. Salinger's The Catcher in the Rye
which always seemed to this reviewer to be the unfunniest
"funny" novel of recent times.

John Hawkes writes brilliantly, but he will probably
never make much of an impression on the general public.
Like Skipper, he is one of the few "honor-bright-men of
imagination" destined to live out their fantasies of friends,
children and possessive lovers.   Except that in his case he
does not live them out, but puts them down on paper in
sentences that are sometimes almost too true to bear.

TO AN EARLY GRAVE

By Wallace Markfield (Simon and Schuster, 1964).

      This has been called an age of criticism, but it is also the age of the Jewish intellectual.   To be specific, it is the age of the Jewish intellectual as literary critic.   Alfred Kazin, Leslie Fiedler, Norman Podhoretz, the late Robert Warshaw, the list is as lengthy as it is formidable. Most of these critics are native New Yorkers who were practically weaned on the Partisan Review, probably the biggest and most influential little magazine of our time.

      With the emergence of these Jewish writers and intellectuals to such a prominent place in our culture, it was almost inevitable that someone would come along and write the definitive satirical novel about them, a book that would poke malicious fun at them and at the same time affirm their ultimate place of importance in the cultural life of our country.   And who could do this better than just such a Jewish writer and intellectual?   Wallace Markfield, the thirty-seven-year-old author of To an Early Grave, has written fiction, criticism and articles for the Partisan Review, Hudson Review, Commentary, Midstream, New Leader, American Mercury and other magazines, the Reader's Digest not included.

      In a sense To an Early Grave is a kind of off-beat elegy to the memory of Leslie Braverman, the idol of the New York intelligentsia, the Naysayer who could spend two whole days over a single sentence or lecture at a writer's workshop in Utah on Lorna Doone.   It is an ode to Brooklyn and Greenwich Village.   It is an epitaph to a New York boy, an American boy, a boy from our century.   A figure, a talent, an original.

      As the novel begins, Leslie Braverman has gone to an early grave, dead of a heart attack.   The news is passed to his friends and disciples who assemble to mourn his passing and attend his funeral.   There is first of all Morroe Reiff, who knew Leslie Braverman when they lived in the Village but has since moved uptown and become a professional fund raiser.   "I am no big intellect," Morroe admits ruefully.   "I am no bargain.   I watch too much

television.   I read, but I do not retain. . . . I am the servant
of no great end.   I follow the recommendations of the <u>Con-
sumer's Research Bulletin.</u> "   There is Felix Ottensteen,
who writes literary articles for a Yiddish daily.   There is
Barnet Weiner, poet, critic, and contributor to the literary
quarterlies.   And there is Holly Levine, an "avant-garde
Tony Curtis. "   Together they set out on an epic journey
through the wilds of Brooklyn in Holly Levine's volkswagon
("To own a car in Manhattan is like towing a camel across
the Sargasso") in search of the funeral parlor where services are to be held for their late idol and guardian spirit.

It is doubtful if this book could have been written
without the presiding spirit of James Joyce and <u>Ulysses.</u>
Morroe Reiff bears a startling resemblance to Bloom as he
might appear as a resident of Brooklyn in the 1960's.   And
although <u>To an Early Grave</u> is ostensibly a satire on middle-
aged Jewish intellectuals and their pretensions, compassion
for individual human beings shines through these pages like
a light in a dark closet.   For ultimately this is an epic
in which the man of feeling and imagination, who only
dreams of obtaining "satisfaction" and someday moving to
Far Rockaway, is pitted not only against his brutish Ne-
anderthal brother in the big city, but against the city itself,
steel-girded, impersonal, reeling under the weight of sky-
scraper and broiling noonday sun.

THE CHILDREN AT THE GATE

By Edward Lewis Wallant (Harcourt, Brace and World,
1964).

Edward Lewis Wallant is the remarkable writer whose
death in 1962 at the age of thirty-six was a great loss to
American literature.   In the last year of his life he completed The Tenants of Moonbloom, published last year and
reviewed in this book, and The Children at the Gate, an
even more amazing novel.

It is clear now that Wallant was more than just
another gifted novelist; he was something of a mystic.   What
this writer at first was inclined to attribute to a certain
morbidity of temperament -- there is an intense preoccupation with death in this book -- suddenly blazes into a rev-
elatory mystical experience in which a Christ-like figure
impales himself on a spiked wrought-iron fence as an act
of love and atonement.   The parallel with Christ who was
nailed to the cross so that we might live is strikingly depicted.   Edward Lewis Wallant wrote simply, but he had
an extraordinary dramatic sense.   The scene in the under-
ground corridor at the hospital ("The air was close and
dusty.   Overhead, great swollen steam pipes wove around
each other and stretched into the murky recesses ... "),
where Lebedov, the old hospital attendant, confesses to his
monstrous crime, is surely one of the most powerful scenes
in recent literature.   The Children at the Gate abounds in
such scenes.

The central figure in the book is Angelo DeMarco,
an arrogant nineteen-year-old youth who works in his cousin's
drug store in a drab New England city.   Angelo comes
from a poor but devout Catholic family, yet he himself has
lost faith in God and man.   Blessed with a keen intelligence,
he uses it to heap scorn on those who take refuge in what
he considers the myths and lies of religion.   Although mo-
tivated by no great purpose in life (he earns thirty-five
dollars for an eighty-five hour week!), Angelo is satisfied
that at least he sees life as it is.   He refuses to be the
dupe of anyone or anything and is strictly his own man.
Or so he thinks.   When someone asks him if he isn't a

Catholic, Angelo replies sardonically: "Sorry ... I'm just a homo sapiens." This seems to best sum up his attitude.

The DeMarco Pharmacy holds the concession at the nearby Sacred Heart Hospital and Angelo regularly makes the rounds of the wards taking orders for ice cream, magazines, cosmetics, cigarettes, sandwiches and other items. In the course of his duties he makes the acquaintance of a strange new hospital orderly, a tall, gangling, wise-cracking Jew named Sammy Abel Kahan. When Angelo is finished making his rounds, he gets in the habit of meeting the older man in the solarium and listening to his obscene, mocking, outrageous stories. For once Angelo has met someone whom he can't quite figure out, someone whose mocking voice seems to be hurling down some intangible challenge.

Of course Sammy is hurling down a challenge and before long Angelo has changed enough to realize what it is. The nature of the challenge is revealed in Sammy's remarks about old Lebedov, who has been arrested for criminally assaulting a little girl in one of the wards. Sammy thinks the old man should be forgiven and circulates a petition to this effect. "...they got to remember Lebedov," he says passionately in one of his more lucid moments. "He's a human- that's all there should be. There shouldn't be anything but people on this earth."

THE OLD MAN AND ME

By Elaine Dundy (Dutton, 1964).

    With her first novel, The Dud Avocado, published
in 1958, Elaine Dundy established a brilliant, vixenish
reputation as a kind of American Françoise Sagan.   Bright,
brash and brittle (rather like the little-girl-lost photograph
of the author looking wistfully out of one eye on the back
cover of the present book), she seemed to be saying to the
bearded beatniks pub-crawling in Greenwich Village and
Soho: "I'll go you one better."

    Miss Dundy's second novel has now made the scene
and the first thing to be noted is that she hasn't reformed
or in any way slackened her pace.   The novel is called
The Old Man and Me.   This is how it begins (it is well
worth quoting): "There is a sort of coal hole in the heart
of Soho that is open every afternoon: a dark, dank, dead-
ended subterranean tunnel.   It is a drinking club called
the Crypt and the only light to penetrate it is the shaft of
golden sunlight slipping through the doorway from time to
time glancing off someone's nose or hair or glass of gin,
all the more poignant for its sudden revelations, in an
atmosphere almost solid with failure, of pure windswept
nostalgia, of clean airy summer houses, of the beach, of
windy reefs; of the sun radiating through the clouds the instant before the clouds race back over it again--leaving the
day as sad and desperate as before."   Perhaps the worst
that can be said of this novel is that, as good as it is, it
never quite lives up to the brilliant promise of the opening
paragraph.

    Miss Dundy is positively uncanny at creating a sinis-
ter atmosphere, but not particularly ingenious when it
comes to putting a story together.   She plumps her heroine,
a clever, sophisticated American Girl named Betsy Lou
Saegessor, down in the middle of London on the trail of a
sybaritic middle-aged Englishman who has come into an
inheritance she considers rightfully hers.   It seems that
Betsy Lou's stepmother, Pauline, went to England after the
death of her husband (Betsy Lou's father) and married C. D.
McKee, the old man of the title.   When Pauline is finally

hounded to her death, C. D. McKee inherits all her money.
Although Betsy Lou will someday be the beneficiary of all
these millions, she feels that she is entitled to it right
away and goes to England to see what can be done about it.
Using the pseudonym of Honey Flood, she tracks down C. D.
and proceeds to ingratiate herself in his affections.   She is
poised for the kill.

Whatever one thinks of the story (frankly it didn't
make too much sense to this reviewer), the stage is set
for an exquisitely demoniacal Dundy comedy of manners
featuring the sly, pleasure-loving, outrageous Englishman
and the equally sly and dangerous American girl who attempts to cut out his heart but ends up wearing it instead.
It is a battle between male and female, love and hate, innocence and corruption, Englishman and American, in which
nobody wins.

It is all quite charming and witty and yet, like the
little-girl-lost photograph by Dick Avedon on the back
cover, it is somehow pathetic too.   There is a slackness,
a kind of self-indulgence in this aggressive, attention-getting
amorality, like walking on quicksilver.

If only Betsy Lou Saegessor were not so patently
Elaine Dundy, the chic blonde photographed by Avedon!   If
only Elaine Dundy would stop capitalizing on her reputation
as a wit and use all the wit and wry disillusionment she
possesses (it's all there in that opening paragraph) to
write a real novel.

Now that would really be something!

A MILLION PESOS!

By José Romero (Doubleday, 1964).

        "Seven thousand five hundred feet above sea level,"
writes José Romero in this gay and uninhibited novel of Mexico City's back streets, "the sun has the power of a million-
watt searchlight focused on Mexico City.   And while that
light makes no hissing sound, its golden rays generate the
energies of young couples so they can fulfill their destiny;
love in its purest form."   I think that in writing this novel
José Romero, the popular Mexican newspaper columnist and
author of an early autobiography, Mexican Jumping Bean,
has also fulfilled the same destiny, for A Million Pesos!
is without any doubt, love in its purest form.

        The main character (and what an eccentric character
he is!) is Señor Emeterio Navarro, head of the Contract
Department at General Energy Corporation.   The reason that
Señor Navarro has attained such a position of eminence is
that he originated a secret filing system which only he understands.   Now an elderly gentleman dressed discreetly in
black with the regal mannerisms of a Grand Duke (at least),
Señor Navarro still dreams of someday winning the million-
peso prize in the weekly National Lottery.   He thinks of himself as a capitalist without money whose funds are tied up in
the lottery.

        Enter Mariano Mora, a handsome youth who ekes out
a bare existence as a lottery vendor.   "Here's the fat prize,"
Mariano calls out in his gay, musical voice.   "Be rich!
With all this money you can buy a house in Acapulco.   Your
sweetheart will become a movie star.   Travel first-class
to Paris.   Own a stable of horses at the Hipodomo de las
Americas.   Buy this ticket and you will be rich.   Here you
are, Señor.   How many series?"   For years Mariano has
been reserving ticket number 2713 for the dignified head of
the Contract Department at General Energy Corporation,
Señor Emeterio Navarro.   Each week he shares the old
man's disappointment when his number fails to be drawn.
They have become very close friends over the years.
Mariano is a product of Mexico City's back streets, orphaned
at an early age.   Señor Navarro once dreamed of marrying
the Widow Patino (as soon as he won the million-peso prize),

but she got tired of waiting and married an Arab who sold
rugs.   Now Mariano is like a son to the old man.

In Mexico City there is a street of guilty men ("a
halftone brushed on the canvas of nightfall") called Organo
Street.   Every Saturday night Señor Navarro arrived on
Organo Street to court his sweetheart, the still handsome
looking middle-aged lady known as "the Queen of Organo
Street."   Invariably they while away an hour or two playing cards.   Meanwhile young Mariano, likely as not, is
doing a good business hawking his lottery tickets on this
same infamous street.

Mariano is a proud, disdainful young man and he
shuns the blandishments of Organo Street.   But one day he
meets the beautiful Paloma and, though she is not unknown
on Organo Street, they immediately fall in love.   "As long
as I can love you, I can change," Paloma assures Mariano.
And Mariano shouts to the whole world: "Listen, world.
Listen, I'm in love.   I'm in love with Paloma, my Paloma
.... Do you hear me?   Yes, and she is in love with me."

As in all ideal love stories, Mariano and Paloma
are too poor to marry.   But wait, there is always the
million peso-prize!   Some one is sure to win!   You will
too if you read this delightful novel.   To borrow Señor
Navarro's own words, it is a Shangri-La where dreams
come true.

GET HOME FREE

By John Clellon Holmes (Dutton, 1964).

          Jack Kerouac is the most famous chronicler of the
"Beat Generation," but it was not Kerouac but John Clellon
Holmes who coined the term "Beat Generation" as early
as 1952 in a novel called Go. Now, reading Holmes' new
novel, his third, Get Home Free, it seems clearer than
ever that this American Sartre is the real philosopher of
the Beats. And if Kerouac's Sal Paradise and Dean Mor-
iarity had all the excitement and fun traveling "on the
road," it is John Clellon Holmes who explained to them
in a fairly coherent manner just what they were seeking
and why.

          Interestingly enough, the character who first philoso-
phized about the "Beat Generation" in Go, Paul Hobbes, re-
appears in Get Home Free. And before long he is philoso-
phizing deeply about the lost America. "I think we're all
going to wear ourselves out here in America," he says
wearily, "just burn ourselves right up. I have this vision
of the nerves of America, all the butchered ganglia, the
flayed tissue, the teeth ground to powder in the night, the
cindery brains that are starting to run amok from the ten-
sions of life here now.... And I find myself thinking that
we'll never make it in this century, because we've lost
touch with something -- something wild and natural, call
it bliss or reality, a capacity for spontaneous love. "

          Dan Verger and May Delano, the main protagonists
of Get Home Free, certainly seem to have lost touch with
reality. As the novel begins, they are living in an old loft
on the West Side of New York. Two years before they
were part of an exciting postwar generation, the "Beat Generation", that was going to discover life anew. But then
Korea came along and suddenly made them obsolete. Now
everything has palled and they are surfeited with too many
bad parties, too much whiskey and too many strangers.
Dan Verger and May Delano decide to break up and, in
order to reassess their life, return to their respective
home towns -- Dan to a small New England town and May
to a small Southern city.

Alas, as Thomas Wolfe said many years ago, "you can't go home again." Dan returns home to Grafton, Connecticut, and realizes that it can only be a way station to somewhere else. He runs into Will Molineaux, the disreputable sixty-year-old town drunk, and together they go on an epic binge. Old Man Molineaux is what Dan would eventually become if he remained in Grafton, "a hell-raiser up and down the valley, an epic eater and singer and horseraround at church picnics, a reckless and adept handler of small boats in all weather, a chronic odd-job man and fire-house lounger, who was always "shipping out next year." This section of the novel describing the tribulations of this harassed old man is a remarkable piece of writing, a real tour de force. John Clellon Holmes isn't a natural novelist -- he writes in spurts -- but no one excels him in capturing the texture and feel of American life. He is in particular a gifted cataloger in the honored American tradition of Walt Whitman and Allen Ginsberg.

May Delano returns to Louisiana and finds that she can no more resume her old way of life than could Dan Verger in Connecticut. She insists on going to Fats', a Negro bar on the shabby edge of town. The boy dating her, a proper Southern boy, tries to dissuade her. He tells her that the South has changed and it is no longer safe to go to a colored bar at night. She goes anyway and, lo and behold!, runs into our old friend Paul Hobbes who just happens to be playing the piano. This may strike the reader as quite a remarkable coincidence, but it does allow the Sartre of the Beats to reintroduce his favorite philosopher.

And as we take leave of Paul Hobbes he is still trying to explain the "Beat Generation," still patiently searching for the lost America: "So I suppose what I'm really doing is searching for the natives, for the lost America. But like a Schweitzer-in-reverse, you see, because I want them to help me. Because, really, only rebels, and oddballs, and outcasts can still feel freshly any more..."

THE NIGHT WATCHMAN

By Simonne Jacquemard (Holt, Rinehart and Winston, 1964).

        John Fowles' The Collector, a strange novel about an
obsequious little clerk named Frederick Clegg who conceives
the horrible idea of kidnapping a lovely young girl, has already been reviewed in this book.   Now I have the honor of
reviewing the prizewinning novel by Simonne Jacquemard
called The Night Watchman, brilliantly translated from the
French by L. D. Emmet, that bears a striking resemblance
to The Collector.   Actually it is an even more impressive
achievement, which is perhaps not surprising when we consider the French genius for philosophical speculation combined with lucid exposition and technical virtuosity.

        Simeon Leverrier, a strange, solitary young man, is
employed as a night watchman at a factory in a small town.
From his glass-walled watchman's cell be surveys a hostile
sleeping world and contemplates his revenge.   For Simeon
is a creature of night, a subterranean being, who is separated from other people by the wrongs and humiliations of
the past.

        In the garden of his private house (behind a nine-foot
wall) Simeon Leverrier has begun to excavate an old well.
He likes to dig in the earth ("Let us take a long journey to
the center of the Earth...") the way Dean Jocelin in William Golding's recent The Spire likes to reach for the sky.
In a sense The Night Watchman is The Spire turned upside
down.   And just as Jocelin's awe-inspiring steeple, an
engineering triumph, rose octagon by octagon, pinnacle by
pinnacle, before our very eyes, so Simeon Leverrier takes
us with him into the depths of the earth as he burrows his
way to oblivion, breathing "the odor of substance immersed
in shadow, touched with virulence like the flavor of damp
bronze and with insipidity like the scent of marsh plants."
Although we stand back appalled, Simeon Leverrier is traveling backward to a condition which preceded the human
one and would probably survive it.

        If Simeon Leverrier did nothing except dig a hole in
his own yard and thereby become interested in geology it
would not be considered a crime and society would leave

him alone.   But Simeon is not content to leave it at that.
He has abducted a young girl at night and locked her up in
his cellar.   During the day he forces her to help dig his
nefarious hole.   Immuned in the cellar at night, she becomes more than just an assistant but an offering to appease
the gods.

When Simeon Leverrier's terrible deed is uncovered,
he is brought before the Judge to answer for his crime.
"I am the Judge, Simeon Leverrier," this awesome power
admonishes, "and I am looking at you.   My attention is
focused on you alone, my entire attention just as you have
always wished and as no one has ever given you." The
Night Watchman is not only the story of a particular crime,
it is a dialogue between the accused and the accusor whoever they may be.   It contains one of the most eloquent
definitions of justice that I have ever read.   "It is justice
which preoccupies us," the Judge remarks, "which holds
us together in tight dependence like two accomplices, so
that our discussion cannot be closed so long as the slightest particle of doubt remains, not about you, but about the
relationship between your act and justice.   Should you object that abstract justice does not exist ... I would answer
that justice is above all that which is good for the conser-
vation of the race.   Because one must choose, must one
not, between defending humanity or losing it in the face of
the universe; it is necessary to choose between man and
the universe, and society chooses man because she is born
of him and he survives solely through her. "

Even the great Albert Camus never said it better!

A MOMENT IN TIME

By H. E. Bates (Farrar, Straus, 1964).

      H. E. Bates, the popular English novelist and author of some of the most masterful short stories in the English language, has now written a novel about that momentous moment in time during the summer of 1940 when England braced itself against the Luftwaffe and a whole nation literally held its breath.   The Battle of Britain was probably the most crucial battle of World War II and it is not difficult to understand the author's desire to offer up this tribute, not only to the brave pilots who sacrificed their lives ("the gay pilots, the young pilots, the foolhardy and the grave"), but to the indomitable courage of the general populace as well.

      Although this was indubitably "their finest hour," this is not H. E. Bates' finest book.   With a few exceptions, the desire to immortalize the courage and sacrifice of the English people and freeze it forever in "a moment in time" has unfortunately conflicted with the story teller's role which is after all simply to tell a good story.   The Battle of Britain is of course a superb story, but Mr. Bates has not told it in this novel.   Seen from a vantage point of nearly a quarter of a century and bathed in a certain nostalgia, the Battle of Britain in these pages seems curiously remote and even unreal.   It is rather like a slightly sinister fairy tale that never actually happened.   And the really curious thing is that H. E. Bates was himself a Squadron Leader in the R. A. F. and personally took part in the epic battle.

      Perhaps this is the trouble.   For A Moment in Time views the Battle of Britain not as a fighter pilot must have viewed it high above the earth, but as a nineteen-year-old girl living twenty miles from the English Channel and married to an R. A. F. pilot views if from the ground.   The story centers about Elizabeth Cartwright Bannister whose grandmother's three hundred-year-old house is suddenly requisitioned by the R. A. F. for an officers' mess.   Elizabeth moves with her grandmother and Uncle Harry into the bailiff's house (they are virtually in the front line of battle) and watches friend, lover and husband go off to fight the enemy overhead.   Not many of them return.

The story is told by Elizabeth in the first person and, quite frankly, Mr. Bates' talents do not include being able to impersonate a young woman.   Elizabeth isn't a real woman, but a man's conception of a real (heroic, suffering) woman.   There is a profound difference between the two and it shows badly in this novel.   H. E. Bates is still not Flaubert.

H. E. Bates may not be Flaubert, but he is still a very gifted writer.   There are flashes of power in A Moment in Time which burst like flak on our surprised senses. Bates is able to impersonate Elizabeth's bumbling, ineffectual (but effective) Uncle Harry with satanic fury that borders on genius.   Grandmother is, well, the way we remember our grandmothers.   The entire first chapter is superb (one is reminded that Bates is basically a short story writer).   And there is a startling scene midway in the novel in which Elizabeth comes upon a dead parachutist in a clearing of chestnut saplings.   For once we are reminded of the horror of war and not merely of the youthful heroics of of war so much like a game of rugby between gentlemen (Pilot-Officers and Flight-Lieutenants) who, despite the war, live in a very neat and orderly world where everything is a "good show" and it is necessary to ask one's Commanding Officer's permission in order to get married.

HERZOG

By Saul Bellow (Viking Press, 1964).

Before reading <u>Herzog</u> this reviewer thought Saul Bellow was probably our best living novelist.   Now I am not so sure.

This is the life story of Moses Elkanah Herzog, Ph. D. , and how in his own words he rose "from humble origins to complete disaster. "   Herzog is an ex-college professor, the author of several articles and a book, <u>Romanticism and Christianity</u>.   On the strength of his early successes, he had never had difficulty in finding jobs and obtaining research grants, but now all his ambitious projects have dried up and eight hundred pages of an incompleted book lie buried in an old valise in the closet -- a testament to his failure.

Herzog has not only made a botch of his teaching career, but his domestic life is a failure too.   Besides going through two marriages, he must endure the added humiliation of knowing that his best friend, Valentine Gersbach, has run off with his second wife.

Now in his forty-seventh year, Herzog undergoes a grave spiritual crisis.   He who has always believed in mercy, compassion and heart now questions the very values by which he has lived.   He begins to act peculiar and has even taken to writing strange philosophical letters to everyone under the sun.   Hidden in an old farm house in the Berkshires, he writes endlessly, fanatically, to the newspapers, to people in public life, to friends and relatives and at last to the dead, his own obscure dead, and finally the famous dead.

He even contemplates murder, but no one reading the book is likely to take him seriously and in the end he doesn't take himself seriously either.   It is one of the weaknesses of this novel that the author saw fit to have his hero -- a civilized, kind-hearted man -- dash off to Chicago with a loaded gun in his pocket in pursuit of his ex-wife, the mother of his child, and his ex-best friend, Valentine Gersbach.

It is a false note and our "best living novelist" cannot afford such false notes.   It is this kind of theatrics that makes Herzog bear such a curious resemblance to James Gould Cozzens' late best-seller.   Herzog is the intellectual's By Love Possessed.

There are a number of false notes in this book.   They are not serious perhaps, but coming from a writer of Saul Bellow's stature, they are certainly disturbing.   On a trip to Martha's Vineyard, Herzog sees a helicopter steering toward Hyannis Port, where the Kennedy family lived. Saul Bellow writes: "Moses felt a sharp pang at the thought of the late President." I don't know why this seemingly innocuous remark rings so utterly false, but it does.   Perhaps it is because one realizes that here Saul Bellow has ceased being the novelist and is instead playing a role that he feels his readers will approve of.

In the end Herzog manages to pull himself together, apparently having weathered his emotional crisis.   He stops writing his long, pretentious, boring, philosophical letters addressed to God and the world.   "Oh, that mysterious creature, that Herzog!" enthuses the author, leading a cheer from the sidelines.   But the trouble is he is not mysterious enough.   He is really a fat-cat professor, after all, who (as he himself acknowledges) can still take the superjet to Chicago when he has the impulse, can rent a teal-blue Falcon (Hertz puts you in the driver's seat!) and drive in style to the old neighborhood.

Saul Bellow is still one of our best novelists, but for real suffering and compassion I prefer the late Edward Lewis Wallant and the Saul Bellow of Seize the Day.   And for real suffering, compassion and humor I prefer Bernard Malamud.

A MOTHER'S KISSES

By Bruce Jay Friedman (Simon and Schuster, 1964).

Toward the end of this zany novel by the author of
Stern, one of the characters (Gates by name) says to Joseph,
the improbable hero: "You're one of those antic New York
guys, slaving away in the wilds of New York's famed Catskills, ready to tear off his busboy's jacket and fill in for
an ailing M. C. Tell the truth, Boss, you've done a turn
in the Catskills, haven't you?"

Now although Joseph denies the charge ("Never admit you've worked the Borscht Circuit"), this is exactly
the way this reviewer felt about the author himself. A
Mother's Kisses is pure Borscht. Bruce Jay Friedman
has put together an act that could follow Allen and Rossi
at the Concord Hotel up in the Catskills. It's that good
(or bad), depending on whether one is interested in literature or vaudeville.

At any rate, the book (or act) features not Joseph
and his Brothers, but Joseph and his Mother. Joseph is a
"tall and scattered-looking boy with an Indian nose" from
the Bensonhurst section of Brooklyn, who has applied for
admission to a long list of colleges and is waiting to hear
from them. As the days stretch interminably into weeks,
Joseph grows increasingly more despondent. His class-
mates go marching off to "wondrous, faraway places such
as Tufts or Coe or S. M. U. " while, bored and stifled, he
waits to hear from the last college of his choice, lackluster
Columbia.

Finally, even Columbia rejects him and Joseph's
mother, a combination of the Wife of Bath and Fanny Brice,
Medea and TV's Hazel, takes things into her own hands.
As the Viennese fabric man remarks, she has "a fullness
of personality. " This is putting it mildly. This latter-day
Wife of Bath drags her seventeen-year-old son off to a
lakeside resort (there follows a very amusing satire on
the American custom of sending the kids off to summer
camp) and eventually inveigles him into Kansas Land Grant
Agricultural College.

Not satisfied with this small triumph, she stays right there to see that our hero (but her son) doesn't catch cold. On the very first day of school she barges into the classroom bearing aloft Joseph's sweater. "I'm terribly sorry," she says to the teacher. "I wouldn't have interrupted for the world. But he ran outside without anything on and you could die from the weather."

"Did your mother ever let you down?" she once asked her son. "Will you please learn to put your last buck down on this baby?"

The book is full of gags and a wild, irreverent, vulgar humor. (One is reminded of Joseph Heller's Catch-22 and similar books which almost seem to constitute a new genre.) What begins tentatively as a surrealistic vision of America -- a grotesque nightmare fantasy -- degenerates into mere buffoonery, Groucho Marx minus the cigar.

In the end it is merely pathetic. When a policeman asks Joseph not to sass his mother, she replies: "That's all right, officer, I'm used to it. I found out that I have a very smart son in college who suddenly developed public speaking. I don't have a boy any more, I have Winston Churchill."

Frankly, I prefer Allen and Rossi.

BIRCH INTERVAL

By Joanna Crawford (Houghton Mifflin, 1964).

Creativity is truly a mysterious phenomenon. There is no telling where it will strike nor whom it will suddenly fail. Saul Bellow can pour everything he knows into a long, complex, stylistic, philosophical novel -- I am thinking of Herzog -- and still leave one feeling vaguely disappointed at the result. How much is art and how much is sheer literary bombast and pretentiousness? On the other hand, an unknown writer will suddenly come along and write an unpretentious first novel of barely 180 pages on the age-old theme of a young girl awakening to the joy and terror of life in an adult world, and her artistry literally leaps from the printed page.

Birch Interval is the story of one year in the life of an eleven-year-old girl in a small village in rural Pennsylvania. Jesse's father is dead and her mother, an artist, wishing to go to Paris, sends her to live with her parents in Birch Interval. Jesse has been there before. When her father was alive he would send her to Birch Interval to learn "humility and the pure spirit of things," as he put it. Jesse's cousins, a nine-year-old boy and two older girls, live at Birch Interval near her grandfather's place and she knows that they will have fine times. There will also be bad times and it is this year that Jesse learns the reason for many things and the truth to her grandfather's words that "life is just a bit of eiderdown and a bit of mealy apple."

Life can be just as cruel in rural Pennsylvania as in the slum areas of Chicago or New York City, perhaps even crueler since the idyllic beauty of the countryside offers an illusion of peace and tranquility. What makes Birch Interval such an especially fine achievement is that the author succeeds in juxtaposing much of the inevitable sadness, disillusionment, cruelty and even horror of life against the rich beauty of the natural world with its manifold blessings.

Jesse certainly reaps a whirlwind of pain and disillusionment at Birch Interval in the twelfth year of her life. Some neighborhood boys teach her a frightening lesson about sex. She sees her beloved Uncle Thomas taken away to the State Mental Institution at Clayburg. Her mischievous cousin Samuel, who has accidentally poked his sister's eye out with a stick, is committed to a corrective school. She becomes privy to a terrible secret concerning her Aunt Marie and the Reverend Watson. And finally she becomes disillusioned with her grandparents who appear to lack strength and to be overcome by events.

The final lesson poor Jesse must learn is that in this life it is necessary to have compassion and to learn forgiveness. It is the most difficult lesson of all. As Jesse's grandfather acknowledges: "And to think that the Bible says, 'Judge not that ye be not judged' ... Everybody pays no attention to it, do they? Everybody is so quick to judge ..."

FUNERAL IN BERLIN

By Len Deighton (Putnam, 1964).

This reviewer is not much addicted to spy stories. John Greene, Graham Ambler, Eric Le Carré--they all swirl around my head like the plot of a Grade B movie starring James Mason in a trench coat.

I have come to the conclusion that the reason I don't enjoy spy stories is that I don't understand them. It's as simple as that. Perhaps there isn't enough guile in my make-up. Spy stories are always neatly cleared up at the end to everybody's satisfaction except mine. "So Vulkan never really existed?" I read hopefully on the next to last page. "Vulkan existed all right," someone else interjects. "He was a concentration-camp guard until a wealthy prisoner (who had been an assassin for the Communist Party) arranged to have him killed. This man was Broum, and an S. S. medical officer named Mohr..." Hmm, I murmur dejectedly, backtracking desperately through three hundred pages of derring-do. Did Vulkan exist or didn't he? Who is Broum? Who is impersonating whom? Who is Cynthia, who is she?

The latest spy sensation is another British import. It is Funeral in Berlin by Len Deighton. Mr. Deighton is already being compared to (you guessed it) Eric Ambler, Graham Greene and John Le Carré. In many ways it is a remarkable book, but it hasn't made me change my mind about spy stories. I still don't understand them. They make about as much sense to me as McGeorge Bundy on his return from Saigon.

Well, as good old straightforward, guileless Jack Webb used to say, "The Facts, ma'am, just the facts." Funeral in Berlin is a novel of international espionage revolving around the abduction of a famous scientist from the East Zone of Germany. Semitsa, the "best enzyme man in the world," will be shipped through Checkpoint Charlie in Berlin in a casket suitably provided with holes. A Russian colonel is involved in the plot. A double agent named Johnnie Vulkan is also involved. The British are involved because they want to keep an eye on Johnnie Vulkan (who doesn't exist?).

Israeli intelligence is involved in the person of a
beautiful blonde named Samantha Steel.   Egyptian intelligence
is involved because Israeli intelligence is involved.   The
Gehlen Bureau or Federal German Intelligence Service is
involved because everybody else is involved.   I think the
Americans are involved too, but I forget why.   Nobody
trusts anybody else in this book, and I don't blame them.

Actually I'm being too facetious.   Funeral in Berlin
is good despite the plot, not because of it.   The plot
doesn't make any more sense than most spy plots.   But the
mirror it holds up to the world!   From Berlin to Prague,
from London to Bordeaux (and the author knows Europe like
the palm of his hand), we are enveloped in an atmosphere
of bureaucratic deceit and double-dealing as thick as the
fog that rolls in over London.

"As a liar, my friend, you are incorrigible," one
secret agent whispers to another, leaning over a balcony
in a great stone building of carefully penned archives and
aged bureaucrats.   "The perspective of the great curves
of balustrade repeated themselves as far as infinity," we
are told, "like the echoes of Grenade's whisper."

The writing is superb in that breezy, sophisticated,
semi-serious Raymond Chandler-ish style we have come to
know so well.   (The blazing gun duel during a fireworks
display in the heart of London at the close of the book is
a spectacular piece of literary pyrotechnics.)   It reflects
perfectly the nightmare world of international intrigue in
which guile is the accepted norm.

THE DEFENSE

By Vladimir Nabokov (Putnam, 1964).

"Of all my Russian books," Vladimir Nabokov writes in a brief foreword, The Defense contains and diffuses the greatest 'warmth' -- which may seem odd seeing how supremely abstract chess is supposed to be. In point of fact, Luzhin has been found lovable even by those who understand nothing about chess or detest all my other books. He is uncouth, unwashed, uncomely -- but as my gentle young lady (a dear girl in her own right) so quickly notices, there is something in him that transcends both the courseness of his gray flesh and the sterility of his recondite genius. "

The Defense was first published under the title Zashchita Luzhina or "The Luzhin Defense" under the pseudonym of V. Sirin in the Russian émigré quarterly Sovremennye Zapiski (Paris) and was then brought out in book form by the émigré publishing house of Slove (Berlin) in 1930. Now, thirty-five years later, it appears in English for the first time, translated from the Russian by Michael Scammell in collaboration with the author.

Nabokov's early novel is about a chess master who loses touch with reality and is destroyed by his own genius. Luzhin is one of the international grand masters. He is cited in all the chess textbooks and is a candidate with a half dozen others for the title of world champion. Luzhin scarcely exists outside of chess and it is this single-minded devotion to the game that ultimately destroys him. For Luzhin the real world is the world of chess, a world that is "orderly, clear-cut and rich in adventure. " The outside world impinges on his consciousness only as a dreary succession of hotels, restaurants and railroad stations, as he travels about Europe playing in one tournament after another.

At one point the outside world does come between Luzhin and the "abysses of chess" long enough for him to marry a young Russian émigré -- or rather to allow her to marry him -- a woman of great gentleness, kindness and

compassion, who marries the taciturn and enigmatical Luzhin against the wishes of her family who prophesy disaster.
Nabokov calls her "a dear lady in her own right." This
does not really do her justice. If The Defense contains and
diffuses great warmth it is because of Luzhin's wife -- I
don't believe we are ever told her name -- who struggles so
valiantly to preserve the remnants of her husband's sanity.

It is apparent that The Defense is an extremely ingenious novel. Midway through the book this writer felt
that it was a little too ingenious, in fact, to be quite convincing. However, these momentary doubts are soon dis-
pelled by the brilliance of the denouement, and one finishes
the novel absolutely convinced of its rightness and credibility and of the genius of its author. Furthermore, one
cannot help reflecting that this novel was written almost
twenty years before Albert Camus' The Stranger and more
than thirty years before Susan Sontag's The Benefactor or
John Fowles' The Collector. Now published for the first
time in English, it has taken us fifteen years to catch
up with Vladimir Nabokov. But he is probably thirty-five
years ahead of us again. Great writers usually are.

THINGS AS THEY ARE

By Paul Horgan (Farrar, Straus, 1964).

Things As They Are by the distinguished novelist and historian, Paul Horgan, is not a novel in the usual sense. It is a loosely organized series of more or less autobiographical episodes chronicling what Winfield Townley Scott calls "the confusion of childhood--its fears and terrors, its half-innocent delights, its intimations realized beyond words." Dorchester, New York, is an American Eden on the Great Lakes. In this American Eden the presence of evil and the loss of innocence manifests itself in cruelty to animals, the suffering of a sensitive youth at summer camp, the foibles and vices of old men, the unalterable fact of death confronted at last in the form of an old work horse lying prone on the asphalt pavement.

Paul Horgan writes rings around most of his contemporaries. This is how he describes a ferryboat ride to Hoboken in a snowstorm: "We went forward into the clear space at the bow just as the boat moved into the blowing curtains of snow. All I could see was the dark green water where we sailed, a little sideways, across to the Jersey shore. The city disappeared. We might have been at sea, as Grosspa would soon be. I felt something like loneliness, to be closed away by the storm from sight of what I knew. Yet I noticed how the ferryboat seemed like a great duck, and the trundling action of her power under water seemed like the engine-work of huge webbed feet. At a moment I could not exactly fix, the other shore began to show through the snow, and we docked with wet, grudging blows against the old timbers of the slip."

There is a scene midway through this beautifully written account of a boy's growing up in the fictional city of Dorchester in upstate New York during the halcyon days before the First World War in which Richard and his parents take the Empire State Express to New York City to see Grosspapa off for Europe on the Kronprinzessen Cecilie. Grosspapa is old and feeble and is returning to Germany to live out his life in the familiar, well-ordered surroundings of his early years.

"Like some old wounded lion crawling home to die,"
Richard's father murmurs sadly, as the huge ocean liner
slowly departs.   It is snowing and bitter cold.   Richard
is too young to understand what the grownups are talking
about.   Caught up in the excitement and wonder of the
occasion, he tugs at his mother's arm and exclaims, "Look,
look, the snowflakes are all black!"

"Richard, why do you say black," his mother replies
angrily.   "What nonsense.   Stop it.   Snowflakes are white,
Richard.   White!   White!   When will you ever see things
as they are!"

But as the author writes in the very first paragraph,
parents are prone to forget that children are artists who
"see and enact in simplicity what their elders have lost
through experience."   The black snow flakes--and seen
against the light, falling out of the sky into the sliding
water all about the Kronprinzessen Cecilie, they were indeed
black--are a metaphor for the loss of innocence.

Writing such as this seems to contain an extra di-
mension.   We feel it to the very marrow of our bones.

It may seem strange but this writer could not help
comparing Things As They Are with Jean-Paul Sartre's
recent autobiography of his early years, The Words.   Sartre
too thought he had been born into Paradise when the century
was still young, but at the age of fifty-nine he could look
back on the happy scene of his childhood and ruefully admit
that he started off with a handicap of eighty years.

In Things As They Are Paul Horgan makes the same
kind of indictment of the "age of innocence" as Sartre.
Apparently it wasn't only in Europe that people strutted
and posed and in general mistook themselves for Victor
Hugo.   Could it be that the halcyon days before the First
World War were not so halcyon after all?

CABOT WRIGHT BEGINS

By James Purdy (Farrar, Straus and Giroux, 1964).

Reading James Purdy's new novel, <u>Cabot Wright Begins,</u> this reviewer was reminded of something Norman Mailer said at the recent National Book Awards (or National Book Best-Seller Awards, as Cabot Wright would say) ceremony in New York. "Four years ago my life went out of control for a time," the bad boy of American letters is reported to have said. "Once you become notorious your personality takes on a legendary quality. I am more and more surprised by what I am supposed to have done in the last two years."

Cabot Wright's life has also gone out of control and his personality has taken on a legendary quality. He is more and more surprised by what he is supposed to have done.

Despite the fact that he is "the mythical clean-cut American youth out of Coca-Cola ads, church socials, picnics along the lake," Cabot Wright is actually a convicted rapist with more than three hundred victims to his credit. Although it all started innocently enough in a branch of the Brooklyn Public Library, Cabot Wright's notoriety is such that upon his release from prison people come from all over the world to interview him and write the story of his life.

One of these would-be authors is Bernie Gladhart, a Chicago car salesman, who is spurred on by his wife to write a documentary novel about the celebrated Robin Hood of rape. He sets out for Brooklyn to seek Cabot Wright in his twentieth century Sherwood Forest, the jungle of New York and environs, U. S. A.

Bernie is joined (and soon surpassed) in this endeavor by Zoe Bickle, his wife's friend from Chicago, and Princeton Keith, a publisher's scout, who conspire to produce a best-selling novel to be entitled <u>Indelible Smudge.</u> "Mrs. Bickle, somewhat to her own amusement," we are told, "saw herself turning into a novelist at a ripe age,

while Cabot Wright's life as fiction sprawled and grew under
her hand, lumbering on in endless corrections and addenda as
it reeled and retraced itself, was interrupted, continued,
ran on over lapses of memory, lies, vague echoes, police-
tapes, gossip-columns and eye-witness stories. It was a
hopeless, finely-ground sediment of the improbable, vague,
baffling, ruinous and irrelevant minutiae of a life.   If she
could not lay down her pen, however difficult her task, it
must have been her realization that all lives were like this
and indeed this was proof of life."

Cabot Wright Begins is a fable for our times; it is
Alice's Adventures in Wonderland come to life in Brooklyn,
U. S. A. , in the middle of the twentieth century. "Do you
mean to say you'd know your story if somebody told it to
you," Zoe Bickle asks Cabot, "but you couldn't tell it to
anybody yourself and be sure you were right?" "How can
you express it so well?" he replies brightly.   "But what
will you get out of it?" Mrs. Bickle persists.   "After all,
when we do get the truth, if it's there, we'll just turn it
into fiction." "Well, Mrs. Bickle," Cabot says unflinchingly,
"let's say I might get my own story straight."

James Purdy is a moralist with the savagery and
bite of a Jonathan Swift.   Which brings this writer back to
something else Norman Mailer said at the National Book
Best-Seller Awards.   "I have great admiration for Herzog as
a novel," the Cabot Wright of American letters is reported
to have said, "but it is not an intellectual book, it has no
ideas in it.   It has about the same relation to ideas that a
cookbook has to good eating." James Purdy's Cabot Wright
Begins has ideas and some of them will make you wince.

GUMBO

By Mack Thomas (Grove Press, 1965).

   This slight book about a freckle-faced boy named Toby
Siler seems to have touched off a series of hosannas from
one end of the country to the other.   Not the least source
of wonder to the exuberant reviewers is that it comes from
Grove Press and contains not a single four-letter word.
Apparently these gentlemen had braced themselves for
another One Hundred Dollar Misunderstanding and the resultant shock temporarily deranged their critical faculties.

   This is an appealing book that Mack Thomas has
written; I do not mean to imply that it isn't.   But it calls
itself a novel and, if literary terms mean anything at all,
it most assuredly is not a novel.   A novel must be more
than just a nostalgic piece of autobiographical reminiscence.
It must be more than a series of episodes held together
by nothing more than chewing gum and a prayer.   "You see,
Toby," Mr. Cunningham says, searching for words, "growing things...living things, that is, are making a trip going
somewhere, on their way from what they are to what they
can be."   A living novel, too, must evolve, and Gumbo
fails to evolve.

   It is true that Toby is five years old at the start
of the book and almost thirteen when it ends, but that is
not what I mean.   Toby's character doesn't change nor
does anyone else's.   Toby's character doesn't change because Toby isn't a real person, but only a vehicle through
which the author reminisces nostalgically about the past in
Texas during the depression days of the 1930's.

   There is much to be nostalgic about and this book
is a kind of celebration.   Even in the worst days of the
depression there was a glow in the American experience
that lit the prairie as far as the horizon and beyond.   The
Silers were poor (Mama and Papa worked in the cotton
mill when there was work), but richer in mind and spirit
than most people today who can boast of a split-level ranch
in the suburbs.   Papa could skillfully peel an apple with
a Sears Roebuck penknife, the peeling coiling around itself

in one piece like a snake shedding its skin.   Papa could
play dominos with Grandpapa and let him win occasionally.
Mama could sew or bake a "good smellin' apple pie."
Toby could play Cowboys and Indians with brother Pud, or
build a tree house in Old Elm Tree, or play his clarinet
as the frogs joined in the chorus of the "evening's starlight
Symphony."   Keeraaawks!   Qooreek! Chitit!   Chitit!

The prose is a bit soft and sticky for my taste, as
if it had been sprayed on with one of those guns that dis-
pense whipped cream in a bakery.   Certainly it was not
written with anything so hard as the sharp point of a pen.
"Papa had a way of narrowing his eyes as he gauged the
fading light of the day," the author writes.   "...And in the
late hours, untying her apron as she came from the kitchen,
Mama liked to say, 'I'll swear I don't know where the day
has gone to!' He'd paid no attention to that, but attention
didn't matter.   He heard it as it happened and the hearing
stayed in his head; slipped into it like a sky slips into a
tree.   The hearing and staying of what he heard made a
knowing that didn't need saying.   Nights <u>come.</u>   Days <u>go</u>..."

They do indeed.

AN AMERICAN DREAM

By Norman Mailer (Dial Press, 1964).

      Norman Mailer's <u>An American Dream</u> first appeared
in serial form in <u>Esquire</u> magazine -- a kind of write now,
pay later proposition (Mailer did not know what he was going to do from one installment to the next), and about all
one can say about the experiment is that it is quite obvious
that Mailer didn't know what he was going to do from one
installment to the next. After a very strong beginning the
novel veers wildly out of control like a weathervane run
amuck. It was rash of Mailer to try to imitate Dickens
and Dostoevsky in the magazine serial sweepstakes. In
his case discretion would definitely have been the better
part of valor. But then Norman Mailer is a modern-day
Don Quixote and probably no one could have persuaded him
not to tilt at this particular windmill.

      The hero is Stephen Richards Rojack, war hero and
ex-Congressman turned college professor who has written
a major work on existential psychology. He also finds
time to star on a popular televison show ("People Are
Ghastly") and murder his wife, the beautiful and immensely
wealthy Deborah Caughlin Mangaravidi Kelly, by strangling
her in her plush tenth-floor East River Drive duplex apartment and then pushing her broken body out the window.

      Norman Mailer is an extremely gifted writer and
for about a hundred pages he keeps us positively enthralled
as he takes us on his existential pilgrimage through the
dark night of the soul from the fashionable East Side to the
Lower East Side, from police precinct stations to gaudy
nightclubs. How brilliantly he conveys the existential
dilemma of mankind trapped between heaven and earth.
Mailer can make us feel what it must be like to stand in a
murderer's shoes. He also exposes every nerve, sinew,
muscle. He takes us out on the street to stand and gape
with the police, newspaper reporters and curiosity seekers.
He knows what the inside of a police station looks like and
doesn't miss a single nuance. He takes us to the morgue
where the light has the color of the "underbelly of a whale,
the denuded white of florescent tubes. "

There is only one trouble and it is fatal.   Mailer
doesn't have a story to tell, only a deadline to meet.   He
gets desperate and tries to befuddle us with meaningless
incidents to cover up the lack of plot.   New characters
emerge like icebergs out of the fog (Shago Martin, Barney
Oswald Kelly, et al.), not to add meaning to the novel but
simply to keep it going.   Even Rojack's new-found love,
the singing thrush Cherry, seems contrived in a vacuum,
and her demise brings back bittersweet memories of <u>A
Farewell to Arms!</u>   Is this what is meant by avant-garde
writing?

As for the prose, it loses its edge and becomes repetitious and monotonous.   The metaphors, so striking and
powerful in the beginning, lose their force.   "I cried within
like a just-cracked vase might shriek for cement," Rojack
exclaims at one point.   It sounds merely silly.   Or, "The
past was like a burned-out field after the blaze has gone
through."   Such metaphors do not illuminate but only add the
requisite number of words to make the inevitable deadline.

And besides, it has all been done before by F. Scott
Fitzgerald in a classic novel called <u>The Great Gatsby</u>, published way back in 1925.   Far from being avant-garde, <u>An
American Dream</u> is <u>The Great Gatsby</u>, reduced to the dimensions of pop art.

THE RECTOR OF JUSTIN

By Louis Auchincloss (Houghton Mifflin, 1964).

Louis Auchincloss' The Rector of Justin explores the life and personality of the Reverend Francis Prescott, D. D., the eighty-year-old headmaster and founder of Justin Martyr, an Episcopal boys' boarding school thirty miles west of Boston. The novel is written mostly in the form of a journal kept by Brian Aspinwall, a shy young English instructor. Brian idolizes the headmaster and hopes that under his wise tutelage he will finally determine whether or not he has a true "calling" and should prepare himself for the ministry.

Dr. Prescott is a wonder. "His schedule is phenomenal for a man of eighty," Brian enthuses. "He rises at six, in the tradition of the great Victorians, and reads for an hour before breakfast. He claims that a mind continually soaked in small school matters needs this daily airing to preserve any freshness. He reads speedily and broadly, with an emphasis on philosophy and history, and although he keeps abreast of modern fiction, he is happiest with the Greek poets. He then officiates at morning chapel, presides over assembly and spends a busy morning in his office at the Schoolhouse. Lunch at the head table is followed by a half hour of faculty coffee, known as the "time for favors," when he is at his most easy and affable. The afternoon is devoted to the physical inspection of his plant, and in the course of a week he visits every part of the school grounds, some of them many times over: the playing fields, the infirmary, the gymnasium, the locker rooms, the dormitories, even the cellars and lavatories. Dinner is at home, with guests, usually with visiting graduates, but after the meal he retires to his study for two more hours of paper work and conferences with boys. At ten o'clock he has a couple of strong whiskies and the day is over."

Because of his special relationship to the headmaster, Brian is made the custodian of a number of hitherto secret memoirs, notes and autobiographical fragments composed by friends and acquaintances of Dr. Prescott. Together with Brian Aspinwall's journal they make up Louis Auchincloss' stuffy novel.

As Dr. Prescott's life and personality begin to emerge it becomes clear that not everybody sees him with Brian Aspinwall's idolatrous eyes. It seems that "the greatest figure in American secondary education" has done some things that are not entirely to his credit. Yet at the end Brian reflects that Dr. Prescott is pretty great after all. At his funeral his coffin, draped in the school colors of red and gold, is borne triumphantly through the packed chapel, followed by the Governor, the Bishop, four senators, eight judges and the headmaster of every boys' school in New England!

Apparently this reviewer failed to grasp the subtle nuances of Dr. Prescott's character and personality. Almost 350 pages of prize Prescottiana proved more than I could bear. Whether he is indeed the greatest figure in American secondary education or merely an old charlatan seems beside the point. In point of fact, he is an unmitigated bore.

And furthermore the fruit of all Dr. Prescott's labor is Justin Martyr, a very select private school for boys. Neither Dr. Prescott, Brian Aspinwall nor anyone else ever gives a satisfactory answer to one extremely pertinent question raised by the wife of the Chairman of the Board of Trustees of Justin Martyr: "It has always seemed to me that a private church school is a contradiction in terms. How can religion be packaged for the privileged and sold to the select?"

THE JEALOUS GOD

By John Braine (Houghton Mifflin, 1965).

It is almost a decade now since John Braine, one of
the original "angry young men" in England, wrote Room at
the Top. Room at the Top delineated the rise and fall of
Joe Lampton, the son of a laborer in a grimy mill town
in the north of England, who takes a job as an accountant
in a pleasant country town and then schemes and lies and
claws his way to the top of the social hierarchy at the expense of his own dignity and self-respect. It was a very
powerful novel, although some of the point was probably lost
on Americans who are apparently much less class-conscious
than their English counterparts and do not kowtow quite so
openly and abjectly to the rich and influential.

With the publication of John Braine's fourth novel,
The Jealous God, it is quite apparent that he has outgrown
the "angry young man" label (if that label ever had any
meaning) and has steadily matured as a writer. He is certainly not the most spectacular novelist writing today, but
he does what he sets out to do in a very professional manner and reminds us that there is still a place for the traditional novel with its emphasis upon story telling and characterization.   The novels of John Braine, like those of
Graham Greene, Evelyn Waugh and Henry Green, will be
around long after Catch-22 is a mere literary curiosity and
catchword.

Vincent Kevin Dungarvan, the main protagonist of
The Jealous God, is a more contemptible character than
Joe Lampton. In a way he is Joe Lampton turned inside
out.   From his privileged sanctuary, he looks down his im-
maculate nose at common humanity ruthlessly fighting its
way to the top of the heap. Vincent Dungarvan, M. A. ,
Senior History Master at Theodoric's Grammar School, is
thirty years old and has never, when it came to the crucial
moment, been able to "march towards the sound of the guns,
not because of fear but because of the desire not to be
drawn in, to lose his freedom, to be forced once and for
all to disclaim his vocation and be like the rest. "

Vincent's strong-willed mother has never relinquished the hope that he will realize his sense of vocation and become a priest. At the age of thirty, however, Vincent's sense of vocation is beginning to seem slightly suspect. As long as the priesthood remains no more than a tantalizing possibility, he is spared the necessity to commit himself irrevocably to God or man.

Suddenly Vincent meets a girl in the reference room of the Charbury Public Library and his whole life is changed. Like his sense of vocation, the library is a kind of sanctuary for Vincent, a place where "no one could make any demands on him...a place where, more often than not, he would simply sit still, a pen in his hand, not thinking, not even sometimes aware of himself as a person." But just as Vincent Dungarvan is a more complicated person than he appears to others ("You're so damn rigid, so black-and-white," Laura Heycliff says heatedly at one point), so the library is more than just a sanctuary. It's a place where there is "nothing to distract the eye and nothing to offend it: only the books and the huge mahogany tables and the catalogue cabinets and the service counter. You emptied your mind of the irrelevant, you sat there quietly and then, sometimes there was a glimpse of the relevant." The Jealous God is a strong and subtle novel.

In addition to being a Protestant, Laura Heycliff has a husband from whom she is separated. Over the violent objections of his mother, Vincent falls in love with Laura. In a rapid-fire denouement, Vincent's complaceny is shattered once and for all and he is forced to a commitment. Five months before, he had asked a girl out for a drink, he had for once in his life acted out a desire, and now everything was changed.

LADIES OF THE RACHMANINOFF EYES

By Henry Van Dyke (Farrar, Straus and Giroux, 1965).

Ladies of the Rachmaninoff Eyes, an unusual first novel by Henry Van Dyke, gently probes the relationship between two elderly widows, a rich Jewish lady and her Negro servant-companion, as well as several other persons dependent upon them.   Over a period of thirty years Etta Klein and Harriet Gibbs have woven a "bickering, bantering tapestry together that was stronger than husband and wife, or sisters or cousins."   Occasionally they have their little differences and refuse to speak to each other for days on end.   The novel is narrated by Harriet Gibbs' precocious seventeen-year-old nephew Oliver whose principal function in life this particular summer seems to be to carry messages back and forth when the two ladies aren't on speaking terms.

In this bizarre atmosphere it is no wonder that Oliver feels woefully isolated and even begins to question his identity.   The situation is further complicated by the fact that Mrs. Klein has lost a son and Oliver is gradually called upon to take his place.

The climax of the novel occurs when a shady character by the name of Maurice LeFleur, who "reads palms, cups, astrological charts, cards, gives seances, and probably steals jewelry," appears on the scene to hold a seance in the hope of resurrecting the spirit of Mrs. Klein's dead son.

In the end Oliver goes off to Cornell, presumably having discovered his true identity.   Ladies of the Rachmaninoff Eyes is unusual and interesting because it attempts to explore problems of race relationships outside the ghetto. Genteel Oliver is certainly a change from James Baldwin's sweaty heroes.   One suspects, however, that those readers to whom Baldwin's shrill polemics are anathema will tend to patronize this novel and its young author, just as in another day the white middle class patronized Booker T. Washington.

Actually Oliver's situation as the favorite nephew of a servant-companion (ambiguous term!) to a million-heiress from Kalamazoo is so unique and special as to be meaningless in any larger sense. Certainly the average Negro living in Harlem would not be impressed with Oliver's refined struggle to find himself. He would probably agree with Della Mae, Mrs. Klein's contemptuous colored maid (if the novel had been about Della Mae instead of Oliver it would be a masterpiece), who says with philosophical scorn, "God gave some people money and talent and the right color skin, but when He came around to Della Mae, well, Our Father Who Art in Heaven ran out of supplies."

I'm with Della Mae.

COLLAGES

By Anais Nin (Alan Swallow, 1964).

Anais Nin is an extraordinary writer.   She was born
in Paris of Spanish-French-Danish parentage.   At the age
of eleven she came to America and started her diary,
which now consists of 103 volumes.   Although an American
citizen, she has spent half her life in foreign countries.
She was the first woman to publish a book on D. H. Lawrence.   In 1934 she wrote a preface to Henry Miller's
Tropic of Cancer.   No one else dared.   In 1949 Olympia
Press published Winter of Artifice.   Unable to find a publisher during the Second World War, she bought an old-
fashioned second-hand press and printed her own works.
Since the war she has been at work on her "continuous
novel" published under the titles of Cities of the Interior and
Seduction of the Minotaur.   She has been a model, a dancer and a psychoanalyst under Dr. Otto Rank.

This reviewer must admit having always been somewhat intimidated by Anais Nin (her name alone is apt to
put one off -- it doesn't have the easy ring of Dodie Smith
or Agnes Sligh Turnbull) and her reputation.   I rather
thought of her as some exotic hothouse plant imbibing an
atmosphere too rarefied for ordinary mortals.   Did she
not use words the way Nina Gitana de la Primavera, the
actress in her latest book, used silver foil paper on the
walls to make them beautiful?

Now like a mouse cautiously nibbling the edges of an
enormous cheese, this writer decided to sample Anais
Nin's new novel, Collages, only to discover to his amazement that this "exotic hothouse plant" is nothing more dangerous or frightening than an original artist.   And like
most original artists, she is not only fun to read but easy
to read.

According to the dictionary, one of the meanings of
collage is "an assembly of diverse fragments. "   If the
author calls her work a novel, she is perfectly right in
doing so, for these remarkable fragments are given unity and
harmony by the luminous quality of the author's intelligence

which one critic has described as "a real shimmering of
light on water." It will also be noticed that the book ends
as it began with the words: "Vienna was the city of statues.
They were as numerous as the people who walked the streets.
They stood on the top of the highest towers, lay down on
stone tombs, sat on horseback, kneeled, prayed, fought
animals and wars, danced, drank wine and read books made
of stone..."

This reviewer would not be so presumptuous as to
try to describe or analyze these collages, as delicate as
spun glass, yet strong as iron hoops. Suffice it to say
there is humor in the tale of the man from Los Angeles
who pampers his car or the misadventures of Count Laund-
romat or the saga of the runaway sailboat. There is terror
in the description of Tinguely's Machine that Destroys Itself in the courtyard of the Museum of Modern Art. (And
if one is searching for a moral, ponder this.) And there
is the beauty and permanence of the prose style which is
inseparable from the content.

To fall under the spell of a book such as this is to
unburden oneself, however briefly, of that accursed puri-
tanical conscience one drags around like a heavy weight. It
is to cast off one's petty preoccupation with jobs, careers,
studies, parents, duties, ties or responsibilities of any
kind. It is an exhilarating experience.

In its liveliness and motion, its poetry in motion,
this novel might be likened to a mobile. Despite what one
reads in the official manuals on writing, one cannot imagine this novel having anything so mundane as a beginning,
middle or end.

A HOUSE ON THE SOUND

By Kathrin Perutz (Coward-McCann, 1965).

Kathrin Perutz' A House on the Sound is one of the wittiest and most devastatingly wicked novels this reviewer has read in a long, long time.   Not everyone will approve of it.   But whether they approve of it or not (and this is really all that matters), they will be affected by it.   In the final analysis, good writers write for effect and not approval.

In outline the novel is very simple.   It describes a dinner party that takes place at a twenty-room house on Long Island Sound during the summer of 1963.   "Whoever came to the Hornbury's house on Long Island," the author begins, "was immediately intimidated by it, or charmed. One ignored the community three miles away, a township which, like so many others, had grown up in the past twenty years to produce suburbia, that lukewarm territory with the affectations of the city and the inconveniences of a village."

Edward Hornbury, a middle-aged published, and his daughter Nickie, a Barnard student majoring in Art History, are host and hostess.   Edward's wife is away on a private tour of music festivals in Europe.   The guests include Sonia Konsitina, an aging Russian beauty, and her young paramour Stanley, and Anthony and Bettina Pond, whose marriage is the setting for war, where "ambush, deceit, truces and concentration camps were part of daily routine." It is a typical marriage says the author with tongue in cheek.   Several young men of Nickie's generation complete the guest list.

The Hornbury's house is "a haven in the midst of barbarism," or so visitors were made to feel.   A Kline hung on the wall only because it was really appreciated, not because it had snob appeal.   The house on Long Island was, in short, a little salon of democracy and liberalism.

The mood of the novel, however, is essentially one of cynicism, disillusionment and despair, and it doesn't

take long for Kathrin Perutz, wielding the most delicate of
scalpels, to rip this cozy facade of democracy, liberalism
and the good life to shreds.   An elegant dinner party becomes a battleground on which modern man unwittingly reveals himself as he is, empty and alone, bereft of those
traditional standards of morality that once gave meaning
to his life.   And although the dinner and bathing party lasts
only a few hours, the author skillfully implies a great deal
more.   The relationships, at first so tentative and uncertain, begin to form a pattern that will continue to exist
long after this particular party is over. It is rather like
some graceful but sterile ballet over which the dancers
have no control and mechanically go through the motions
of an absurd and ritualistic choreography.

Like the people who cavort on its shore, the Sound
itself, this "proud, cruel body of water," has become
tamed by suburbia, made docile and boring, and can do no
more than "drag itself weakly towards land to lap at a few
dead crabs or broken beer bottles."

NINA UPSTAIRS

By Beverley Gasner (Knopf, 1964).

It is interesting to compare <u>Nina Upstairs,</u> a first
novel by Beverley Gasner, with Kathryn Perutz' <u>A House on</u>
<u>the Sound.</u>   Miss Perutz' imaginative and technically ac-
complished novel, a dazzling virtuoso performance, could
conceivably have been written by either a man or woman,
but <u>Nina Upstairs</u> could only have been written by a woman.
It is written in that aggressively feminine manner (the Jean
Kerr syndrome) that women feast on but men sometimes find
embarrassing.

There are other differences.   Miss Perutz is an extremely witty writer; Miss Gasner has "a sense of humor."
One simply cannot write a first-class novel with "a sense
of humor," no matter how wholesome, appealing and girlish
it may be.   And finally Kathryn Perutz is a most original
writer whose wry individuality permits her to view the world
objectively and dispassionately, whereas Beverley Gasner
(and no one would deny this is part of her charm) is a very
conventional writer.   She <u>is</u> Nina upstairs, a New York City
"career girl" from a good, solid, middle-class family in
Westchester.

Nina is employed as a copywriter in the grubby advertising department of a large department store called
Blaner's, the "favorite emporium of the Metropolitan
Square."   (She should know.)   As the novel begins, she has
just broken off her engagement to Robert and gone home
to live with her parents in the suburbs.

One day a mysterious older man is introduced to her
at the office and she promptly falls in love with him.   His
name is Julien Dennis and he is the new buyer in furniture;
to be specific, chairs.

Now Nina upstairs has dropped Robert because she
has discovered that he is a terrible snob.   Perhaps it is
her conventional upbringing, but she cannot help wondering
what a refined looking gentleman like Julien Dennis is doing at Blaner's.   When she gets to know him better, she

is emboldened to ask, "...who <u>are</u> you? What is someone
like you doing at Blaner's?" It turns out that Julien isn't
really a buyer in chairs after all (just as Joe the bellhop
out on the Island isn't really a bellhop, but a senior at
Yale), but an ex-college professor who has written part of
a novel.

But although Julien is eminently suitable for our
heroine, alas, there are complications. The poor man has
a wife (shades of <u>Jane Eyre</u>). I won't divulge any more
of the plot, except to say -- and this is all to the good --
that the book doesn't end the way I feared it would.

No doubt Julien will some day complete his novel
and resume his teaching career at that nice women's college
in Connecticut (imagine, a buyer in chairs!), but he and
Nina upstairs are not destined to live happily ever after.

I thought it was rather touching.

THE GARDEN OF THE FINZI-CONTINIS

By Giorgio Bassani (Atheneum, 1965).

In recent years a number of books have appeared
testifying to the terrible catastrophe that overtook European
Jewry some twenty-five years ago.   Some of these books
have been fiction, some nonfiction, but almost without exception they make harrowing reading.

Most of these books are set in Germany and Poland
where the worst atrocities were committed and indeed where
the most notorious and infamous extermination camps were
located.   However, Giorgio Bassani's prizewinning novel,
The Garden of the Finzi-Continis, translated from the Italian
by Isabel Quigly, is set in the ducal town of Ferrara in
northern Italy.   On the surface a love story about two ad-
olescents in the years just prior to the Second World War,
it is actually a profound and deeply moving indictment of
man's inhumanity to man (if that is not too mild a phrase)
that spread like a cancer over the entire Continent.   For
whether the setting is the Warsaw ghetto or the garden of
the aristocratic Finzi-Continis in the north of Italy, the
ending is the same: deportation and death.

The Finzi-Continis are a rich, refined landowning
family which occupies the preeminent place in the Jewish
community of the picturesque town.   Moise Finzi-Contini
who died in 1863 shortly after the northern provinces had
been annexed by the Kingdom of Italy, was known as the
"reformer of Ferrarese agriculture," according to the
plaque erected by the Jewish community on the synagogue
wall in via Mazzini, commemorating his virtues as "an
Italian and Jew."

The narrator of the story, whose family also belongs
to the small Jewish community of Ferrara, has been fas-
cinated by the Finzi-Contini family as far back as he can
remember.   Then one day he meets Micol, a thin, fair,
thirteen-year-old child, over the garden wall of Barchetto
del Duca.   He is invited back to play tennis with Micol
and her brother Alberto and other members of their circle.
He is received cordially by Micol's father, Professor

Ermanno, who takes a personal interest in his studies.   The
magna domus, the big ancestral estate of the Finzi-Continis,
becomes a second home to him.

Inevitably he falls in love with Micol, but, alas, it
is a hopeless love.   The Finzi-Continis instinctively know
what it takes the youthful narrator many years to discover.
It is neither the time nor the place for the kind of relationship Micol's suitor envisages.   For in the years before the
war in fascist Italy there is no time for youthful dreams of
love and marriage.   At least not in the Jewish community.
There is only time to prepare for the holocaust.

The first signs and portents come with the introduction of the racial laws in the summer of 1937.   Gradually
the everyday life of the Jewish community is subtly and not-
so-subtly altered and there follows "a kind of slow, progres-
sive descent into the bottomless funnel of the maelstrom."
As the narrative proper (there is a brief, heart-rending Epilogue) comes to a close, we have reached the fatal last
days of August 1939 and the Nazi invasion of Poland.

This is a haunting story of what might have been if
the world had not been what it was, written by a novelist
whose beautiful prose style is reminiscent of such masters
of an earlier, more literary era as Marcel Proust and
Henry James.

In the years preceding the war the noble and aristocratic Finzi-Continis are already a "desperate and grotesque
gathering of ghosts."   The narrator himself finally realizes
that it is late, terribly late.   And Micol, foreseeing her
own coming death and that of her family, cares nothing for
the democratic future her idealistic friend Malnate is already forging in his mind's eye; in fact, she abhors the
future and truly loves the "dear, the sweet, the pious past."

THE (DIBLOS) NOTEBOOK

By James Merrill (Atheneum, 1965).

Although he is the author of one previous novel, James Merrill is known primarily as a poet. In The (Diblos) Notebook, an extremely clever and imaginative work of art, he has written what might be described as a poet's novel. "I wanted a tale light as air," the narrator writes in his notebook, "lightly breathed out, two or three figures only, in clear, unexpected colors." The (Diblos) Notebook is just such a tale.

Much of the beauty of the novel can be attributed to the beauty of the setting, the Greek island of Diblos. In such a place the elementary things are important: rock, sea, sun, wine, goat, sky. "From the moment of my arrival," the narrator writes, "the world was transfigured for me, the language, the landscape, both of which I had pondered, as it were, in reproduction, now overwhelmed me with their (truth) and (beauty). I was more at home than I could ever have dreamed... thanks, say, to little more than a ray of sun entering the honey-cells of marble, I felt my whole person cleansed and restored."

The keeper of the notebook is a young American writer of Greek extraction named Sandy. The central figure of the notebook is not Sandy himself, however, but his older half-brother Orson, a brilliant "man of letters" who has gone back to Greece in search of his roots.

It all started seven years before on Sandy's first visit to Diblos where Orson has formed a close friendship with a cultivated older woman, a Greek widow named Dora. It is on his second visit to the island that the younger brother begins to keep a notebook. He intends to write a novel based on Orson's liaison with Dora. The (Diblos) Notebook consists not only of Sandy's notes, but of his first tentative gropings to transform these notes into a novel. Included also is Part Three of the novel itself which tells about the experiences of Orson and Dora in America, their marriage and ultimate separation. At the end we are back in Diblos with the narrator, reading his notebook. All at once there

is a dramatic confrontation between the two brothers.
Events have finally caught up with the "notebook"; they merge
and become one and the same, just as in real life fact and
fiction (appearance and reality) have a tendency to merge
imperceptibly together.   In a classically Greek denouement,
we await developments along with the narrator (a native of
Houston) to see how it will all turn out.   Although the bizarre ending is humiliating for Orson (Orestes), it does enable him to begin the task of exorcising (Diblos) and Greece
from his mind and conscience.

The (Diblos) Notebook is so subtle and imaginative
a novel that it defies easy interpretation.   Technically it
would seem to represent a startling advance in the novel
form.   The use of the notebook to tell the story, with all
the "false starts, contradictions, interruptions of self"
which this entails, is a striking departure from the traditional narrative represented by the "finished pages" of
Part Three of the novel which, though they have their own
movement and are often believable, "have become fiction,
which is to say, merely lifelike."   Technically the novel
would almost seem to begin where James Joyce left off a
quarter of a century ago.

As far as the subject matter is concerned, The
(Diblos) Notebook has its antecedents in the work of Marcel
Proust and Henry James.   "In form and tone the book must
derive from the conventional International Novel of the last
century," the narrator writes, "full of scenery and scenes
illustrating the at times comic failure of American and European manners to adjust to one another."   And again: "It
strikes me as I write that this national theme could be most
espressively illuminated by the story of Orestes & (Dora)--
the one coming to Greece athirst for his past, unaware of
how it is his coming, and that of others like him, that will
in the end obliterate what he has come for; the other asking nothing better than to be changed, to take on the fancied
independence and glamor of the American woman."

The (Diblos) Notebook is not a novel one is likely to
forget.

OF THE FARM

By John Updike (Knopf, 1965).

John Updike's new novel, Of the Farm, recalls this writer's review of The Centaur. "John Updike is unquestionably a brilliant stylist," I wrote at that time, "...but there is a nagging suspicion of excess, a tendency toward over-elaboration in the prose that inevitably runs counter to the simple and effective story line. A boy perched on top of a stack of folding chairs in the school gym is 'riding on this rickety raft the ocean of tummult.' One hesitates to use the word pretentious."

Now, after reading Of the Farm, I no longer hesitate to use the work pretentious, for this is pretentious writing at its worst. The "nagging suspicion of excess" has become 'excess' pure and simple. Of the Farm can scarcely be considered a novel at all (a novel says something), but only a vehicle for Updike to exploit those stylistic gifts that everybody says he has in abundance.

The novel, or whatever it is, describes the weekend visit of a thirty-five-year-old advertising consultant, his second wife and eleven-year-old stepson, to the southeastern Pennsylvania farm where he grew up and where his aging mother still lives alone. Anybody else would have called the book simply The Farm, but Updike must constantly embellish the most obvious things and so, with a Shakespearean flourish, it becomes Of the Farm.

In the evening while Joey Robinson is reading Wodehouse (during the day he cut the grass), his mother and wife of a few weeks talk from eight-thirty to ten ("eddies of disagreement nonsensically dissolved... suffocating tunnels of tension broke onto plateaus of almost idyllic reminiscence that imperceptibly narrowed again"), and this is the real climax and purpose of the visit. There is bitterness and resentment on all sides and the air must be cleared once and for all. Unfortunately this is not easy to do in an Updike novel and, instead of clearer, the atmosphere gets murkier by the minute.

Instead of Of the Farm, why not read Freud? He is a much better writer, even in translation.

THE LITTLE SAINT

By Georges Simenon (Harcourt, Brace and World, 1965).

"At long last I have done it!" With these words ring-
ing triumphantly from the back cover, Georges Simenon introduces his latest novel, The Little Saint. "With each
successive novel for at least twenty years," he continues,
"I have been trying to exteriorize a certain optimism that
is in me, a joie de vivre, a delight in the immediate and
simple communion with all that surrounds me, and to at-
tain, in order to describe such a state, to some kind of
serenity."

Let us admit at the outset that Simenon's joie de
vivre is a rather solemn affair. One can be sure it will
not end up on the Broadway stage in the form of a musical
by Lerner and Loewe! But what is it that the usually modest and reticent M. Simenon is suddenly so excited about?
For the first time (we are told) he has depicted a life that
develops serenely rather than disintegrates.

The novel tells the story of Louis Cuchas, an illegitimate child whose mother, a street vendor, earns a meager
living selling fruits and vegetables in one of the most notorious sections of Paris. Louis is an odd child who stands
apart from the street urchins of the neighborhood and from
his own brothers and sister. Before very long he is being called "the little Saint."

Simenon is very good at creating the world of the
poor people of Paris around the turn of the century, the
promiscuity and degradation which are as much a part of
their lives as the air they breathe. And as Louis grows
to manhood in this sordid environment, we witness the
growth of Paris itself and the passing of an historical and
cultural epoch. The automobile replaces the horse-drawn
carriage. The subway is built. Streets are being torn up.
Electricity is being installed everywhere.

Little Louis takes it all in, the color and excitement
of the streets as well as the degradation and despair, and
begins to translate these images into works of art. He
becomes a famous artist who lives to a ripe old age. He

is particularly fond of painting cabbages. "Most people eat vegetables," Simenon gently admonishes us, "without ever having watched a cabbage or leek or young carrot actually live." It just about sums up his entire philosophy.

"At long last I have done it!" For Simenon this book seems to represent a tremendous breakthrough. Like Louis Cuchas, he does not merely wish to copy reality, but would like to get down on paper (canvas) reality itself as it composes itself spontaneously in his mind. Simenon has visions of transcending reality to discover the essence of things in all their pristine clarity. He has visions of obtaining sainthood through a mystical experience.

Alas, I think he is the same old Simenon, extremely good in his way, but no mystic. The prose drones methodically on, always seeming to suggest more than it delivers. "What I can't manage to get," Louis says to M. Suard, the art dealer, "is a certain sparkle that I'm after, the quivering space between objects. You understand?" "I understand," M. Suard replies. "Monet spent his life trying to do that."

It is precisely this sparkle that Simenon has not been able to capture.

SLOWLY, BY THY HAND UNFURLED

By Romulus Linney (Harcourt, Brace and World, 1965).

For such a young country, America carries on a great love affair with its past. Colonial furniture is all the rage. Whole villages are restored to look as they did back in Colonial times. (But try to get someone to clean up the litter in the shopping centers!)

These philosophical reflections are inspired by a remarkable novel entitled Slowly, By Thy Hand Unfurled by Romulus Linnney. Mr. Linney, the author of Heathen Valley, would seem to be one of the most talented young writers to appear in some time.

Slowly, By Thy Hand Unfurled is written in the form of a diary kept by an almost illiterate woman sometime during the nineteenth century. The diary covers a period of a year and some odd months. As we begin to read the diary, our sympathies are all with the writer. She is a respectable, God-fearing soul, no doubt of the same pioneer stock as those who tamed the wilderness and baptized the heathen. She is as American as apple pie.

Gradually the following picture emerges. The writer of the diary is married to a patient, good man, a storekeeper named David. David is her second husband. Of her four children, two are by her first marriage. The oldest girl died three years before. Two months after beginning the diary she loses her youngest girl, Evie. This leaves two grown sons, Ed and Charlie, who are both working in a nearby city.

It soon becomes apparent that this respectable, God-fearing woman out of the American past has a number of very bad character traits. She is petty, small-minded, vindictive, a malicious gossip. She has spoiled her sons and destroyed her daughters. She has killed off one husband and is working hard on the second. She has done everything except commit murder and there is even some question about that. Her youngest son, Charlie, finally driven mad, goes around accusing his mother of murder.

Now this is not a pretty picture of our American
heritage (actually the diary has its comic moments and
contains some very eloquent writing too), but Romulus Linney is an ambitious writer who wants to say something new
and vital about the American experience. In order to do
this he must ruthlessly destroy the family album view of
our past. It is not a question of being cruel. None of us
is perfect. But how are we to live a better life unless we
try to come to some understanding of our faults and fail-
ings?

In a sense this is just what this poor, nameless
woman is attempting to do in her diary. In her humble way
she is trying to pierce through the self-limitations of her
time and place, the hypocrisy and self-deceit that have hitherto sustained her, to come to some understanding of her
life.

Unless I misunderstand the author, she does not
succeed; however, she does survive and this is no small
accomplishment. "Yes this monument is swaying but still
standing," she writes toward the end of her travail. "Will
it fall I don't know And what after all is it a monument of
Answer me that Journal answer me that..."

THE EVENING OF THE HOLIDAY

By Shirley Hazzard (Knopf, 1966).

The Evening of the Holiday by Shirley Hazzard is a
slight but beautifully written tale set in the north of Italy.
It describes the bittersweet love affair between a cultivated
English woman and an Italian architect in his forties.

Sophie is half Italian (on her mother's side) and is
spending a few weeks visiting friends and relatives and enjoying the civilized delights of the picturesque countryside.
Tancredi is separated from his beautiful and troublesome
wife. "He has the qualities," we are told, "that are attractive about Italy itself -- grace and the lack of earnest-
ness." The romance is conducted against the background
of the annual summer festival to celebrate an ancient victory, a victory gained by the opposing side! Appropriately
enough, it begins with tea and ends with tears -- restrained
tears.

In The Evening of the Holiday not much happens and
yet everything happens. An idyllic picnic in the lush countryside is described in lavish detail. A violent thunderstorm
occurs while Sophie and Tancredi are having lunch at a
restaurant on the way back from Florence and leads Sophie
to reflect portentously on the course of events.

The festival itself, which reproduces in miniature
"all the rancor and intolerance of the world," comes between the lovers. During the height of the celebration,
Tancredi calls Sophie from out of town and asks her to
join him outside the main gate. Sophie finds that her way
is barred. She slips into the side door of the church bap-
tistery nearby and passes through the transept of the cathedral. Someone approaches in the dimly lit church. A
small elderly caretaker in black coveralls nods to her polite-
ly, as if it were the most natural thing in the world to
find her there that evening. Without a word he unlocks a
door and she runs out into the deserted square to keep her
appointment with Tancredi.

Their love is doomed from the start. Sophie thinks:

"Tancredi has a wife and children.   And in Italy there is
no divorce.   It could only end badly for everyone concerned.
What a fuss about nothing."   "No," she corrects herself,
"not about nothing.   If it was a fuss, it was a fuss in the
way that life itself is a fuss."

        Tancredi thinks: "Her love is perfect.   What one
always hears about -- perfect love."   He tells himself,
with relief and a certain satisfaction: "I am not worthy
of that, not up to it at all.   I am an ordinary person -- a
fallible, inconsistent, mortal man."

        If the story is slight (and I suspect that it is not so
much a novel as a long short story), the artistic conscience
behind it, the sensitivity to beauty and subtle intelligence,
is not.   Let us treasure it while we may.

THE MANDELBAUM GATE

By Muriel Spark (Knopf, 1965).

Freddy Hamilton is a fifty-five-year-old foreign service officer assigned to the British Embassy in the Israeli
sector of Jerusalem.   His weekends are usually spent with
his good friends Matt and Joanna Cartwright who live in a
neat bungalow in Jordan.   It is his habit to leave his office
on the Israeli side of Jerusalem early on Friday afternoon
and walk through the Mandelbaum Gate with his diplomatic
pass in one hand and his zipper-bag in the other.

The year is 1961.   Even as Freddy Hamilton walks
through the Mandelbaum Gate in the pages of this enthralling
novel, the Eichmann trial is taking place.   Eichmann sits
expressionless in a bulletproof box.   The Mandelbaum Gate
is a symbol of all the hatred and intolerance of the world.

To the already explosive situation (for this land
knows no peace) add one young English woman, a half-
Jewish Catholic convert who insists upon entering Jordan
through the Mandelbaum Gate to complete a pilgrimage to
the Holy Land.   The young woman's name is Barbara
Vaughan.

If it were not so dangerous it would be ludicrous.
The English have a wonderful knack for seeing the funny
side of things and Muriel Spark is a past master of the
art.   "Quite absurd!"   On the strength of this phrase Freddy has struck up friendships in all parts of the world.
"The intensity at the Gate was quite absurd," Freddy thinks.
"One could understand the border incidents where soldiers
would flare-up an incident suddenly and unaccountably.   But
there at the Gate the precautions and suspicions of the
guards were quite absurd.   No Israeli money allowed into
Jordan, no Israeli postcards, the Jordanian police almost
biologically unable to utter the word 'Israeli'.   The Israeli
police were inordinately dramatic: 'Safe crossing,' they
would say as one left the emigration hut."

Freddy is in all respects a subdued, obedient civil
servant who walks a safe, narrow path between extremes of
any kind.   In one gloriously romantic episode, however,

Freddy throws caution to the winds.   Barbara Vaughan is
in Jordan and she is in danger.   Freddy has friends on
both sides of the Mandelbaum Gate and together they devise
a plan to rescue Barbara from a convent where she has
sought refuge.   Disguised as an Arab servant woman, she
completes her pilgrimage to the Holy Land.   A beautiful
and vivacious blue-eyed Arab girl leads the way.

It is all quite absurd (as Freddy would say) and yet
in her delightfully zany and painless way the author points
up a moral.   In a land where it is necessary to construct
a bulletproof cage inside a courtroom and erect a Mandelbaum Gate, one free individual (half-Jewish Catholic convert or whatever) can travel across frontiers of hatred
and intolerance on a holy pilgrimage and return unscathed.
It would take a gate higher than the Mandelbaum Gate in
Jerusalem, Muriel Spark seems to be saying, to deter the
human spirit or restrict the human heart.

AN ANCIENT ENEMY

By Pierre Moinot (Doubleday, 1965).

"I have not often written what I am going to say to
you," Albert Camus wrote to Pierre Moinot upon publication
of the French novelist's The Royal Hunt.   "You have everything that is necessary to accomplish a very important body
of work; to become what is foolishly termed a great writer.
Your work already possesses a tone which belongs only to
you, a forthright approach, good red blood, and especially
-- especially -- a warm humanity, without sentimentality:
in sum, the style of a man.   Now you can go ahead with
anything you may want to do; don't hesitate any longer."

Camus died tragically in an automobile accident in
1960, but fortunately Pierre Moinot is still living and writing novels that have more than fulfilled the late Nobel prize-
winner's faith in him.   An Ancient Enemy, Moinot's fourth
novel, may well be his best.

Two couples are enjoying an idyllic holiday on the
island of Corsica: Jacques Lortier, an archeologist, his
wife Françoise, Jacques' friend Jerome Valdès, a photographer by profession, and their mutual friend Celia.   The
men spend much of their time hunting wild boar with a
shrewd native guide by the name of Cardoni.   When not
hunting, they are likely to be found sun bathing and swimming with the girls at the beach.

Such is the pervasive nature of evil, however, that
even in this idyllic spot one cannot escape it, whether it
appears as an act of cruelty to animals or in the form of
a wild boar marauding the valley in search of food.

Jerome Valdès in particular has been touched by evil
in the way few men have.   For thirteen years he has conducted a fruitless search for the two men who subjected
him to torture and, after having murdered his friend Charles,
left him for dead.   For thirteen years he has thought of
that moment when, suddenly, he would become the dark
angel of atonement, the avenging arm of justice.

What happens, then, when Valdès does come upon his ancient enemy in the midst of an idyllic holiday in Corsica? And what questions does this raise about the nature of evil and the nature of justice? Does the act of justice not contain within itself an infection as corrosive as the taint of original injustice?

Even Cardoni, for whom there is nothing more vital, insistent or natural than the hunt, realizes that this particular hunt between a man and his ancient enemy is at last over.

THE SAILOR WHO FELL FROM GRACE WITH THE SEA

By Yukio Mishima (Knopf, 1965).

In The Sailor Who Fell from Grace with the Sea the
Japanese novelist, Yukio Mishima, has written a brilliant
allegory of man's fall from grace.

The sailor in question is Ryuji Tsukazaki, Second
Officer on the freighter Rakuyo. Ryuji reached manhood
just as the Second World War was drawing to a close and
his memories of life on shore are of poverty and sickness
and death. Whereas most men choose to become sailors
because they like the sea, Ryuji has been guided by an
antipathy to land.

The second mate's fall from grace begins when he
meets an attractive widow named Fusako Kuroda, the owner
of an exclusive gift shop in Yokohama. Ryuji is already
beginning to tire of the sea anyway. He knows better than
anyone the loneliness and boredom of a sailor's existence.

In the eyes of Fusako Kuroda's thirteen-year-old
son Noboru, however, Ryuji Tsukazaki is cast in an heroic
mold. The wailing of a ship's horn in the harbor pierces
Noboru to his very soul. The phantoms of the sea and
ships and ocean voyages existed only out there in that glist-
ening green drop. Someday he would have an anchor tat-
tooed on his chest.

And so when the freighter Rakuyo sails from Yokohama without Ryuji Tsukazaki, Noboru is absolutely crushed.
He brushes his teeth furiously until the gums bleed. The
smell of peppermint makes "a purity of his rage."

"The child is father of the man," Wordsworth has
written. When a sailor retires from the sea to marry the
attractive owner of a swank specialty shop, never under-
estimate the fury of an idealistic thirteen-year-old boy.
Noboru belongs to a gang whose youthful members reject
the adult world as materialistic, false and hypocritical.
They have taken a secret oath to destroy that world.

"Of course, living is merely the chaos of existence," the chief exclaims heatedly, "but more than that it's a crazy mixed-up business of dismantling existence instant by instant to the point where the original choas is restored, the taking strength from the uncertainty and the fear that chaos brings to re-create existence instant by instant. You won't find another job as dangerous as that. There isn't any fear in existence itself, or any uncertainty, but living creates it. And society is basically meaningless, a Roman mixed bath. And school, school is just society in miniature: that's why we're always being ordered around. A bunch of blind men tell us what to do, tear our unlimited ability to shreds."

The Sailor Who Fell from Grace with the Sea could be described as an existentialist novel in the sense that Camus' The Stranger is an existentialist novel. It compares very favorably indeed with The Stranger.

In a way the thesis of the novel is the direct opposite of that posed in William Golding's popular Lord of the Flies in which a tribe of so-called civilized boys revert to a savage and primitive state. As far as this reviewer is concerned, Yukio Mishima has built a much more convincing case.

THE EMPEROR OF ICE-CREAM

By Brian Moore (Viking Press, 1965).

Ever since his first novel, The Lonely Passion of Judith Hearne, was published in 1956, Brian Moore has been steadily winning recognition as one of the outstanding novelists of the day. Born and educated in Belfast, he emigrated to Canada in 1948 and now lives in the United States. One of his novels, The Luck of Ginger Coffey, was recently made into a fine motion picture.

In The Emperor of Ice-Cream, Brian Moore returns to the Belfast of his youth to write about seventeen-year-old Gavin Burke who comes to manhood during the critical early days of the Second World War.

Like so many of Brian Moore's protagonists, Gavin is a self-acknowledged failure who does not quite seem to fit in. "Failure is a more interesting condition than success," Moore once said. "Success changes people; it makes them something they were not and dehumanizes them in a way, whereas failure leaves you with a more intense distillation of that self you are."

Gavin belongs to a Catholic family in predominantly Protestant Belfast. His father is a lawyer, a practical man, whereas Gavin is a reader of new poetry (e. g., Wallace Stevens' ironic "The Emperor of Ice-Cream"). Gavin's father is bitterly anti-British, whereas Gavin dons the hated British uniform of the A. R. P., the Air Raid Precautions.

Enlisting in the A. R. P. is a desperate bid for freedom on his part. Having failed his London the A. R. P. represents a kind of marking time for Gavin. It also means that he will be able to get out from under his father's roof and escape the "pretenses and compromises which had helped keep him becalmed in indecision between adolescence and adult life."

Of course the A. R. P., "the front line of Home Defense," is a joke, a sham. Gavin is under no illusions about that. It is made up of a motley collection of old reprobates, the dregs of humanity, who spend their time training in first-aid and stretcher-bearing in the very unlikely event of a German air raid on Belfast.   For a writer noted for his compassion and understanding, incidentally, Brian Moore would seem to take a very harsh view of humanity.   But then I suppose the point is that he is compassionate and understanding despite his harsh view of humanity.   In this sense he is merely being realistic and intellectually honest.

The sense of Ireland as a backwater during these momentous days is brilliantly conveyed in this novel.   In the end, of course, Belfast is bombed and Gavin comes fully into his own.   He wins over not only his girl but his father as well.   If Gavin's ultimate triumph seems almost too pat to be entirely credible, this doesn't alter the fact that the bombing of Belfast is one of the most vivid and powerful descriptions of war that this reviewer has ever read.   It makes H. E. Bates' A Moment in Time, also about the Battle of Britain, seem like a mock battle waged by boy scouts.

And yet The Emperor of Ice-Cream is really not a war novel.   It is the story of adolescence and youth and the difficult and lonely struggle that must take place before youth arrives at manhood.   This too is a kind of war and in delineating it Brian Moore brings to the task all the attributes of a four-star general.

THE MAKEPEACE EXPERIMENT

By Abram Tertz (Pantheon, 1965).

On February 14, 1966, the Russian Supreme Court sentenced two writers to hard labor after judging their writings harmful to the Soviet regime. In so doing the Soviet Union pronounced judgment on itself in the eyes of the world.

With this trial the identity of Abram Tertz, the gifted author whose works were smuggled out of Russia and published abroad, has now been revealed to the world. As has been suggested, more than this has been revealed to the world. But for the moment let us merely state that Abram Tertz is Andrei D. Sinyavsky, a forty-year-old literary critic and teacher.

The Makepeace Experiment, originally published in France in 1963, surpasses anything we have yet seen by the author of The Trial Begins. Even when judged by the highest standards, it is an extraordinary work of art, a dazzling tour de force. It is a book that the author of Finnegans Wake surely would have admired.

The novel describes the brief reign of Leonard Makepeace, "our best mechanic and bicycle repairer in town," who learns the secret of "Psychic Magnetism" (Norman Vincent Peale, please note), a powerful force that enables him to win friends and influence people to such an extent that he is able to proclaim himself ruler of Lyubimov, an obscure market town in Central Russia.

Lenny proceeds to create a model communist state in Lyubimov, a Utopia, even going so far as to improve on Lenin who said that socialism (the new outlook) plus electrification (the scientific revolution) equals Communism. "Behold the fulfillment of the people's century-old dream," exclaims Lenny's amanuensis, Proferansov. "Behold the rivers of milk and honey, the Kingdom of Heaven which in scientific terms is the great leap forward! Never before in the history of the world has the individual received such care, never before..."

Despite his grandiose plans, Lenny Makepeace goes the way of all dictators and Lyubimov, his ideal communist state, comes crashing down on his head.   What has happened?   What has gone wrong?

There are three things which Lenny has failed to take account of in his ideal state.   They are (1) the Power of Evil, (2) the Power of God, and (3) the Power of Love. In one brilliant scene after another Abram Tertz makes it clear that these three powers cannot simply be wished away by governmental decree.   Indeed they come back to ruin Lenny Makepeace and his experiment.

Throughout this satirical, often hilarious novel runs the plaintive, haunting echo: "Who will restore love to the human heart?"   "Who will encompass the mysteries of creation?"

Not Stalin nor Khrushchev nor Kosygin nor Lenny Makepeace.   Who then?   Just possibly an old peasant woman, "so old and humped and tottering it was a wonder she was still alive," who drags herself to church amid the ruins of Lyubimov to worship as her ancestors did before her.

THE COMEDIANS

By Graham Greene (Viking Press, 1966).

The Comedians is Graham Greene's first novel since
A Burnt-Out Case, published in 1961.   It is even better than
A Burnt-Out Case.   It is probably as good or better than
anything he has written since The Power and the Glory.

The Comedians is set in Haiti, "the Nightmare Republic," and of course the setting is all-important in a
Graham Greene novel.   For in addition to being a master
of English prose, Graham Greene is a renowned world-trav-
eler, a cosmopolite, a man who seems to be at home anywhere in the world.

"It was by accident that I first came to Haiti more
than twelve years ago...," the author tells us.   "It was
then a happy period, at least for the tourists; only after
my second visit a year or so later did the shadow of Doctor Duvalier descend.   I made my third visit in August
1963, and now it was to the Haiti of The Comedians, of
the Tontons Macoute, the searches, the roadblocks, the
rebels in the hills.   I would have liked to return yet a
fourth time before completing my novel, but I had written in
the English press a description of Doctor Duvalier's dic-
tatorship, and the best I could do in January 1965 was to
make a trip down the Dominican and Haitian border -- the
scene of my last chapter -- in the company of two exiles
from Haiti.   At least, without Doctor Duvalier's leave, we
were able to pass along the edge of the country we loved
and to exchange hopes of a happier future."

Although the author himself was not able to return
to Haiti in January 1965, the narrator of The Comedians
whose name is Brown, does return after a three-year absence, though not without grave misgivings.   Brown is the
owner of a hotel located outside the capital of Port-au-
Prince, the Trianon.   Like Haiti itself, the Trianon has
fallen on evil days.   Once the center of Haitian intellectual
life, it now lies virtually abandoned, its fate uncertain.
Brown has returned to the Haiti of "Papa Doc," the Tontons
Macoute, the searches, the roadblocks, the rebels in the
hills.   He has also returned to Martha, the ambassador's

wife, with whom he is carrying on a half-hearted love affair.   In a chaotic world the Trianon and Martha are about
all he has left.

Brown's fellow-passengers on the ship carrying him
back to Haiti include Mr. and Mrs. Smith, an idealistic
(even naïve) American couple, who hope to establish a vegetarian center in "the Nightmare Republic," and a soldier
of fortune named Jones who is bent on exploiting the situation in Haiti for private gain.

Brown, Smith and Jones: they are all comedians,
their names as interchangeable as comic masks in a farce.
The Smiths do not last long in Haiti (it is not a likely place
for a vegetarian center).   Jones gets into trouble with the
authorities and goes over to the rebels in the hills.   Brown
smuggles him out of the capital and in so doing finally
commits himself to a cause.

This novel has special meaning and relevance for
Americans.   Graham Greene likes Mr. and Mrs. Smith,
but there is an implied criticism of our foreign policy running all through The Comedians.

But most of all it is a superb novel by a writer who
seems incapable of writing a bad sentence or of leaving a
single loose end dangling disconcertingly at the end.   The
Comedians has already been purchased for the movies.   It
should make a good one.   Graham Greene writes novels
with the discipline, the economy and the skill of a first-
rate dramatist.

ABSENT WITHOUT LEAVE

By Heinrich Böll (McGraw-Hill, 1965).

Heinrich Böll, the author of <u>Billiards at Half-past Nine</u> and <u>The Clown</u>, is one of the finest German novelists to emerge since the war. <u>Absent Without Leave</u> is in a different vein from the author's previous novels. It consists of two short, ironic novellas, <u>Absent Without Leave</u> and <u>Enter and Exit</u>.

"As long as I can remember," says the forty-eight-year-old narrator of <u>Absent Without Leave</u>, "... my aim in life has been to become unfit for duty... I would like to encourage suspicion as well as misunderstanding... I urge everyone to go absent without leave... You become human when you go absent without leave."

Wilhelm Bechtold is a casualty of the war. As he wanders about the thriving city of Cologne, observing the fruits of his country's "economic miracle," he is reminded of the past. His young wife was killed in an air raid in 1942. Her mortal remains were never found. His best friend was killed in 1939 by a French sentry who must have thought he was going to attack, although all he wanted to do was to give himself up. His father-in-law was executed by the Nazis as a traitor against the regime.

Now no one understands him except possibly his mother-in-law with whom he is planning to live as soon as his son-in-law finishes swindling him out of his coffee business. Not that he cares about the coffee business. He is a tea drinker.

<u>Enter and Exit</u> is a novella in two parts: "When the War Broke Out" and "When the War Was Over." The first part takes place in an army camp toward the end of August 1939. The hero is an undisciplined twenty-year-old draftee who is preoccupied mainly with calling his girl friend in Cologne through the post switchboard. It is hot, the barracks square deserted.

In the second part the same man is seen as he returns to Germany, a battle-scarred veteran of six years of

war, after being released from a prisoner of war camp.
He returns to a Germany that lies in rubble. In Bonn he
finds a telephone with great difficulty (they are reserved
for doctors and priests) and somehow manages to place a
call to his wife.

In these two novellas Heinrich Böll encompasses
"the whole Armageddon of World War II" without describing
a single battle or firing a single shot. Only a very
gifted writer could have achieved so much with so few
words.

IN COLD BLOOD

By Truman Capote (Random House, 1966).

On November 15, 1959, Herbert W. Clutter, a prominent Kansas wheat grower, his wife and two children, were
brutally murdered in their home in the small town of Holcomb. "Of all the people in all the world," everyone agreed,
"the Clutters were the least likely to be murdered."

Alvin Dewey, an agent of the Kansas Bureau of Investigation and a long-time friend of the Clutter family, was
put in charge of the investigation. "...I've seen some bad
things," Dewey remarked. "...But nothing so vicious as
this. However long it takes, it may be the rest of my
life, I'm going to know what happened in that house: the
why and the who."

As everyone must know by now, the killers were
Richard Eugene Hickock, aged thirty-three, and Perry Edward Smith, aged thirty-six. They had become acquainted
at the Kansas State Penitentiary where they plotted to rob
the Clutters and, if necessary, to kill them so that there
would be no witnesses.

There were virtually no clues and for weeks Al Dewey and his men seemed to get nowhere. While they methodically tracked down every possible lead, their fellow townspeople locked and bolted their doors. ("Howdy, Stranger!"
the sign in nearby Garden City says invitingly. "Welcome
to Garden City. A Friendly Place.") But then suddenly
there was a break in the strange and puzzling case. Now
Al Dewey and his men knew who they were looking for.
All they had to do was find them.

After leaving the Clutter farm, Dick Hickock and
Perry Smith went on a long hegira in which they covered
ten thousand miles in the space of six weeks, a hegira
composed of highways and hotels, motels, rivers, towns,
and cities, a chorus of entwining names: Apache, El Paso,
Corpus Christi, Santillo, San Luis Potosi, Acapulco, San
Diego, Dallas, Omaha, Sweetwater, Stillwater, Tenville
Junction, Tallahassee, Needles, Miami, Hotel Neuvo Wal-
dorf, Somerset Hotel, Hotel Simone, Arrowhead Motel,

Cherokee Motel and many, many more.

Eventually they returned to Kansas and Al Dewey and his men were waiting for them. On December 30, 1959, they were apprehended in Las Vegas, Nevada. More than five years later, they were executed by hanging in the Kansas State Penitentiary in Lansing.

In his account of the crime, In Cold Blood, Truman Capote claims to have invented a new form of literature which he calls a "non-fiction novel." Frankly, I do not think it is any such thing. It is a true account of a multiple murder and its consequences. It is only because Truman Capote writes nonfiction so much better than anyone else that gives him the temerity to think he has invented a new form.

If In Cold Blood is not a "non-fiction novel," it is more than just the true account of an especially gruesome crime. It is a profound social document. Perry Smith was first arrested in 1936 at the age of eight! Moreover, it is the intimate story -- an existentialist nightmare, really -- of the dark side of the American dream, the tragedy and heartbreak that lies always just beneath the surface of our cozy "Howdy, Stranger" America. And how ironic (somehow) that the man who wielded the gun should be the half-Indian, half-Irish offspring of professional rodeo performers, Flo Buckskin and Texas John Smith. Tex and Flo!

In the very first pages of the book we are given a glimpse of the master of River Valley Farm, broad-shouldered, healthy-hued and youthful, munching an apple at break of dawn. "It was apple-eating weather," we are told. But nobody -- least of all Mr. Clutter -- suspected that the apple was forbidden fruit and River Valley Farm in Holcomb, Kansas, near Garden City, anything but the Garden of Eden.

TOO FAR TO WALK

By John Hersey (Knopf, 1966).

John Hersey is a journalist who happens to write
novels.   In 1945 he won the Pulitzer Prize for his first
novel, A Bell for Adano.   The following year he wrote
Hiroshima, a sort of (with apologies to Truman Capote)
"nonfiction novel."

Now twenty years later this man with a real talent
for journalism is still plugging away at his profitable trade.
He has virtually made a career of writing "thesis novels."
They are not very good.   But that does not prevent him
from being good at it.

Hersey's latest "thesis novel" is Too Far to Walk.
The hero of this American fable is John Fist, a student at
Sheldon College in New England.   At first Fist is imbued
with his father's ideas about education.   This is all tied
in with the "ineluctability of the educational conveyor belt
... the relentlessness of the journey from grade school to
high school to college to graduate school to military service
to a Good Job to a suburb in Megalopolis, where one
would beget children and pass on to them the priceless lesson of life: --Learning equals earning!"

In his sophomore year John Fist tires of the academic "rat race" and is drawn to the campus radicals.   He
takes part in campus demonstrations.   He lets his hair grow
long.   He even stops going to classes.   "I don't know exactly why," he admits to his family.   "I didn't mind them so
much... I can't exactly say I wasn't interested.   It just
seems too far to walk to class a lot of the time."   Too far
to walk.   Was there ever a lamer excuse for a title?

Poor John Fist.   (Poor John Hersey!)   He doesn't like
the academic conveyor belt, but he doesn't like all this
ferment on campus either.   It seems he has made a contract with the devil (friend Breed) to sell his soul for experience.   "What a cheat his contract had so far proved to
be!" he thinks.   "Where were the soaring ecstasies Breed
had promised, where even were the acts of nihilism, deviltry, destructiveness?   John felt that, far from shooting

back and forth to the sharpest extremes of experience, he was, rather, drifting sluggishly through life, like a waterlogged log. He had lost the sense of control over his existence without gaining anything in its place."

But pact with the devil aside, surely John Fist (John Hersey) has got it all wrong. It is just the other way around. It is the student placidly riding the academic conveyor belt who is "drifting sluggishly through life, like a waterlogged log" (inelegant phrase). Conversely one does not lose one's sense of control over existence by taking part in a demonstration. The opposite is more likely to be true.

John Fist's pact with the devil is a failure. (After trying LSD Fist exclaims: "Not anything at all could be like this. The colors!" A pretty flat reaction, it must be granted.) But then so is author John Hersey's pact with his readers.

CRAZY FEBRUARY

By Carter Wilson (Lippincott, 1965).

After his graduation from Harvard in 1963, Carter
Wilson lived for a year among the Mayan Indians of southern
Mexico. Now at the age of twenty-four, he has written a
novel based on his experience in Mexico that novelists
twice his age might well envy.

If Truman Capote writes nonfiction that reads like
fiction, Carter Wilson writes fiction that reads like nonfiction. Indeed, Crazy February, written in a flat, under-
stated documentary style, sometimes reads more like a
sociological study of an impoverished Mexican town than
a real novel. But whatever it is, it is good. And Mr.
Capote, if he has done nothing else, has taught us to re-
examine our traditional attitudes and assumptions concerning the novel as a literary form.

The title refers to the fiesta of Carnaval held in February, the great fiesta of the year. There are bands, pro-
cessions, a huge market, and even skyrockets. No one can
escape the excitement of it. They are like crazy dogs, all
the men and boys, the young chasing the bulls, the old
snorting with pleasure like old dogs asleep in the sun and
dreaming.

For the Indians of the remote village of Shomtik,
the fiesta represents only a momentary respite from the
harsh reality of their daily lives. For these humble people
reality is the unrelenting struggle merely to exist. It is
going to the fincas in the north to work all day under the
hot sun in the fields for seven pesos.

The predicament of the Indians is summed up eloquently
in an exchange between Juan Lopez Osa and his brother
Miguel. When Miguel tells his brother that he intends to
stay in Arriaga and look for work, Juan replies that the
hot country isn't good for Indians. "We get sick here,"
he says, "you know that yourself." Miguel is silent for
a long time. At last he says, "Then we have to stop being Indians."

The Indians live in virtual bondage to their Mexican overseers and Carter Wilson has written with great sympathy and understanding about their struggle to find some measure of dignity and meaning in a world that seemingly rejects them.

He writes with sympathy and understanding, but he does not sentimentalize them.   His attitude is somewhat akin to that of Doctor Mendez who is of the opinion that all Mexicans who made beautiful pronouncements about the Indians were foolish.   "The Indians were men and they suffered like everyone else," Doctor Mendez reflects.

It remains to be seen whether this young writer will some day be reckoned among the best novelists of his generation.   One thing is already clear.   In his first novel he has had the wisdom and foresight to choose a universal theme.   That in itself is a considerable accomplishment.

THE MAGUS

By John Fowles (Little, Brown, 1966).

John Fowles is the English-born author of The Collector, a widely acclaimed first novel that has recently been made into a fine motion picture.   In The Collector a psychopathic young man kidnaps a beautiful girl and holds her prisoner.   He does not intend any harm, but simply wishes to worship her at his leisure.   Despite the fact that he treats her with extreme gentleness and respect, she withers away in her prison and dies.

The Collector was such a brilliant tour de force that it must have posed a problem for the author when it came to writing a second novel.   In The Magus John Fowles has met this problem head-on by elaborating in depth on the theme of The Collector.   One may have some doubts as to whether it succeeds, but if it does not it is still one of the most ambitious and honorable failures to come along in many years.

In an epigraph at the beginning of the novel, the author quotes from The Key to the Tarot by Arthur Edward Waite: "The Magus, Magician, or Juggler, the caster of the dice and mountebank in the world of vulgar trickery." John Fowles' Magus is Maurice Conchis, an elderly English-born Greek who lives in a luxurious villa on the beautiful island of Phraxos.

Conchis is also a "collector."   He does not collect beautiful girls, but rather misguided Englishmen who have made a mess of their lives.   On these unwitting subjects he conducts "an experiment in mystification."

The story is told by Nicholas Urfe, a young Oxford-educated Englishman who, bored, at odds with himself and the world, accepts a teaching position at an English boarding school in Greece.   Nicholas soon learns about the mysterious occupant of the villa at Bourani.   One day he goes there and introduces himself to Conchis.   In so doing he has unwittingly entered "the domaine."

At Bourani "every truth...was a sort of lie, and
every lie... a sort of truth." <u>The Magus</u> is an attempt
to shed light on the ultimate questions of illusion and reality and to do so in an entertaining way.   Nicholas calls
it "the godgame."

The godgame is an elaborate hoax, a masque (or
rather a series of masques) performed by Conchis, this
latter-day Svengali, and a cast of forty or fifty others, including two beautiful twin sisters named Lily (Julie) and
Rose (June).

"I am Theseus in the maze," poor bewildered Nicholas thinks, "let it all come, even the black minotaur, so
long as I may reach the center."   He thinks this on page
285 and there are still 297 pages to go!   In truth the reader
began to weary of the godgame even before page 285.   Like
Nicholas himself, I badly needed to "shout something de-
bunking, something adolescent and healthy and English..."
There are times when one suspects that the godgame has
gotten a little out of control.

And yet one is reluctant to put the book down and
thereby end the game.   John Fowles has great powers of
persuasion.   He invests so much effort and enthusiasm
into his godgame.   Note the detail in the following paragraph: "I walked over the gravel and under a brick arch.
There were two garages, and a little further down I could
see and smell stables.   A small boy appeared from a door
holding a bucket.   He saw me and called, 'Mummy! There's
a man.'   A slim woman in jodhpurs, a red headscarf and a
red tartan shirt came out of the same door.   She seemed to
be in her early forties; a still pretty, erect woman with an
open-air complexion."   Can anyone doubt that Nicholas was
there?   Or that John Fowles is not a Magus of sorts himself?

WARD 7

By Valeriy Tarsis (Dutton, 1966).

Valeriy Tarsis' Ward 7 is one of the most amazing documents ever to come out of the Soviet Union. Thinly disguised as fiction, it is not so important as a literary work as it is for what it tells us about what is going on inside Russia. Abram Tertz, the author of The Trial Begins and The Makepeace Experiment, is a much more accomplished novelist than Valeriy Tarsis. Both writers are critical of the regime. Both writers smuggled their dangerous works out of the Soviet Union. But consider this difference. Abram Tertz chose to remain anonymous and his books were published under a pseudonym, whereas Valeriy Tarsis has chosen to write under his own name and to accept the consequences.

Tarsis' novel, The Bluebottle, was published in England in 1962. Wishing to protect him, the publisher brought the book out under the name Ivan Valeriy, even though Tarsis insisted that his real name be used. Tarsis made no secret of the fact that he was the author of The Bluebottle. Even before its publication, he was arrested and committed to an insane asylum. After a great furore in the Western press, he was released in March of 1963. Undaunted he wrote an account of his experience as an inmate of Ward 7 and managed to smuggle it out of the country to be published, this time, under his own name.

Actually there is only one real lunatic among the 150 inmates of Ward 7 in this Moscow asylum known as the Kanatchikov Villa. Built to hold a maximum of one thousand patients, it is bursting at the seams with six thousand. No real attempt is made at treatment. The patients are merely stuffed with "happiness pills." The Kanatchikov Villa is not really a hospital at all, but a prison. It represents a convenient way for the authorities to stifle dissent.

Some of the inmates laughingly suggest that they are well off compared to the people outside. "Personally I'm very happy," exclaims Samdelov. "I'm fed, I'm clothed,

nobody preaches communism at me.   Do you realize?   No
propaganda, and you can say what you like!   Where else can
you do that?   I put down Remarque's <u>Black Obelisk</u> on my
library list and all I got was a reprimand!   How much more
can anyone ask?   And the company couldn't be nicer -- I
wouldn't at all mind spending the rest of my life with you
people!"

        Most of the book is taken up with an account of the
daily routine of Ward 7, as well as the individual histories
of Valeriy Tarsis (called Valentine Almazov) and his fellow
prisoners who comprise three main groups: the failed
suicides, the "Americans" (those who have tried to get in
touch with a foreign embassy), and finally the less clearly
defined category of young people who have failed to adjust
to life in the so-called "Socialist Paradise" and who reject
all its standards.

        All of this is quite illuminating to the Western reader,
but what is most impressive, even awe-inspiring, about this
unpretentious book is the author's single-minded and passionate commitment to the cause of freedom is his native land.
There is even something messianic about it and, goodness
knows, the Russians need a Messiah.   "Freedom is the one
unarguable good on earth," Valentine Almazov says.   "Almazov thirsted for action," we are told, "he saw it as sacra-
mental.   His duty as a writer was to speak new words, and
his worst fear was of uttering words which failed to become
acts, failed to become God transfiguring our wretched, terrifying, bankrupt world."   <u>Ward 7</u> is Valeriy Tarsis' sacra-
mental act.

A GENEROUS MAN

By Reynolds Price (Atheneum, 1966).

A Generous Man is a new novel by the author of A Long and Happy Life. As in the earlier novel, Reynolds Price writes about the Mustian family of Afton, North Carolina, though the novel takes place at an earlier point in time. The Mustians are hard-working and respected tobacco farmers who are as droll of speech as they are hard of muscle.

Actually this is not so much the story of the Mustian family as it is the story of the coming-of-age of fifteen-year-old Milo Mustian. The novel covers a period of three days and at the end of that time Milo can say, "My learning's just started but I've learned some things."

It all begins on the morning after Milo's return from the Warren County Fair where he manages to see the "hootchy-kootchy show" and meets Lois Provo, a sixteen-year-old carnival girl from Clearwater, Florida. The plot gets very complicated indeed (Reynolds Price throws out all the stops in this one), but suffice it to say that before the day is over a 280 pound python has gotten loose and is being pursued by a dog (believed mad) belonging to Milo's mentally retarded younger brother, Rato. Rato has in turn vanished in search of his dog.

Sheriff Rob Pomeroy organizes what can only be described as an "epic hunt." "...I've had a full life," Sheriff Pomeroy says at the start of the hunt, "I'm honored to have it -- but this job today is the height of my life. And I've got a strong feeling...that all of us here, every man and boy with a part in this day will end bigger men in the eyes of their loved ones and enemies if they play that part the Lord has given them."

As if a twenty-foot python, a mad dog and a retarded fourteen-year-old boy were not enough to contend with, the novel is further enlivened by the presence of a mysterious wanderer from out of the past and by the Sheriff's love-starved wife. There are plots within plots, mysterious revelations and strange coincidences, that somehow all seem to fit together to form an extraordinarily vivid, if not quite convincing, canvas.

Convincing or not (and Reynolds Price apparently has a higher purpose in mind than merely to be convincing), A Generous Man would seem to be an important novel by a young man destined to become a major novelist. Reynolds Price reminds this reviewer of John Updike and A Generous Man compares very favorably with The Centaur. Both writers possess a very individual and poetic prose style, but Reynolds Price's style seems to flow more naturally out of his milieu -- I understand people still speak a pure, almost Elizabethan English in some parts of Appalachia -- whereas John Updike's style often seems self-consciously "literary," even pretentious. Both writers lean heavily on symbolism. The python in A Generous Man, for example, is named Death.

There is a very eloquent passage near the end of the novel in which Milo mourns his poor lost brother. In speaking these sentiments Milo gives expression to the kind of moral world he envisages as good and healthy. They sum up the theme of the novel better than anything this reviewer could write. "To be born with half the mind that most people get," Milo says, "...to stand in your life and never look forward to being grown, giving somebody something -- their food and their pleasure; to think you would sleep every night of your life a dog in winter, curled on yourself to save your own little heat...I know I'm a child but I hadn't stood still. I have learned some things, and this is one thing --if Rato's dead he's in Heaven, all right. He's had all the Hell he ever could have earned in four hundred years much less fourteen."

DESPAIR

By Vladimir Nabokov (Putnam, 1966).

      Vladimir Nabokov's publisher has recently been bring-
ing out English editions of his early Russian novels. Despair
was written in 1932 in Berlin and serialized in the émigré
review Sovremennye Zapiski. An English version published
by John Long Limited of London first appeared in 1937.
The book sold badly, Nabokov tells us in a brief foreword,
and a few years later a German bomb destroyed the entire
stock. Interestingly enough, Nabokov himself did the English
translation. "Although I had been scribbling in English all
my literary life in the margin, so to say, of my Russian
writings," he writes, "this was my first serious attempt...
to use English for what may be loosely termed an artistic
purpose."

      Despair is probably not one of Nabokov's more im-
portant novels, but somehow this does not seem to make
much difference where he is concerned. His genius lies
not so much in what he has to say, but in the way he says
it. A novel by Vladimir Nabokov cannot be mistaken for
anyone else's.

      Hermann Karlovich, the protagonist of Despair, is
every bit as mad as Humbert Humbert. Hermann, a sales
executive for a chocolate concern, lives a comfortable
middle-class existence in Berlin with his doting but rather
scatter-brained wife, Lydia. On a business trip to Prague,
he comes across a tramp in a deserted field. To his
amazement he discovers that the man looks enough like him
to pass for his twin brother. The tramp's name is Felix.

      Hermann returns to Berlin, but he cannot put Felix
out of his mind. Despite everything, he keeps seeing himself in the sorry disguise of a tramp, his face motionless,
with chin and cheeks bristle-shaded, as happens to a dead
man overnight.

      As happens to a dead man overnight. A diabolical
plan begins to form in the dark recesses of his mind. He
will commit the perfect crime. "Let us discuss crime,"
Hermann says, "crime as an art...Oh, Conan Doyle! How

marvelously you could have crowned your creation when your
two heroes began boring you! What an opportunity, what a
subject you missed! For you could have written one last
tale concluding the whole Sherlock Holmes epic; one last
episode beautifully setting off the rest: the murderer in that
tale should have turned out to be not the one-legged book-
keeper, not the Chinaman Ching and not the woman in crimson, but the very chronicler of the crime stories, Dr. Watson himself -- Watson, who, so to speak, knew what was
Whatson. A staggering surprise for the reader."

"But what are they -- Doyle, Dostoevsky, Leblanc,
Wallace," Hermann continues, "what are all the great novelists who wrote of nimble criminals, what are all the great
criminals who never read the nimble novelists -- what are
they in comparison with me? Blundering fools! As in the
case of inventive geniuses, I was certainly helped by chance
(my meeting Felix), but that piece of luck fitted exactly into the place I had made for it; I pounced upon it and used
it, which another in my position would not have done."

This reviewer will not divulge any more of the plot.
Despair is Hermann's story and he should be allowed to
finish it. "As a rule I have always been noted for my exceptional humorousness," Hermann writes, "it goes naturally
with a fine imagination; woe to the fancy which is not accompanied by wit." He might have been talking about his
creator, Vladimir Nabokov.

THE GATES OF THE FOREST

By Elie Wiesel (Holt, Rinehart and Winston, 1966).

Elie Wiesel was born in Hungary in 1928. While still a child, he was deported to Auschwitz. Somehow he managed to survive the holocaust. But of course one can only survive such an experience in a physical sense. For Elie Wiesel the clouds have not always been clouds, but Jews driven from their homes and transformed into clouds. Stars have not always been stars, but the eyes of Jewish children killed in the transparent light of dawn.

Elie Wiesel has survived to write about what happened and ask why it happened. Now in his fourth and perhaps finest novel, The Gates of the Forest, beautifully translated from the French by Frances Frenaye, Elie Wiesel asks how it is possible to go on living in a world that God would appear to have abandoned.

As the novel begins, Gregor is hiding out in a cave in a forest in Transylvania. Another youth stumbles upon his hiding place and Gregor takes him in. Gregor asks him his name and the youth replies that he does not have a name. Gregor's real name is Gavriel, but he cannot risk using a Jewish name. "Your name left you and mine has gone into hiding," Gregor says, "like myself. On that score we're even, you and I."

In a symbolic gesture, Gregor gives the nameless youth his name. "I don't need my name any more," he says. "I'm giving it to you; it's yours. Take it, Gavriel." Gavriel literally means 'Man of God.' The novel takes place during the last year of the war. With the liberation of Europe, Gregor emigrates to America. Although still not able to exorcise the past, he is able to walk freely among men as Gavriel.

Between the time he gives his name away (Spring) and the time it is restored (Winter), a great deal happens. Gavriel sacrifices his life for Gregor. Gregor leaves the cave and takes refuge with the kindly old family servant, Maria. He poses as Maria's deaf-mute nephew. When his identity becomes known, he flees to the forest where he joins a band of partisans. In attempting to rescue Gavriel

from his captors, Gregor inadvertently betrays his friend
Lieb the Lion. This episode is a kind of parable based on
the betrayal of Christ in the Bible.

Elie Wiesel carries a terrible weight on his shoulders,
a weight such as few men have lived to bear. This terrible
weight, this knowledge, gives to his utterance a passionate
intensity almost unique in modern literature. In trying to
alleviate this terrible burden, he goes right to the point
and asks the fundamental questions of God and man. "And
Auschwitz?" Gregor asks the Rebbe in America. "What
do you make of Auschwitz?"

"Auschwitz proves that nothing has changed," the
Rebbe replies, "that the primeval war goes on. Man is
capable of love and hate, murder and sacrifice. He is
Abraham and Isaac together. God himself hasn't changed."

Gregor is angry. "After what happened to us, how
can you believe in God?" With an understanding smile on
his lips the Rebbe answers, "How can you not believe in
God after what has happened?"

THE PREMIER AND THE TRAIN

By Georges Simenon (Harcourt, Brace and World, 1966).

Georges Simenon, the world-famous creator of Inspector Maigret, does not like the idea of being regarded only as a brilliant writer of detective stories. In recent years he has turned his attention to the serious novel. La Bicêtre and The Little Saint were generally well received, though this reviewer found them somewhat disappointing. They seemed rather stodgy after the excitement of the Maigret stories.

Simenon's latest book contains two short novels entitled The Premier and The Train. The Premier is about one of the most powerful men in France who at the age of eighty-two learns that he has merely been manipulated by those around him. The Train is about a quiet, rather dull radio engineer who, when the Germans invade Belgium in 1940, is abruptly wrenched from his comfortable, humdrum existence and hurled into the excitement, terror and delicious irresponsibility of war. The Premier is Simenon at his pompous worst; The Train, a minor masterpiece except for the ending, is probably one of the finest stories he has ever written.

The main trouble with The Premier is that, if ever a writer had the common touch it is Simenon, and yet we are asked to believe that this lonely old man living in retirement on the Normandy coast was once one of the five most powerful men in the world whose "faintest frown on emerging from a meeting, would be reported in press communiques with banner headlines in all the newspapers." We are also asked to believe that this great man of France has for years been hiding incriminating documents in his library in the event that one of his unscrupulous ex-colleagues should rise to power. But of course the aging former head of state has not counted on the cunning of the governmental bureaucracy in the person of Superintendent Dolomieu, who with the cooperation of the Premier's servants has taken the precaution of having the incriminating documents secretly copied and returned. All these absurd contretemps are apparently meant to illustrate the thesis that power is an illusion. All this reviewer can say in conclusion is tell it to General De Gaulle!

    The narrator of <u>The Train</u> is Marcel Féron who
lives with his wife and small daughter in a neat house with
garden in the village of Fumoy in the Ardennes. When the
Germans attack Belgium, Marcel and his family join the
stream of refugees fleeing before the German advance.
They manage to board a train, but are soon separated.
Marcel finds himself alone with a motley group of refugees
in an old cattle car. He has no idea where they are going
nor does he care. All at once he is experiencing a sense
of freedom that he has never known before. He is no longer
responsible for his actions. He is just "one man among
millions whom superior forces were going to toss about at
will."

    He falls in love with Anna, about whom he knows
nothing except that she has just been released from prison.
But of course they both know that their love has no future.
Marcel has a family with whom he must soon be reunited.
Anna has merely attached herself to him for the duration
of a long, meandering train ride. A break has occurred,
but that does not mean that the past has ceased to exist or
that he has repudiated his family and stopped loving them.
It is just that, for an indeterminate period, he is living
on another level, where the values have nothing in common
with those of his previous existence.

    Unfortunately Simenon adds a postcript that is more
dramatic than convincing. Anna turns up again with an
English airman at a most inappropriate time. Suddenly a
classic story of war and its disruptive as well as exhilarating effect on individuals in particular and society in
general becomes merely a vehicle for an aspiring novelist,
an erstwhile writer of detective stories, to point a moral.

OLD POWDER MAN

By Joan Williams (Harcourt, Brace and World, 1966).

Joan Williams' first novel, <u>The Morning and the Even-</u>ing, received enthusiastic praise when it was published in 1961. "To her simple materials," wrote Robert Penn Warren, "Joan Williams brings the art of the born storyteller, subtlety of psychological insight, and a deep clarity of feeling. She has, in fact, that last and greatest gift: to move the heart."

The hero of Joan Williams' first novel was a mute named Jake, considered "not quite right in the head" by his fellow townspeople. The hero of Miss Williams' second novel, <u>Old Powder Man,</u> is a tough self-made man, Frank "Dynamite" Wynn, who perfected the use of dynamite for the construction of levees and roads, clearing borrow pits, draining swampland and other industrial purposes. "Dynamite" Wynn is not a very sympathetic character and does not easily "move the heart."

It would have been easy for the author to caricature "Son" Wynn (as Sinclair Lewis caricatured Babbitt), but this she has refused to do. Her object is not to make fun of him, but rather to try to understand him, to place his life in the context of his time and place. It is a tribute to her integrity and skill as a novelist that she has succeeded in this difficult task as well as she has.

The story of Frank "Dynamite" Wynn is a uniquely American one. He literally blasted his way to success. When the Flood Emancipation Act of The Mississippi Valley was passed in 1928, it was "Son" Wynn who furnished the dynamite and the know-how to build the great levee from Cairo to New Orleans. In writing about the levee camps of those days hacked out of the American wilderness and of the rough men who occupied them, Miss Williams has contributed a superb portrait of one aspect of our American past. It is, after all, the Frank Wynns who settled the West and tamed the Mississippi. Whether we like them or not, we cannot disown them.

By the early 1940's the job was done and the levee

stretched, unbroken, from Cairo to New Orleans. Son
termed what began then "the second go-round." For the
next ten years his work would be enlarging, rehabilitating,
reinforcing work already done. The Engineers would widen,
deepen and change the river's channels, making more cut-off
until the Mississippi River would flow the way men wanted
it to, not the way it was intended.

But still only in his fifties, Frank "Dynamite" Wynn
is a broken man. Having looked forward all his life to retirement, he is not prepared when ill health forces retirement upon him. "I started out working when I was fourteen
years old," he confides to his friend Buzz. "I never have
known how to do anything but work." This is the tragedy
of Frank Wynn.

Son's college-educated daughter, Laurel, surely
speaks for the author when she eloquently sums up his
epitaph. "He had always said he came along at the right
time in the right place," she thinks, "seen the business
there when he was. Beyond fame, the mark he had left
on the countryside would last. So would his mark on her...
Directions her life would take would be because of him.
She had even begun to believe she would find out some of
the things he never could. She would not make exactly his
mistakes. In turn her children would know more than she.
It made everything all right."

A COUNTRY OF STRANGERS

By Conrad Richter (Knopf, 1966).

A Country of Strangers is the companion novel to
Conrad Richter's classic The Light in the Forest. The
Light in the Forest told the story of True Son, a captive
white boy adopted at the age of four by an Indian chief of
the Lenni Lenape tribe. Eleven years later True Son is
reunited with his white parents, but finds that he is more
Indian than white. True Son returns to the tribe. When he
refuses to take part in a raid against his own people, however, he is condemned to death. The Indians spare his life
on the condition that he return to the whites.

Although True Son appears briefly toward the end of
the novel, A Country of Strangers is the story of Stone
Girl, another white captive of the Lenni Lenape tribe of
what is now Ohio, but was then still part of the Northwest
Territory. "When I was young I was also taken captive by
the Lenapes," Stone Girl relates. "My cowardly white skin
was washed away. I was made a daughter of Feast Maker.
He took out my pale Yengwe heart and gave me the brave
heart of the Indian. I was shown how to plant and hoe corn,
to make meal, to cut up the deer and cook it and dress and
tan the skin. The great hunter and warrior Espan became
my husband."

Never Laugh, the white woman taken captive on the
same raid as Stone Girl, has never let her forget who she
is. "You must remember, Mary, who you are," she would
say. "Not Stone Girl, daughter of Feast Maker and granddaughter of Machilek, but Mary Stanton, daughter of Captain Peter Stanton, assemblyman and friend of the proprie-
taries of Pennsylvania."

One day the word flew like Tskinnak, the blackbird,
among the cabins of the village. It was that the Lenni
Lenape must give up all children who had once been white,
captives taken in raids across the Ohio and adopted into the
tribe, even those who had married Indians, and their children. The white captain at the Forks had decreed it. He
had come into the Indian forest with more warriors than
leaves on a tree. Should the Indians refuse, his army would
never depart, but settle here in the heart of the Indian

country, cutting down the Indian forest, shooting the Indian game, and growing like a white cancer in the heart of the red man.

A Country of Strangers tells what happens when Stone Girl is returned to her parents. It is not a happy story, but rather a story of exile and wandering, of an alien in a "country of strangers." It is an American tragedy.

"In The Trees and The Town," Conrad Richter writes in a brief foreword, "I have written of the Indian from the white man's point of view. Here I would like to continue the design of The Light in the Forest, which observes the white man from the viewpoint of that not ignoble race which once called this continent home but whose people were deprived, often rooked, of their rights and lands; their native conceptions of primitive justice and national defense cried out against; their very presence hated and despised; their reduced numbers, never large in the first place, driven from exile to exile; their solemn treaties with us repeatedly broken by their "white fathers"; their poetic, generally honorable and childlike savage nature corrupted by the white man's perfidy, liquor, and disease until their fate today remains a blot on our national conscience."

LANDSCAPE IN CONCRETE

By Jakov Lind (Grove Press, 1966).

Landscape in Concrete is a first novel by the author of the highly acclaimed collection of short stories, Soul of Wood. Born in Vienna in 1927, Jakov Lind was only eleven years old when the Nazis took over Austria. He managed to escape to Holland where forged papers enabled him to survive the war. At the present time he lives in England.

Landscape in Concrete is an allegory about Nazi Germany. The hero of the tale is Sergeant Gauthier Bachmann of the Eighth Hessian Infantry Regiment. At Voroshenko on October 22, 1941, Bachmann's regiment was decimated by the Russians. "My regiment, Herr Major, it vanished off the face of the earth in Voroshenko," he tells Major von Goritz, "it drowned in the mud as if it had never been there. It was simply gone. When I woke up in the hospital in Oppeln, it was gone."

Sergeant Bachmann's private war begins when he goes AWOL in 1943. Having apparently lost his sanity at Voroshenko, his superiors request that he be discharged as mentally unfit for service. The one thing that Bachmann cannot bear is not to be able to serve the fatherland. In desperation he goes off, like Don Quixote, on a fool's errand in search of his regiment and his reason. His travels take him from Palermo, Italy, to Narvik, Norway. In essence he is a terrifying caricature of the Good Soldier Schweik.

There would seem to be little doubt that Sergeant Gauthier Bachmann is a personification of Nazi Germany in particular and modern Germany in general. Standing well over six feet tall and weighing three hundred pounds, as physically healthy and strong as an ox, Bachmann is referred to as "this pedantic gorilla." Bachmann is from an old, respected family, as he is fond of pointing out. There are Bachmanns in every district council and school board. "We even have a bishop in the family," Bachmann says proudly. Bachmann himself is a highly skilled craftsman in civilian life, a gold silversmith who can admire the exquisite chasing on a tea set.

Conceiving it to be his duty as a soldier, Bachmann does not flinch from murdering an entire Narvik family in cold blood, but he refuses to steal the Carl Erzmann tea set that he admires so much. Good upbringing is stronger than greed. "I say shoot and you shoot," the quisling Hjalmar Halftan laughs disbelievingly. "I say cut him open and you cut the poor kid open. I say knock him out and you pretty near kill him. You're quite a number. You've really let yourself be made an ass of, ha-ha-ha! Lord, what lunatics there are in the world today!"

Even Bachmann, out to dispel the last vestiges of his guilt, begins to perceive the truth. "I honestly thought the world had conspired against me. I was absolutely convinced that everybody was out to humiliate me and push me aside, but now I know it. They wanted to humiliate me and push me aside, they knew what I didn't know, but know now. And they were banking on it. That I'm sick. And they all used the sick man for their own ends. They abused me!"

One can only hope that this sick giant, described in this harsh but brilliant allegory, will recover, and there are signs that he will. But that is not the message of this despairing and fanatical book. What can one expect, however, from a novel that begins with the words: "There is a plague called man."

NORWOOD

By Charles Portis (Simon and Schuster, 1966).

Norwood Pratt, the twenty-three-year-old hero of Charles Portis' fresh and altogether captivating first novel entitled Norwood, is in the tradition of such memorable literary characters of the past as Huck Finn, Holden Caulfield and Captain Yossarian. He is unique. He is disarming. He is winning. He may well be the fictional discovery of the year.

Norwood is an ex-Marine who lives with his sister Vernell in a tumble-down house on Route 82 in Ralph, Texas, just the other side of Texarkana in Bowie County. He works at the Nipper Independent Oil Co. Servicenter which features dishes and cheap gasoline and where the rest rooms are locked for the protection of the customers.

Although Vernell is not too bright, Norwood gets a job for her as a waitress at the New Ralph Hotel Coffee Shop. The job works out too well. Money and position go to Vernell's head. Some weeks, with the tips, she made more money then Norwood. It was a terrible state of affairs. Then with absolutely no warning Vernell marries a disabled veteran named Bill Bird and brings him home to live in the little house on the highway.

At the local roller skating rink, Norwood meets Grady Fring, the Kredit King ("You can't convince Grady your credit is bad"), and they make a deal. Norman will drive two cars in tandem to New York for fifty dollars and expenses. Norwood wants to go there anyway as his ex-Marine buddy, Joe William Reese, owes him seventy dollars. As an extra added attraction, a Miss Yvonne Phillips is to go along for the ride.

All dressed up in his best black hat, the brim curled up in front to defy wind resistance, and his thirty-eight-dollar stovepipe boots, coal-black fourteen inchers with red butterflies emblazoned on the insteps, Norwood takes off for the big city. At the last minute he decides to take along his guitar made in West Germany. Norwood has ambitions of some day becoming a star on the Louisiana Hay-

ride, the celebrated hillbilly show, presented Saturday nights on KWKH in Shreveport.

New York is a disappointment and Norwood learns that Joe William has left his Eleventh Street apartment to return home. In the subway the air smells of "electricity and dirt." (Has anyone else ever described that peculiar smell so well?) On the way back to Texas Norwood meets Rita Lee and they fall in love on a Trailways bus.

In Jacksonville the two lovers make the acquaintance of Edmund B. Ratner, "The world's smallest perfect man," and Joann the wonder hen. "She's plenty smart for a chicken," Norwood says. "There's no question about it." Edmund replies. "I'm sure a good agent could get her something. Perhaps some small role in an Erskine Caldwell film."

To rectify whatever impression this reviewer may have given that Charles Portis, a newspaper man from El Dorado, Arkansas, is only a jokester, I would like to quote a paragraph to convey the underlying realism, the sadness and beauty, of his prose style:

"They reached Jacksonville in the very early morning. The sun was not hot yet but it was bright and painful to their grainy eyes. A dozen or so Marines in limp khaki and with ruined shoeshines were hanging about the station waiting for the last liberty bus back. Fatigue and unhappiness were in their faces, as of young men whose shorts are bunching up. A city cop and an MP sat together in a squad car outside, slumped down in the seat, not talking, and too bored or tired even to go to the trouble of looking mean. Inside the station on a bench some mail-order baby chicks were cheeping away in a perforated box."

THE LATE BOURGEOIS WORLD

By Nadine Gordimer (Viking Press, 1966).

One sometimes feels guilty about reading novels other than as a form of escapism (reading mysteries is generally acknowledged to be quite harmless.) Should not a grown man be reading histories and biographies? Everyone knows that public men who admit to reading at all admit only to reading histories and biographies. Then history itself, the naked act, explodes in the headlines. The Prime Minister of South Africa is killed at the hands of an assassin's knife. The historian and journalist furiously scribble their notes to make the next deadline or edition. But even before the act was committed, the novelist had coolly and intelligently analyzed the situation and put it all down in the form of a novel. The mind and vision of the artist (not the pundit) is the prophecy of things to come.

In a short, eloquent novel entitled The Late Bourgeois World, Nadine Gordimer, a resident of Johannesburg, has sounded the death knell of apartheid in South Africa. In 120 tightly-knit pages she has succeeded in penetrating behind the headlines to bring us a glimpse of "a nation in transition." She has described the social and political forces that divide the country. Moreover, she has not only described how these forces relate to each other, but how they act upon each other. In The Late Bourgeois World she has done no less than write the history of her country.

The title, with the emphasis on late, is purely ironic. The late bourgeois world is represented by the narrator's eighty-seven-year-old grandmother, an inmate of the Home, who lives entirely in the past. In her room with the signed photographs of famous artists hanging on the walls (and the framed menu of the lunch where she met Noel Coward in 1928), it always seems that nothing has happened. Or that everything has already happened.

The old lady was proud when Elizabeth married Max Van Den Sandt, the son of the wealthy M.P. Of course it was taken for granted that Max would follow in his father's illustrious footsteps, but things did not work out that way.

Espousing the cause of African nationalism, Max Van Den
Sandt failed his parents, just as in the end he failed the
cause to which he had dedicated his life by turning state's
witness (no one knew under what pressure) after serving
fifteen months of a five-year sentence. There was nothing
left for him to do but commit suicide.

Now left alone with her young son to provide for,
Elizabeth must make up her mind what part she will play,
if any, in the continuing struggle for the liberation of the
Black majority. She must decide at a time when it takes
more courage than ever before to work for the movement.
The challenge is put to her by Luke Fokase. Luke knows
what he wants, and he knows who it is he must get it from.
He knows almost by instinct that a sympathetic white woman
always retains some footing, no matter how tenuously, in
the "good old White Reserve of banks and privileges."

Elizabeth is both an idealist and a realist, as the
author herself must be. There must be other Elizabeths
in South Africa and elsewhere. They are idealists because
they know that apartheid can have no place in an ideal
world. They are realists because they recognize that when
segregation is practiced everybody loses, the Whites as
well as the Blacks. One of the most moving things in this
novel is the sense of desolation and loneliness it conveys
in regard to the unnatural and enforced separation of the
races. The Blacks -- ten million strong -- are always on
the other side of the fence with their delivery bicycles, or
in working overalls, the "legends of firms across their
backs."

THE FIXER

By Bernard Malamud (Farrar, Straus and Giroux, 1966).

In the Summer of 1911 in the city of Kiev, Russia,
an employee of a small brickworks named Mendel Beiliss
was arrested and accused of the murder of a thirteen-year-
old boy.   In the Russia of Tsar Nicholas II with its long
anti-Semitic history, its pogroms and Pale of Settlement,
Mendel Beiliss was an unfortunate scapegoat whose only
crime was being a Jew.   For two years Beiliss was held
in prison while the prosecution tried desperately to build
a case against him.   But despite bribery, lies and threats,
they could not even convince a prejudiced jury of Beiliss'
guilt and he was finally exonerated.

Although Bernard Malamud has said that his novel,
The Fixer, is an imaginative piece of work and should not
be tied to the Beiliss case, there are many points of similarity.   The Beiliss case has obviously given the author
the idea and inspiration for his novel.   It also seems to
have furnished the moral.   The one thing that suffering
teaches Malamud's fixer is that there is no such thing as
an unpolitical man, especially a Jew.   "You can't be one
without the other," he realizes, "that's clear enough.   You
can't sit still and see yourself destroyed."   The fixer refuses to be destroyed and this is his salvation.

Like Mendel Beiliss, Yakov Bok, a simple handyman,
is imprisoned for more than two years for a crime he did
not commit, the murder of a Russian youth.   Accident and
history have involved Yakov Bok as he never dreamed he
could be involved.   "Veh is mir," he intones.   "I'm a fixer
but all my life I've broken more than I fix."   The Beiliss
case has many ramifications, but what seems to have impressed Malamud the most was the depth of the man's suffering.   At least this is what he has emphasized in The Fixer.

Whenever Yakov Bok thinks that he has been through
the worst, there is always worse to come.   Almost the
entire novel takes place within the narrow confines of
Yakov's cell, although this is not strictly true since one
cannot always imprison a man's mind.   "The cell is your
woods and sky," Yakov thinks.   "Vanzetti went mad and

was confined to Massachusetts General," Malamud told an interviewer. "I incorporated that into Yakov. When I leave him, he is at the next step to commitment. The reason is that he has suffered injustice. What has happened to Yakov and how he changes is the story. But what happens to Yakov after I leave him, I don't know."

What happens to Yakov Bok is that he suffers. When he intones dolorously, "Veh is mir," he has told us everything, but this does not constitute a novel. Bernard Malamud must tell us over and over again, "Veh is mir." As fine a novelist as he is (and until this novel, I thought he was just about the best there was), he cannot bring it off. The author of that wonderfully inventive, wild and witty novel, A New Life, with its extraordinary feeling for nature, has limited himself too severely.

What Malamud has probably demonstrated in The Fixer is that it is just about impossible to convey the experience of suffering by writing about it in the third person. One can describe a series of calamities that overtakes a man, but suffering itself continues to elude one. No matter how sincere his intentions, Bernard Malamud cannot really put himself in the place of Mendel Beiliss, alias Yakov Bok. The difference between what Mendel Beiliss, alias Yakov Bok, must have gone through and what Bernard Malamud is able to convey of this man's suffering is too great.

THE NOWHERE CITY

By Alison Lurie (Coward-McCann, 1966).

In reviews of The Nowhere City Alison Lurie has been
compared to Jane Austen. This reviewer was reminded not
so much of Jane Austen as Henry James. In such novels
as The American and The Ambassadors, Henry James
dramatically juxtaposed two different ways of life, the American and European. Now almost one hundred years later,
Alison Lurie has shifted her gaze westward and focused on
southern California. With the Americanization of Europe,
there is probably a greater difference between the mores of
southern California and New England than between those of
New England and Western Europe. Miss Lurie, an extremely gifted young novelist, has exploited this difference with
a vengeance.

The "Nowhere City" is of course Los Angeles,
better known as L.A. As a novel about Los Angeles and
environs, The Nowhere City compares quite favorably with
F. Scott Fitzgerald's The Last Tycoon, Nathanael West's
The Day of the Locust and Evelyn Waugh's The Loved One.
But it is more than just a novel about Los Angeles. It is
also a shrewd and witty study of the clash of cultures when
a young Harvard historian and his shy and refined wife move
to Los Angeles from Cambridge, Mass.

Paul Cattleman, his Ph.D. thesis still incomplete,
takes a year's leave from teaching to accept a high-paying
position with the Nutting Research and Development Corporation, one of the largest electronic companies in southern
California. Paul, with his degrees in history and literature,
and his Navy radar training, is just the person they are
looking for to write a history of the company.

Paul and Katherine Cattleman feel differently about
the move to L.A. and their new home in Mars Vista-on-the
Freeway. Paul is enthusiastic about the move. For him
Los Angeles expressed everything toward which our civilization was tending. As one went to Europe to see the
living past, so one must visit southern California to observe the future. He liked to think of this city as the last
American frontier. Whoever has some little interest, even

faith, in man must ask what he might do if he were set
free of a restrictive tradition, a hostile climate. Why
condemn his first extravagances? As for Katherine, the
whole idea of southern California is anathema to her. She
hates everything about L. A. , the climate, the smog (which
irritates her chronic sinus condition), the monstrous flora
and fauna, even the people.

    The plot takes some surprising twists and turns,
like L. A. itself; the partners change hands as in some
kooky ballet, and when they are reunited, they are no longer
what they were. Katherine gets a job as a research assistant to Dr. Isidore Einsam, a bearded Beverly Hills psychiatrist, and obtains a free analysis. Her sinusitis im-
proves and people are soon calling her Kay. Paul discovers
Ceci O'Connor, a far-out waitress who digs Beckett, and
has a brief fling with a gorgeous Hollywood starlet in an
outsized swimming pool. It is perhaps no coincidence that
the starlet's husband is none other than Dr. "Iz" Einsam.

    While Paul and Katherine adjust (or fail to adjust)
to their new life, our talented author-guide takes us on a
dazzling tour, a genuine spectacular, of the L. A. scene,
from Bohemian Venice to Beverly Hills, from the U. C. L. A.
campus to the corner of Hollywood and Vine. The Nowhere City is not only a brilliant satirical novel, but a marvelously entertaining one as well, a combination that suggests (Henry James, please move over) Mary McCarthy at
her irreverent, free-swinging best.

THE SECRET SWINGER

By Alan Harrington (Knopf, 1966).

Alan Harrington is the author of one previous novel,
The Revelations of Dr. Modesto, and a scathing indictment
of corporate life in America, Life in the Crystal Palace.
In his new novel, The Secret Swinger, the author once
again attacks (among other things) conformism in American
life and demonstrates that he is one of the ablest practi-
tioners of that difficult genre, the "novel of ideas."

The hero of The Secret Swinger is George Pectin,
a member of the editorial staff of Forecast magazine
George is a slender, youngish man with dark circles under
his eyes. A pale descendant of a prominent old New England family, he has become habituated to failure as other
men are to success. Now forty-three has struck for him
like a warning bell. He thinks: Get going, time is short.
Warning flags were up all over the course. No more promises. Nearly everybody he knew had surpassed him,
leaving the obscure staff reporter behind. The wild and
rebellious, seemingly impractical friends he had knocked
about with in his Greenwich Village days had become famous.
Other stodgy ones with less ability had persisted and somehow made reputations. He had moved indecisively in neutral
ground between the rebellious and the stodgy.

Haunted by pale ancestral ghosts -- his staid New
England family -- and hounded by the bitter taste of failure,
George Pectin becomes obsessed with an idea. "Something
has been withheld from me," he tells a stranger on a train.
"I'm speaking of true love. Yes, I know. It fades, supposedly. But I refuse to believe that I've been left out
emotionally. I think it's just because I haven't met her."
Her is George Pectin's feminine double, the one woman in
this world waiting for him, the ideal mate whom he must
seek out no matter how long it takes. "Most of us lack the
guts to keep on searching for our counterpart," George exclaims. "That's why there are so few happy marriages.
We settle. . . " George almost seems to think of this
feminine double in messianic terms, as a substitute for
religion as it were, and this is undoubtedly part of what
ails him.

At any rate, George Pectin obtains a Mexican divorce from his pale, sickly wife, Mary, and goes out into the world in search of his feminine double and a new life. The author has used a series of train rides with imagination and wit as a literary device to bridge the ominous gap between his hero's old life as an obscure staff reporter on Forecast and his exciting new life as "the secret swinger."

As the secret swinger, George inevitably gyrates to Greenwich Village where he meets his old nemesis, George Muchnik, and a girl named Serena who has instructions to "turn him on." "Why don't you live!" Muchnik bellows in his ear, while George ponders the question, "Why can't a man over forty ignore his years?"

In the end, George Pectin learns that he cannot escape those pale, ancestral ghosts. The tragedy of George Pectin is that he is fundamentally a schizophrenic personality for whom a train ride is the only reality. But this is also the tragedy of America, the author seems to be saying. Schizophrenia is the sickness of our times. There are too many George Pectins riding indecisively back and forth in neutral ground between the rebellious and the stodgy.

THE SEEDS OF HIROSHIMA

By Edita Morris (Braziller, 1966).

Before the Second World War Edita Morris was known primarily as a writer of light fiction. Typical of this period was My Darling from the Lions which became a best-seller in several countries. "New experiences were to change my writing," Edita Morris has written. "I saw Auschwitz. I saw Greece after its civil war. I saw Hiroshima. My book, Charade, which tells of exhausted children singing and acting their way through shattered Poland, was inspired by Auschwitz. My Greek experiences resulted in the short novel, The Toil and the Deed. My three lengthy stays in Hiroshima, each a revelation on a new level, were followed by the writing of The Flowers of Hiroshima, and now The Seeds of Hiroshima. "

The Flowers of Hiroshima was published in twenty-six countries and received the Albert Schweitzer Literary Prize. It told the story of Yuka Nakamura, her husband Fumio, and younger sister Ohatsu, all survivors of the atom bomb attack on Hiroshima.

When a young American, Sam Willoughby, comes to stay with the Nakamura family, with typical Japanese delicacy and courtesy Yuka tries to protect him from the knowledge that she and her family are victims of the holocaust. Despite her good intentions, however, Sam becomes involved in their personal tragedy. Fumio eventually dies of radiation poisoning and Small Sister, about to marry, runs away in terror of the taint she may pass on. The tragedy of Yuka Nakamura and her family is the tragedy of the whole world.

In The Seeds of Hiroshima, Edita Morris continues the story of Yuka and Small Sister. It is a story of love and hope in the midst of hatred and despair. Sam Willoughby, who has fallen in love with Yuka, flies to Tokyo from California where he is attending the university on a science scholarship. Meanwhile, Yuka accompanies Professor Morioka, the celebrated radiation physicist, and his adopted son to Tokyo to attend a giant peace rally.

While Yuka and Sam are enjoying a carefree reunion in the big city, Small Sister remains at home in Hiroshima preparing for the birth of her baby. Ohatsu has built a safety-wall between herself and her memories. She has shrunk her whole world to the size of a bird's nest, inhabited by herself, her husband Hiroo and their unborn child.

Edita Morris possesses no extraordinary literary gifts. She succeeds through her total dedication to the cause of peace. Her sincerity shines through the simple prose and illuminates it from the heart.

The Seeds of Hiroshima is not a realistic novel such as Bernard Malamud's recent The Fixer. The one thing that suffering teaches Malamud's fixer is that there is no such thing as a nonpolitical man, especially a Jew.

On the contrary, what Edita Morris seems to be saying is that there must be a conscience in mankind that is above politics. It is this simple nonpolitical, humanitarian nature of her writing that makes it so universal and appealing. Although she uses the techniques of the popular writer of fiction, Edita Morris still manages to address herself to the conscience of mankind. It is this humble conscience which may yet save us all.

INDIAN SUMMER

By John Knowles (Random House, 1966).

The hero of John Knowles' third novel, Indian Summer, is named Cleet Kinsolving and he just happens to be
part Indian. Cleet is not very bright but his instincts are
good. "All my life I have had this somewhat foggy mind,"
he confesses. ". . . I can't remember what the capital
of Russia is or who the second President of the United
States was or things like that, or trigonometry and physics
and things like that. But all my life I've had a certain
thing inside my head like a beacon in the fog. Once in
a while it cuts right through the fog and lights something
up very clearly, clearer than most people would see something because it comes out of a fog."

As the novel begins, it is the year 1946 and Cleet
has just been discharged from the Army Air Force after
serving in the South Pacific as a gunner. Cleet has no
immediate plans or prospects (and very little money), but
he feels sure of one thing. Some kind of magnanimous,
complete way of life was opening for him. He has one
great overriding ambition or dream and that is to start an
airline carrying freight between Seattle and Alaska.

Discharged in Wichita Falls, Texas, Cleet starts to
hitchhike home. Home is Wetherford, Connecticut, a
typical New England town on the Connecticut River between
Hartford and New Haven. Cleet spends one night in a small
Kansas town and falls in love with the landscape. Straight-
laced, perpendicular, Colonially oriented Wetherford seemed
especially cramped next to country like this. Cleet decides
to settle down and go to work for Al Eubanks doing odd
jobs around a small airport for forty dollars a week.
Wetherford never seemed so far away.

Just when it seems that Cleet Kinsolving has nothing
more to fear from Wetherford, who turns up by sheerest
chance but Neil Reardon whose multimillionaire father
practically owns Wetherford. This is what is known as a
coincidence. But of course the author simply has to get
our honest injun back to Wetherford or there won't be any
novel. It seems that in the old days the rich and powerful

Reardons practically adopted Cleet.   Neil Reardon is Cleet's
best friend.   This is a polite way of saying that the Reardons
have a habit of dominating and using for their own ends anyone who happens to come within their orbit.   Unfortunately,
Cleet Kinsolving happened to come within their orbit at a
very early age.   The Reardons are also very possessive
and cannot bear the thought that one of those whom they
have befriended should wish to live outside their orbit.   The
Reardons entice Cleet back to Wetherford with a vague promise to help finance his airline to Alaska and a flunky job
that pays two hundred dollars a week.   At this juncture,
poor Cleet's beacon isn't working very well.

        The big climactic scene of the novel is the annual
ball at High Farms, the Reardon estate.   It is a veritable
war between the haves and the have-nots -- the rich and
powerful Reardons against all the other poor slobs.   In addition to Neil and Cleet, the combatants include Neil's wife,
Georgia, who never had it so good, and her parents, Genevieve and Ken Sommers, who have been flown to the ball
in the Reardons' private plane.   Ken Sommers is that most
hackneyed of characters, the attractive failure who drinks
too much.   Genevieve Sommers just likes to play such
oldies as "I Feel Like a Feather in the Breeze" on the
piano.   After assessing the situation, Cleet decides to pack
his duffel bag and take off for the West.   Of course he
should have stayed there in the first place.   But if he had
there would not have been any big climactic scene or any
novel either.

THE WRECK OF THE CASSANDRA

By Frederick Prokosch (Farrar, Straus and Giroux, 1966).

In his introduction to a special edition of Frederick
Prokosch's The Asiatics published by The Readers Club in
1941, Carl Van Doren wrote: "Nowhere in American literature is there another book quite like The Asiatics by
Frederick Prokosch .. It merely tells the imagined story
of a young American who finds himself in Beirut and makes
his zigzag way across Asia to the southern border of China.
Perhaps no American has ever been over this precise
route, and Mr. Prokosch had not been over it in flesh-and-
blood. It was his mind, eager and sensitive, which made
the journey through that ancient continent, as historians
explore the remote past and the writers of fiction study
the characters they have created." "The Asiatics," Carl Van
Doren concluded, "is original in its conception, beautiful
in its execution. It belongs with the most notable modern
American books."

As a reader who vividly remembers The Asiatics
but has not followed the author's subsequent career perhaps as closely as he should have, this reviewer was disappointed in Frederick Prokosch's latest novel, The Wreck
of the Cassandra. Mr. Prokosch has resorted to that most
hackneyed of themes about shipwrecked passengers marooned
on a desert island. Despite his obvious stylistic gifts, he
has not been able to salvage much from the wreckage in
the way of a novel. The author himself seems to be apol-
ogizing for foisting this hackneyed theme on his readers
when he has Baron Hugo von Wolfhausen note in his diary
that "this spectacle of a bunch of masqueraders landing on
a palm-fringed peninsula . . . seems like a rather banal
novelistic contrivance."

Apparently Mr. Prokosch decided that the end would
justify the means. How else is one to get nine people of
widely dissimilar backgrounds cast on a primitive island
somewhere between Hong Kong and Australia except by
means of a shipwreck? (Since the story takes place in
1938, the Boeing 707 is automatically ruled out.) Thus
to be fair to the author, his novel should be judged on the

basis of what happens after his nine disputatious passengers
become stranded on their proverbial tropic island.

At first everyone gets along fine and there are intimations of a Garden of Eden. Shapes, colors, even sounds
take on an exaggerated vividness. Everything swings into
being with a sharp, prismatic exactitude. The nine stranded
beachcombers cooperate beautifully and divide up the chores.
They become very philosophical. "Civilized life is nothing
more than a feverish kaleidoscope," the Baron exclaims.
". . . One illusion after another, seductive, empty, infinitely boring. The sea, the sand, and the stars! Will
they give us a new perspective? We will see. It all depends. Do we want reality? Do we want the truth? Do
we really desire the healing blandishments of nature?"

The Garden of Eden, alas, turns out to be an illusion. The fundamental reality is neither the feverish
kaleidoscope of civilized life nor the new Utopia built out
of palm leaves, sea shells and coconuts. The fundamental
reality is the Power of Darkness that lies at the heart of
existence. The universe is inhabited by sharks, vultures,
pestilence and death. There is no God. If only we would
recognize this fact, Mr. Prokosch tells us reassuringly in
this confused and banal fable, everything will be all right.

In his introduction to The Asiatics more than a quarter of a century ago, Carl Van Doren noted that Frederick
Prokosch "never seems disposed to make lovely things
lovelier than they are, or ugly things uglier, for the sake
of some bias already in his mind. He seems to be concerned purely with the things themselves." In The Wreck
of the Cassandra the bias is all too evident.

THE ANTI-DEATH LEAGUE

By Kingsley Amis (Harcourt, Brace and World, 1966).

In The Anti-Death League Kingsley Amis has combined a number of special talents to produce one of the
most entertaining novels of the year.   Kingsley Amis will
be remembered as the author of that hilarious first novel
about a young history instructor in a provincial English
university, Lucky Jim.

As one would suspect from the title, The Anti-Death
League is more than just an entertainment.   Underlying the
general spirit of fun is a deeply (if not profoundly) serious
examination of religious faith and of man's place in the
universe.   As Lieutenant James Churchill of the Blue How-
ards expresses it, "You don't have to believe in God or
fate or the hidden powers of the mind to believe that there
are such things as runs of bad luck."   The particular run
of bad luck which is instrumental in the formation of a
chapter of the Anti-Death League begins with the apparently
accidental death of a dispatch driver while delivering classified documents to an army unit engaged in a highly secret
operation in the English countryside called Operation Apollo.

An anonymous typed notice, smudged but legible,
mysteriously appears on the recreational bulletin board
outside the canteen.   Beneath the heading, "THE ANTI-
DEATH LEAGUE, incorporating Human Beings Anonymous,"
is the following message: "It has been decided to form a
branch of the above organization in this Unit.   We want
you to join us if you agree with our attitude.   There is no
other qualification for being a Member, no entrance fee or
subscription, and any activities you may see fit to carry
out on behalf of the League are entirely up to you.   You
will not be given orders of any kind..."

The notice drops into an atmosphere already tense
with excitement.   The officer in charge of security arrangements, Captain Brian Leonard, has his hands full trying
to apprehend a spy suspected of having infiltrated into the
unit.   Captain Leonard, a conscientious but unimaginative
officer, is a character worthy of the creator of the bumbling,
likable protagonist of Lucky Jim.

There are a number of other colorful and mixed-up characters in the novel. There is the Adjutant, Captain Ross-Donaldson, who speaks as if he had been programmed by a computer. There is Dr. Best, a psychiatrist at a nearby mental hospital, who is crazier than most of his patients. There is Major Ayscue of the Army Chaplains Department who delivers several extraordinary sermons. To put it as discreetly as possible, the men are not always what they seem and neither are the women. It is indeed an odd conglomeration that Kingsley Amis has assembled.

The author does introduce one fairly normal character, Lieutenant Churchill, who immediately falls in love with Catherine Casement. Their love affair is perhaps the only normal relationship in the novel and is all the more moving and beautiful for being so. Toward the end, Catherine is taken away from the young officer and he begins to crack under the strain of his manifold problems. (For some time the whole idea of Operation Apollo has been anathema to him.) "You're falling off a cliff," he says despairingly, "and yesterday you saw something beautiful. Now you're falling off a cliff and so yesterday you didn't see something beautiful. She wasn't really here. Because she's gone."

But the novel does not end on this unhappy note. Lucky Jim was able to bounce back from adversity and so does Lieutenant Churchill in The Anti-Death League. Catherine isn't gone. She was here and will be again. Life is more than just a lethal node, "a bit of life it's death to enter," over which man has no control. We are all charter members of the Anti-Death League.

TWO TALES

By Shmuel Yosef Agnon (Schocken Books, 1966).

Edmund Wilson has called Shmuel Yosef Agnon, the Hebrew novelist recently awarded the Nobel Prize for literature, "a man of unquestionable genius" whose writing is "distinguished, poetic, and strongly personal." Two Tales, translated from the Hebrew by Walter Lever, is the first major work in fiction by Agnon to appear in English translation since 1948.

"Betrothed," the first of these tales, takes place in Palestine in the years before the First World War. It is a kind of idyl even though the setting is the port city of Jaffa, "busy at trade and labor, at shipping and forwarding." The protagonist of "Betrothed," Jacob Rechnitz, is exempt from this busyness by virtue of the fact that he is a scholar. Rechnitz is a botanist whose special field is marine vegetation. "The stars adorn the sky and provide light for the world and those who live in it," the author writes, "the flowers adorn the earth and give off their good scent; for this the stars and the flowers were created. But those weeds of the sea, which have neither scent nor taste -- what good is to be found in them?" As far as Rechnitz is concerned, he has subordinated everything to the cause of pure knowledge. All seasons were the same to him. A storm outside or blazing sunshine never held him back. With the strength of youth, with keen intellect and a discriminating eye, Rechnitz studied, investigated and assembled minute details as well as general principles, constructing from these a complete system.

Jacob Rechnitz was indeed a tranquil and happy young man. Perhaps only in the halcyon days before the First World War when life was leisurely and unexacting could such a life be lived. Before he became so absorbed in his work, Jacob had called upon Rachel Heilperin, or taken Leah Luria for a stroll, or visited Asnat Magargot, or gossiped with Raya Zablodovsky, or chatted with Mira Vorbzhitsky, or now and then seen Tamara Levi. Sometimes they would all go for a stroll along the beach at night. Because they were often seen together, the townspeople called them the "Seven Planets."

One day Jacob's great benefactor, Herr Ehrlich, writes that he will be traveling to the Holy Land on an extended visit with his daughter, Susan, with whom Jacob played as a child. As a matter of fact, Jacob and Susan are secretly betrothed. As children they pledged to remain true to each other as long as they lived. Now Susan is grown up and Jacob will see her again after a long separation. In Palestine Jacob courts Susan after his fashion, but they do not seem able to come to any understanding. Jacob is inclined to let events run their own course. Susan becomes afflicted with a strange malady, a kind of sleeping sickness. The climax of the tale is a strange race that is run along the moon-blanched shore for the affections of Jacob Rechnitz. The winner is crowned with a wreath of garlands. As for Jacob, he finally becomes wedded to a human commitment.

In "Edo and Enam" the setting is no longer the halcyon days before the Great War, but the post-World War II period, a time of trouble and turmoil. In this poetic and mystical story the past comes back to haunt the present. In both "Betrothed" and "Edo and Enam" there is a polarity between science and scholarship on the one hand and intuition and alchemy on the other. In these tales the moon is a great magnet which exerts a force on man which no man can fathom. The genius of Agnon is that he encompasses science and alchemy and weaves them into his fiction so subtly that it is difficult to know where the one begins and the other ends. He has taken for his province the mystery of creation and all the natural spendor of the universe.

TWO VIEWS

By Uwe Johnson (Harcourt, Brace and World, 1966).

A resident of West Berlin since 1959, Uwe Johnson has written a novel about the city he knows best. Already well known for his prizewinning first novel, Speculations about Jakob (1959), Uwe Johnson's Two Views, translated from the German by Richard and Clara Winston, should catapult him into the front rank of German writers alongside his more celebrated contemporaries, Heinrich Böll, Günter Grass and Peter Weiss.

Much has been written about the Berlin Wall, but this reviewer cannot imagine anything more affecting than this poignant story of two lovers separated by the Wall. It is perhaps not too fanciful to say that Two Views is the Romeo and Juliet of the 1960's.

On the surface the narrative is anything but romantic in the conventional sense of the word. For one thing, the lovers do not belong to the aristocracy, but are ordinary members of the rising middle class. Dietbert is a photographer from a provincial town in the north of Germany. Beate is a nurse from East Germany. Dietbert and Beate do not "fall in love at first sight," but are drawn together as much out of loneliness as anything else. Their relationship is a very tenuous one. Beate thinks of it as an affair, a flirtation, a beginning. She does not know what to call it or why.

Dietbert met Beate during one of his frequent trips to Berlin in March of 1961. As the novel begins, it is August and Dietbert has just returned to Berlin in a flashy new sports car. The day after he arrives his new car is stolen right from underneath his hotel window. He had planned to drive to East Berlin where he was to meet Beate. Sick at heart over the theft of his car, Dietbert rents another one and drives to the border crossing. The East German guards turn him back because the rented car has a West Berlin registration. After reporting the theft of his car to the police and vainly trying to contact Beate by telephone, Dietbert takes a plane out of Berlin for Hamburg and returns to his provincial town.

Dietbert would like to forget Beate whose face he can
scarcely remember, but he cannot. He tries to phone the
hospital where Beate works, but does not succeed in penetrating beyond the switchboard. He writes to her. Then
he receives a letter from her asking him not to write anymore. Her tone is polite, without allusions, as if addressed to a stranger. To all intents and purposes, Beate
has been swallowed up in the vast impersonal bureaucracy
of East Berlin. Without even a plan in mind, Dietbert
flies back to Berlin. It has suddenly become very important for him to find her.

There is a great deal of pathos in this simple tale
of two individuals caught up in the bureaucratic machine of
the state. The style is deliberately set in a minor key,
without flourishes, as befits the humble protagonists who
must struggle to reach each other across the barrier of a
divided city. "Was the hotel in Schoneberg, Wilmersdorf,
Steglitz?" Dietbert wonders. "His memory disowned the
district. Dust sparkled in the bright night above the street.
Frequently the air boomed from low-flying planes coming
in. Between the shopwindows the busses passed, swift
and empty; under the neon signs couples stood before the
glass hopefully studying the displays..."

It is probably no accident that Dietbert is a photographer by profession. Uwe Johnson's plain, objective
style recalls Christopher Isherwood's "I Am a Camera"
stories set in Berlin prior to the rise of Hitler. There is
a certain poetic justice in the fact that the literary ren-
aissance of the 1960's in Germany is not unconnected with
the great period of the late 1920's and early 1930's when
Berlin was one of the great literary capitals of Europe
and attracted writers and artists from all over the world.

THE PAINTED BIRD

By Jerzy Kosinski (Pocket Books, 1966).

A paperback edition of Jerzy Kosinski's terrifying account of a small boy's experiences while wandering from village to village in Eastern Europe during the Second World War entitled <u>The Painted Bird</u> has just been published. Since the publication of the hard-cover edition last year, <u>The Painted Bird</u> has achieved the status of a minor classic. The paperback edition contains three pages of critical comment extracted from the reviews, all testifying to its eloquence and power.

Shortly after the beginning of the war, the boy's parents, who resided in a large city, were forced to go into hiding from the Nazis. They sent their son away to a distant village in the hope that he would be safe there. In the confusion of the times they lost contact with him. Two months after his arrival in the village, the boy's foster mother died and he found himself homeless and alone. He was six years old.

The story is told in the first person, but the narrator is never given a name. There seems little reason to doubt that he is the author himself. Like the child protagonist, Jerzy Kosinski was six years old at the beginning of the war. He was born in Poland in 1933. Although <u>The Painted Bird</u> is classified as fiction, the reviewers have studiously avoided calling it a novel.

The child is an outsider. In the humble villages in the eastern part of the country, the peasants are fair-haired and blue-eyed, whereas the child has dark hair and black eyes. The peasants, isolated and inbred, are deeply superstitious and wary of strangers. The child speaks the language of the educated class, a language virtually unintelligible to the ignorant and fear-ridden peasants. Olga the Wise calls him simply the Black One. A twentieth-century Robinson Crusoe, the Black One survives by his wits. When he is forced to flee one village for another in the middle of winter, all that is required is a comet — a small portable fire carried in a preserve can -- and a pair of skates fashioned out of thick wire and wood.

The Black One is as much of an outcast as the dun-colored birds which Lekh, the bird seller, paints in vivid colors. Just as the painted birds are viciously attacked as imposters when they try to rejoin the waiting brown flock, so the Black One is brutally maltreated at the hands of the peasants. Not only do they believe him to be imbued with evil spirits; they are convinced that he is a Gypsy or Jewish stray. In German-occupied Poland harboring a Gypsy or Jewish stray is a crime punishable by death.

Jerzy Kosinski recounts such a catalogue of horrors in The Painted Bird that one rejects the idea that it is meant to be taken as a literal account of a small boy's experiences. What it apparently is meant to convey is a child's heightened impressions of man's inhumanity to man. Whether meant to be taken literally or not, however, The Painted Bird is a deeply disturbing book. (Anyone doubting the book's relevance to our own day need only reflect on the Liuni adoption in which a fair-haired, blue-eyed child is ordered removed from its foster parents who happen to be dark and of Italian descent.) Although the author tries to make allowances for the peasants because of their hard lot, one is not too impressed by these demurrers. As Elie Wiesel points out, The Painted Bird is "a moving but frightening tale in which man is indicted and proven guilty, with no extenuating circumstances."

A DREAM OF KINGS

By Harry Mark Petrakis (McKay, 1966).

        The middle-aged hero of Harry Mark Petrakis' heady
and exhilarating novel, <u>A Dream of Kings</u>, Leonidas Matsoukas, is a modern-day Icarus.   According to Greek legend. Icarus flew too close to the sun while attempting to
escape from Crete.   The sun singed his wings and he
plunged into the sea.   There is one important difference
between Icarus and Matsoukas, however.   Whereas Icarus'
ambitious scheme ended in disaster, the outcome of Matsoukas' daring scheme remains in doubt.   One suspects that
the irrepressible Matsoukas will succeed in realizing his
absurd dream, a dream of kings, and that the healing sun
of Greece will indeed work a miracle.

        Leonidas Matsoukas is President and sole proprietor
of the Pindar Master Counseling Service.   Operating out
of a modest office above Akragas' grocery store in Chicago,
Matsoukas specializes in the following services: palmistry,
astrology, omen analysis, inspiration to overcome drinking,
bedwetting and impotence, Greek poems written for all
occasions, real estate bought and sold, wrestling instruction
(Hellenic champion of Pittsburgh, 1947-1948), vocabulary
tutoring, personality improvement, and talent agent for
Banzakis restaurants.

        As if this were not enough for one man, Matsoukas
yearns for the love of the beautiful widow, Anthoula, who
runs a small bakery.   "From these warm cloisters she
made sweet the bitter hungers of the world," Harry Mark
Petrakis writes.   "The racks of fragrant pastries, the
trays of luscious honey and nut sweets, the warm fresh
marrow of dark and light breads were as much a landscape
for a Goddess as any sylvan setting by a sparkling pool. "
When Anthoula tries to reject Matsoukas' passionate advances on moral grounds, he says simply, "There are
laws of the heart which transcend the laws of man."

        Although his heels are run down and his collar frayed,
Matsoukas never forgets that the blood of heroes and giants
runs in his veins.   After fighting with the Partisans against

the fascist depredators of his beloved Greece in World War
II, Matsoukas emigrated to America and prepared to conquer the New World. "You have never learned to accept
boundaries," his old friend Cicero tells him. "The boundaries in which human action and human judgment are en-
closed. You give life the offering of an undivided heart."

Loving the sun and cursing the darkness, Matsoukas
would be a happy man if it were not for one thing. His
only son, Stavros, is not like other children. His frail
body is wracked by dreadful struggles. Apparently there
is nothing anyone can do for the dying child whose body
bears an affinity to shadow. Nevertheless, Matsoukas
fervently believes that the sun of Hellas can do for Stavros
what all the doctors in their wisdom cannot do. "You
have never seen a sun like that," he whispers into the
child's ear. "It warms the flesh, toughens the heart,
purifies the blood in its fire. It will make you well, will
burn away your weakness with its flame, will heal you with
its grace."

It is a dream fit for a king and to make it come true
Matsoukas will do anything. He will even come down from
those Olympian heights which are his natural habitat and
rejoin the race of mortal men. But then, holding Stavros
tightly in his arms, this modern-day Icarus will board a
wild-winged plane and fly straight into the sun.

THIS JANUARY TALE

By Winifred Bryher (Harcourt, Brace and World, 1966).

In This January Tale the distinguished poet and novelist who writes under the name Bryher goes back nine hundred years to the winter following the Battle of Hastings when the Norman invaders drove hundreds of loyal Englishmen into exile in a foreign land.

Bryher refuses to accept the popular view that Norman culture was superior to that of England and her sympathies lie completely with the vanquished. She quotes the historian, Stenton, who wrote: "It can at least be said that for the ordinary Englishman who had lived from the accession of King Edward to the death of King William, the Conquest must have seemed an unqualified disaster."

"What is there to add to these words other than to underline a few facts?" Bryher writes. "There can have been hardly a family in the country who did not lose all or most of their land to a foreign intruder. Hundreds of English went into exile, some to join the Varangian Guard, others to Ireland, the North or France. Art and learning virtually disappeared. A magnificent language was largely destroyed; we have to learn the words of Beowulf today as if they were a foreign tongue. There is economic evidence that a hundred years after the Conquest many estates were supporting fewer cattle and men. The free peasant of King Edward's time lost his stature and became bound to the soil."

Bryher recreates the turmoil and tragedy of those shadowy times by describing the fortunes of an ordinary Englishman, Eldred. (Alas, even the talented Bryher cannot pierce the remoteness of nine hundred years!) Eldred is a former hausecarl in Earl Harold's army, who was wounded in a border skirmish against the Welsh. Eldred reluctantly returns to his native city of Exeter on the Exe River in Devon and resumes his former trade of smith. He marries the widow Elfreda and becomes the stepfather of Goda, Elfreda's impetuous daughter by her first marriage.

Eldred is loyal to his family and a good provider, but something went out of his life forever when he left the Earl's army. From the moment he returned to Exeter he knew that "the unity of life was over, the wild cat crouching in the bracken, the smell of a peat fire, the bond of the Earl's service."

In 1067 the Normans launch an offensive against the West and lay siege to Exeter. The brave citizens man the walls and repulse the attack. Eldred does what he can to help despite his wounds. Eventually the Normans breach the wall and the defenders are forced to capitulate. The Queen along with the Godwins and her other loyal supporters flee the city by ship. As in all wars, however, some citizens elect to remain behind. "Coming with us, mother?" Eldred jokingly remarks to an old woman who comes to the door of her hut. "Coming?" she replies. "Why? The fighting has stopped and that is all that matters. It's the same to me whether a Duke or an Earl rules Exeter. Men want eggs and I know how to hide them till they pay me."

And so Eldred and his wife and daughter round the edge of the world during the winter of their discontent ("It will make a January tale for our descendants...") and set sail for Ireland to settle in a strange land among alien people. Years later -- after her husband's death and Goda's marriage -- Elfreda returns to Exeter to live out her life under the Normans. "Whatever he was," she says of her husband, "he was loyal, loyal to the Godwins and to us." In the eleventh century it was the best compliment anyone could receive.

SATURDAY THE RABBI WENT HUNGRY

By Harry Kemelman (Crown, 1966).

Harry Kemelman, whose best-selling first novel,
Friday the Rabbi Slept Late, was named the best mystery
novel of the year by the Mystery Writers of America,
should win some kind of award for fostering the ecumenical
spirit. Certainly he has done it in a most unusual way by
combining Jewish theology with the conventional detective
story. In Saturday the Rabbi Went Hungry, an unorthodox
mystery, Mr. Kemelman is back again with the redoubtable
Rabbi David Small of Barnard's Crossing, Massachusetts.

Rabbi Small's troubles begin on the evening of Yom
Kippur, the "Sabbath of Sabbaths." Isaac Hirsh, a mathematician at the Goddard Research and Development Laboratory, is found dead of carbon monoxide poisoning in his
car. The police call it an accidental death. Hirsh was a
known alcoholic. An empty whiskey bottle confirms the fact
that he was drinking on this particular night.

Isaac Hirsh was not a member of Rabbi Small's congregation, but at the request of Hirsh's attractive widow, a
gentile, he is buried in the small Jewish cemetery. Despite the official police verdict, it is widely believed that
Hirsh committed suicide. A controversy ensues over the
propriety of burying Hirsh in the temple cemetary. A
wealthy member of the temple threatens to withdraw the
gift of a new building if the matter is not resolved to his
satisfaction.

When the president of the congregation asks him to
do something that runs counter to his principles, Rabbi
Small has no alternative but to submit his resignation. "I
am not a tool of the congregation to be used any way they
see fit," he says indignantly. "I cannot be asked to do
something that runs counter to the principles of my profession any more than you can ask a CPA to cover up some
discrepancy in the books. The CPA has loyalties to the
entire business community that transcend his loyalties to
the person who engages him. In the same manner my
loyalties cannot be commanded completely. Transcending
my loyalties to this congregation are my loyalties to the

Jewish tradition, to the Jews of the past, and to Jews as
yet unborn. In certain areas, and this is one, my authority
is supreme and not subject to question by the congregation."

    Rabbi Gordon's wife is expecting their first child
and they do not relish the prospect of having to leave Barnard's Crossing.   Under the circumstances the only way
the rabbi can retain his job is to do a little private detective work and prove that Isaac Hirsh did not commit suicide.
Not only does he prove that Hirsh did not commit suicide,
he proves that the late mathematician was the victim of
foul play.   Rabbi Small then proceeds to track down the
killer.   "You see," he tells Police Chief Hugh Lanigan,
"the whole pattern of the crime was laid out before me
in our Yom Kippur service."   Chief Lanigan admits somewhat sheepishly that be bungled the case from the beginning.

    Saturday the Rabbi Went Hungry is replete with hu-
man drama illuminating people and their problems.   Harry
Kemelman is not as wise as Solomon, but he has an all-
embracing curiosity about human beings and enough of the
pedant in his nature to make him want to explain to the
uninitiated all the intricacies of Jewish liturgy and theology.   He is rather garrulous and pompous in the manner
of that other Harry named Golden, but like Harry Golden,
he is so sincere about it all and communicates so much
simple joy in what he is doing that we are inclined to forgive him his trespasses.   He is one part Harry Golden,
one part Sholom Aleichem, and one part Mr. Anthony.

LA CHAMADE

By Francoise Sagan (Dutton, 1966).

    The French term la chamade signifies the particular
roll of drums by which the inhabitants of a besieged city
acknowledged their defeat. In her latest novel, La Chamade, a sensational best seller in France, Françoise Sagan
sounds the muted roll of drums as background music to a
passionate love affair doomed almost from the start to end
in failure. La Chamade is one of the best books she has
written since Bonjour Tristesse made her an international
celebrity at the age of eighteen.

    The lovers are Lucile, a beautiful but spoiled woman
of thirty, and Antoine, an impoverished young editor of a
Paris publishing house. They become acquainted at a dinner party at Claire Santré's, one of "the small brave regiment of middle-aged women who somehow manage, in Paris,
to live and to remain fashionable and sometimes even to
set the fashion."

    For a while the lovers steal precious moments to be
together without disturbing the basic tenor of their lives. In
Paris beautiful but unattached young women are likely to
attach themselves to wealthy, older men. For the past
two years Lucile has shared the luxurious apartment of her
wealthy protector, Charles Blassans-Lignieres. Charles is
genuinely in love with Lucile. Lucile is genuinely fond of
Charles. That she had not left him was already beyond
his hopes. Security was the only thing he could offer her.
Or so he thinks. Lucile has no intention of leaving him,
however. She is quite pleased with her life.

    Shortly after the dinner party at Claire Santré's,
Lucile and Antoine are thrown together by accident. They
drive from the theatre in her convertible through the Bois
de Boulogne and along the Seine. "They must have looked
like specimens of gilded youth," Françoise Sagan writes,
"two sweethearts in a purring sports car: she the daughter
of Dupont Steel, he, the son of Dubois Sugar, they would
marry next week in the cathedral, with the families' con-
sent. They would have two children."

This is an ironic comment on their relationship. This svelte, pampered woman who stubbornly refuses to do anything with her life is neither a courtesan nor an intellectual nor the mother of a family; she is nothing. As Claire Santré's devoted escort, Jean (or Johnny as he is called), has discovered, worldly society kills everything, even vice. And as for Antoine, even the sports car belonged to another.

And so this unlikely pair fall in love. Physical passion turns what might have been a passing fancy into a real love affair. Eventually Antoine asks of Lucile more than she is capable of giving. Not that she does not try. She leaves Charles and for Antoine's sake even takes a job in an office. It is one thing to drive through the Bois de Boulogne in a sports car, however, and quite another thing to wait for a bus on some drab Paris streetcorner in the November rain. Lucile begins to discover that even her beloved Paris can become terrifying with only some bus tickets and two hundred francs in one's pocket.

If a minor writer is one who has a limited range, then Françoise Sagan is undoubtedly a minor writer. However, she is infinitely wise and sagacious about her admittedly narrow Paris milieu. She has sharpened and honed her gifts over the years. She has a fine aphoristic prose style with a cutting edge. She makes up in irony what she lacks in power.

Françoise Sagan is the novelist of Paris par excellence: warm, tender, incomparable Paris. One cannot imagine this very feminine novel taking place anywhere except Paris. In another fifty years it probably could not even happen there. Part of the curious nostalgia one derives from the novels of this talented writer is no doubt engendered by the suspicion that the Paris milieu she describes so well is already doomed to extinction.

MOSS ON THE NORTH SIDE

By Sylvia Wilkinson (Houghton Mifflin, 1966).

Sylvia Wilkinson's Moss on the North Side is a first novel by a former student of the late Randall Jarrell at the University of North Carolina who called her "the best prose writer I have ever got to teach." Miss Wilkinson, who was born in North Carolina in 1940, is a prodigiously gifted writer. There is no other way to describe it. She writes prose the way Dylan Thomas wrote poetry. She has a direct, personal way of looking at the world around her and this is probably the essence of poetry. She does not use words as counters to translate her inner vision, but plunges directly into the world of the senses where the green snake weaves around the rocks, "rolling like a liquid in hot glass." The world she describes is a very physical and immediate world. There is nothing remote or intellectual about it. It is the world bounded by childhood and adolescence.

Moss on the North Side tells the story of Cary, the illegitimate child of a Cherokee tenant farmer and a promiscuous white woman. Cary's childhood is spent in an orphanage, but as she nears adolescence she is sent home to live with her father in one of the Strawbrights' scattered tenant houses. Although he never learned to read or write, Cary's father is possessed of deep natural wisdom. Cary loves her father as dearly as she despises her mother. As the novel begins, Cary's father dies of rabbit fever and she is left to fend for herself in a predominantly hostile world.

Cary is sent to live with her mother in town and this is more than the frail, sensitive creature with an affinity for the wild creatures of the fields and forests can bear. She withdraws increasingly into herself. She is morbidly attracted to the perversities of nature that she sees all around her. She seeks the friendship of a mentally retarded albino Negro boy named Jasper. She is haunted by a mad squirrel in a cage. A dirty old man, the blacksmith Maurice, fills her with loathing. She observes a half-witted hired man performing a strange rite in the Strawbrights' barn.

In the spring Cary goes to live with Mrs. Strawbright
to help with the farm chores. Gradually with the sympathetic understanding of Mrs. Strawbright and the compan-
ionship of Mrs. Strawbright's two sons, Sam and Johnny,
Cary begins to find the strength to overcome the terrible
trials of the past. She discovers the positive joys of
nature as well as the perversities of nature. Instinctively
she falls back on her rich Indian heritage, a knowledge and
love of the land and of all living creatures.

"When she reached the top of the hill near the house,"
Sylvia Wilkinson writes, "the freshly plowed garden stretched out before her. Two starlings scurried in and out of
the upturned clods, making black dashes in the dirt. Around
the edge of the garden the ground swelled and cracked
where the moles ran their veins outward, crawling from
the plowed earth. The air smelled of rotten potatoes the
plow had upturned from the dead garden; they lay in broken chunks across the ground. On their sides were white
patches where the moles had eaten and the plow had
slashed across. She put her foot on a zigzag mound leading from the garden, and when she pressed her weight
downward the mound folded like dry ashes beneath it."

Near the end of the novel Cary returns to the abandoned house where her grandmother lived. In one of her
grandmother's old books she comes across the following
passage: "We will not be hunted like wild beasts; when
we are forced from our orchards and cornfields, our un-
milked cow will cry as hard as that of the white man and
in the snow our feet will freeze and our poetry will sing
like things of the earth, the rain in the trees, the thunder
in the mountains, and the water against the rocks." Sylvia
Wilkinson's prose sings eloquently of things of the earth.

THE SHAMIR OF DACHAU

By Christopher Davis (New American Library, 1966).

The Shamir of Dachau is Christopher Davis' contribution to the genre made famous by Ian Fleming and John Le Carré. the spy thriller, even though it is not about spies or espionage agents in the usual sense. The author of such distinguished novels as Lost Summer and First Family easily demonstrates his competence in this field. To the list of names which includes the Messrs. Fleming and Le Carré, as well as Len Deighton and Adam Hall, may be added the name of Christopher Davis. The Shamir of Dachau is a very readable, if rather implausible, adventure novel. Plausibility has never been a prerequisite of the spy thriller.

In Hebrew legend the shamir is a useful sort of dragon that by its persistent glance splits rock and hews its stubborn way through mountains. Heinz Karl has earned the title of "the Shamir of Dachau" because of the many acts of heroism he performed while a prisoner in the infamous concentration camp. Twenty years after his release from Dachau by the United States Seventh Army, Heinz Karl is the successful proprietor of a string of Frankfurt nightclubs in the heady atmosphere of the German economic miracle. Heinz Karl's friend and fellow prisoner at Dachau, Bodo Cohen, who emigrated to America in 1950, rejoins the Shamir in Frankfurt to help run his nightclubs. Bodo owes his life to the Shamir.

"You can fit any sort of story into the filth that Dachau was and it looks possible," Heinz Karl remarks, "because in the boiling lake of madness, of men who had become beasts, of turned-around morality, of animal survival, anything was possible." This fantastic story that Christopher Davis has concocted from equal parts of the German guilt-laden past, the "new" Germany of the present day and his own vivid imagination, begins with a routine visit to a veterinary hospital on the outskirts of Frankfurt. Bodo Cohen carries out this act of mercy in behalf of Pierrette, a singer at the most successful of Heinz Karl's nightclubs, the Monchskutte. While at the hospital, he recognizes an old enemy, the notorious "Butcher of Dachau,"

Franz Kuhn. Kuhn had reportedly been killed in a train
wreck near Barcelona in 1956. But here he was very much
alive in 1965 not far from the scene of his horrible crimes
against humanity. Ironically, the Auschwitz trials were
being conducted at that very moment in the Gallushaus or
Community Center in the city of Frankfurt. In two months,
on May 8, the War Crimes Statute of Limitations would go
into effect. Not only Kuhn, but every ex-Nazi criminal at
home or in exile would be free to come out of hiding.

Bodo Cohen reports his incredible discovery to the
Shamir and together they go into action. The password is
Nekamah, the Hebrew word for revenge. The chase leads
from the Monchskutte, to a women's prison in Berlin, to a
Jewish cemetery desecrated by neo-Nazis, to the bizarre
veterinary hospital complete with gas chamber and crema-
torium that is a front for an illegal organization that helps
ex-Nazis wanted for war crimes to escape from Germany.
The action is extremely fast-paced and full of surprises.
Characterization is weak, but that is almost inevitable in
this kind of adventure story where the exigencies of plot
must take precedence over character development.

Graham Greene uses the term "entertainment" to
distinguish his own unique brand of "spy thriller" from his
serious novels. The Shamir of Dachau is a kind of entertainment. It isn't likely that Christopher Davis meant it
to be anything more than this. Heinz Karl remarked that in
the filth that was Dachau anything was possible. Anything
is not possible in a novel, however, even in a novel about
Dachau. Truth is stranger than fiction only because fiction
cannot be stranger than truth.

A SEASON IN THE LIFE OF EMMANUEL

By Marie-Claire Blais (Farrar, Straus and Giroux, 1966).

Marie-Claire Blais is a French Canadian writer of genius whose first novel, La Belle Bête (translated as Mad Shadows), was published in 1959 when she was only eighteen. In his foreword to Mlle. Blais' latest novel, A Season in the Life of Emmanuel, Edmund Wilson writes that "the appearance of such a book as this--so far, it seems to me, much the best of Mlle. Blais' novels and the best I have read from French Canada except some of those by André Langevin--would seem to show that French Canadian literature, after producing a good deal of credible work of merely local interest, is now able to send out to the larger world original books of high quality."

Emmanuel is the sixteenth child born to an impoverished French Canadian family in Quebec Province. It is winter and Emmanuel has just come into the world. Grand-mère Antoinette's feet dominate the room. "Born without fuss, this winter morning," the author writes, "Emmanuel was listening to his grandmother's voice. Immense and all-powerful, she seemed to be ruling the whole world from her armchair." Emmanuel's father is an ignorant farmer who cannot even read his own name. In the minds of the smaller children he exists only as a brutal silhouette who comes between them and their patient, silent, long-suffering mother, always great with child. Even their mother exists only as a dim figure on the edge of their consciousness. During the day she is usually outside helping to run the farm. It is Grand-mère Antoinette who rules the teeming household with her heavy cane and sharp tongue.

In this babble of children of every age and description, two do manage to stand out above the rest. They are Jean-Le Maigre and Héloïse. Jean-Le Maigre, refined and lewd by turns, is the poet of the family. He is an extremely precocious youth with a certain propensity for evil. He is certainly one of the most engaging characters to emerge from modern fiction since Stephen Dedalus in James Joyce's A Portrait of the Artist As a Young Man. Unfortunately he is suffering from tuberculosis and is not destined for a long life. This season in the life of Emmanuel, brief though it is, is still

long enough to see Jean-Le Maigre buried in the cold earth.
Unlike her mocking brother, Héloïse seems to have a religious vocation.   After several months in the convent, however, Héloïse is sent home with a letter from the mother
superior.   The letter speaks of nervous exhaustion and attacks of hysteria.   Soon afterward Héloïse is "miraculously
earning a great deal of money" at the Public Rose Tavern
in a nearby town.   A religious vocation in French Canada
does not always mean what it seems.

Among Jean-Le Maigre's numerous writings which
come into Grand-mère Antoinette's possession after his
death is a work entitled "Family Prophecies."   In it Jean-Le
Maigre predicts that his brother Pomme will end up in
prison, Fortune (known as Number Seven) on the scaffold
and Héloïse in a brothel.   He also predicts that his grandmother will die of immortality at an advanced age and that
his brother Emmanuel, "now weeping the bitter tears of the
newly born," will end up in the Noviciat and succumb to the
same honorable disease that afflicted Jean-Le Maigre himself.   One season in the life of Emmanuel is like another.
This is the bitter legacy handed down from generation to
generation among the poor in French Canada.   This is the
tormented vision of Marie-Claire Blais in this extraordinary
novel.   But this vision is also broad enough to encompass
Grand-mère Antoinette who remains indestructible to the
very end.   As the novel closes, Grand-mère Antoinette
rocks Emmanuel in her arms and whispers in his ear:
"Everything is going well; we mustn't lose heart.   It's
been a hard winter, but the spring will be better."

THE QUILLER MEMORANDUM

By Adam Hall (Simon and Schuster, 1965).

Published little more than a year ago, Adam Hall's The Quiller Memorandum is already an acknowledged classic in the field of the spy thriller. Adam Hall is the pseudonym of a well-known English writer whose previous books have sold over two million copies in paperback form. Apparently his novels are providing something which ordinary people desperately crave. Perhaps what they provide is a vicarious outlet for the killer instinct. Mickey Spillane, Batman and Adam Hall; they all prey on the psychological weakness of man. If man did not find it necessary to create them, perhaps there would be peace on earth, good will toward men.

Quiller is a secret agent working for the British in Berlin. The primary mission of the bureau for which Quiller works is to round up ex-Nazis suspected of war crimes and bring them to trial with the end in view of safeguarding human life against the risks of a resurgence of Nazi militarism and its war potential. Quiller is especially good at this because of his experience in Germany during the war when he masqueraded as a camp guard at Auschwitz and personally saved hundreds of Jews from certain death.

But now it is the 1960's and, according to the "Quiller Memorandum," Germany is still seething with Nazis. There are more Nazis in Adam Hall's Germany than Communists in Senator McCarthy's America of the 1950's. The government is infested with them and there are at least two under every bed. They are not just ex-Nazis either, but paid-up members of the Nazi Party dedicated to the overthrow of the Federal Republic and the reestablishment of the Third Reich in the name of Adolph Hitler. They are madmen. Berlin itself is "the capital of a sometime hell on earth, split by a wall and writhing, as a cut worm writhes." The author uses the phrase "the rot setting in" to describe what is happening in Germany. To put it mildly, Adam Hall seems obsessed with the notion of German guilt. Deep in the heart of Deutschland is the jungle.

The memorandum addressed to Quiller directs him
to learn the details of a gigantic conspiracy involving a
secret Nazi organization called Phönix. The lives of millions hang in the balance. "There are two opposing armies drawn up on the field," the bureau chief tells Quiller,
"each ready to launch the big attack. But there is a
heavy fog and they can't sight each other. You are in the
gap between them. You can see us, but so far you can't
see them. Your mission is to get near enough to see
them, signal their position to us, giving us the advantage.
That is where you are, Quiller. In the gap."

The Quiller Memorandum is a fantasy, a brooding
sex-and-Götterdämmerung nightmare that reveals more
about the soul of man than about the state of contemporary
Germany. It is a kind of how-to book of espionage, which
explains how messages are coded and decoded, how contacts
are made, the art of tagging, flushing a tag and switching,
how a man reacts to truth drugs, and a great deal more.
It would make an exciting game by Parker (a spy thriller
version of "Monopoly," say, complete with paper money),
but a game recommended for adults only. We could not
in good conscience expose children to such violence and
depravity. Children would have to continue to watch "Batman."

MOUCHETTE

By Georges Bernanos (Holt, Rinehart and Winston, 1966).

Originally published in France in 1937, Mouchette
is a tragic story of human loneliness and longing by the
author of The Diary of a Country Priest.   Evidently this
is the first English translation of Bernanos' daring and
compassionate novel.   Georges Bernanos was born in Paris
in 1888.   Like the other French Catholic writers of his
generation, Bernanos reflects in his novels his deep preoccupation with moral and spiritual values.

Mouchette is a fourteen-year-old peasant girl who
lives in a mud house in the tiny village of Saint-Venant
on the edge of the Manerville woods.   Mouchette's father
is a shiftless drunkard.   Her mother, who holds the
family together as best she can, is already worn out in
middle life.   Mouchette is treated as an outcast in the
village.   Everywhere she is surrounded by a "treacherous
zone of silence."   No one will have anything to do with
her.

One day Mouchette runs away from school and wanders into the woods.   It begins to rain and she desperately
tries to find shelter.   A rough poacher by the name of
Arsene, an epileptic, stumbles upon her huddled beneath
a tree.   Arsene tells her a bizarre story about his having
killed a game warden in a drunken brawl.   It is the first
time anyone every confided in her.   She who has learned
to mistrust others gladly becomes Arsene's accomplice
in crime.   The need for warmth and human solidarity is
stronger than any fear of wrongdoing.   Ultimately this
need is disappointed and Mouchette is brought face to face
with her terrible solitude.

"It takes centuries to change the rhythm of life in
a French village," Bernanos writes.   Mouchette offers
a profound glimpse into the life of a simple French village.
We learn that the hour before High Mass is a time of with-
drawal and peace.   The main street is empty and silent
as people prepare for church at nine o'clock.   Men put
on their starched shirts, cursing as they push their heads
through the crackling cloth.   Preparing vegetables for the

soup, the women have already carefully laid out the black
pleated woolen dresses and stockings on the bed.

The day after her experience with the poacher in
the woods, Mouchette's mother dies. Until now Mouchette
has thought of death as something as "strange and unlikely
as winning a big prize in the lottery." At her age, dying
and becoming a lady were "equally fantastic adventures."
In one of the most moving passages in the novel, Bernanos
describes the death vigil of the local veilleuse, an old servant of the Marquis de Champains. Besides being about
the terrible loneliness of a rejected peasant girl, Mouchette
is about poverty and death.

It is a somber, fatalistic study. "She was obedient
to a law as fixed and implacable as that which governs the
fall of a body in space," the author writes, "for some kinds
of despair have their own acceleration. Nothing could stop
her now. She would follow her anguish to its end." "My
pity was stronger than her revulsion," the old servant lady
tells Mouchette while relating something that happened to
her. There is both pity and revulsion in this novel, pity
for a victim of society and revulsion at the conditions
that produced her. Perhaps the best compliment one could
pay him is to say that Georges Bernanos' pity is stronger
than his revulsion.

THE MAN WHO KNEW KENNEDY

By Vance Bourjaily (Dial Press, 1967).

In this excellent novel by Vance Bourjaily the man
who knew Kennedy didn't know him very well (they were
both patients in a navy hospital during World War II), but
of course this is unimportant.   The important thing is that
Dave Doremus--the man who knew Kennedy--and his friend
Barney James are members of the same generation as the
late President.   Vance Bourjaily is attempting to say something important about this generation and the assassination
of President Kennedy provides the focal point.   Like the
ill-fated Kennedy family ("that great, doomed family,"
Dave Doremus calls it), the Kennedy generation that lived
through the Depression and the Second World War is also
ill-fated, doomed.

Barney James had known Dave Doremus since his
high school days in St. Louis.   Elected to Tribune in his
sophomore year and a straight-A student, Dave was the
most popular boy in school.   After graduation he went on
to Harvard.   When the Japanese attacked Pearl Harbor he
enlisted in the Marine Corps. Commissioned in the field,
Captain Dave Doremus won a silver star leading his company's advance at Iwo Jima.   After the war Dave returned
to Harvard and obtained a law degree.   Talented, personable and ambitious, he became a candidate for political
office in Massachusetts on the Republican ticket.   He had
high hopes of taking on Kennedy himself for national office.
While Kennedy went on to become President, however, Dave
Doremus became involved in a notorious scandal which put
an inglorious end to his political career and ultimately
destroyed him.   He fell in love with a nightclub singer
named Sunny Brown who was a hopeless drug addict.

The novel begins on the day of Kennedy's assassination.   Barney James, the head of a small manufacturing
concern in Connecticut, and his wife, Helen, receive word
of the assassination while on their way to the Virgin Islands to cruise for a week with Dave Doremus and meet
his new wife, Connie.   The news changes their plans and
they return to Connecticut to be with their children ("into
the cave children.   Get back against the wall, while I roll

the stone up against the door. Something is moving around
out there in the night that makes the earth tremble with
its weight"). The charter cruise aboard the fifty-two-foot
schooner is abruptly canceled.

A year later the two couples, all amateur sailors
with considerable experience, are able to get together for
an ocean cruise on The Bosun Bird with Captain Kelso
Clark and his assistant, a young man from Dartmouth,
Art LaBranche. They plan to sail from the Virgin Islands
to Connecticut via Nassau and the inland waterway. This
cruise, the climax of the novel, is a brilliant piece of
writing. One by one the passengers and crew of The Bosun
Bird are forced by events to leave the boat until only Barney James is left to sail the schooner into port at Essex,
Connecticut. A cable from Sunny Brown waiting for Dave
Doremus in Nassau changes a happy voyage into a tragic
one. After crossing the Gulf Stream, Art LaBranche
gives himself up to the Coast Guard (he is a fugitive from
justice) and the indomitable Captain Kelso Clark is physically stricken and removed to a hospital in Saybrook,
Connecticut.

The novel ends appropriately at Arlington National
Cemetery. "No, little Ozark buddy," Barney James thinks
"... You can be witty, charming, married to the prettiest
girl...You can be the son of a strong man, surrounded by
fierce brothers, father of lovely children...survivor of a
dozen deaths...but if the finger of diseased imagination
presses a real trigger, you will, in the next moment,
be truly and terribly dead."

Born in 1922, Vance Bourjaily is one of the most
gifted novelists of his generation. Hemingway has praised
him and this novel shows why. He writes in the great
novelistic tradition of Hemingway and F. Scott Fitzgerald.
The Man Who Knew Kennedy is The Great Gatsby of the
1960's.

THE SOLDIER'S ART

By Anthony Powell (Little, Brown, 1967).

The Soldier's Art is the second novel in the wartime trilogy within Anthony Powell's ambitious and highly praised "Music of Time" series. The time is 1941 and Nicholas Jenkins, still a second lieutenant, is serving with a divisional headquarters unit as an assistant to his old friend, Widmerpool, a major on the staff. The division is in training in a remote backwater of England where it is afforded an excellent opportunity to practice "the soldier's art" of "think first, fight afterwards," as immortalized by Robert Browning.

Although The Soldier's Art will not detract appreciably from the series as a whole, it does not represent Anthony Powell at his best. The famous Powell wit is somewhat subdued which is not very surprising considering the circumstances. These are the dark days of the war and England is literally battling for her life. The Germans are on the offensive everywhere and an invasion of the island fortress seems imminent.

If Mr. Powell's wit seems subdued, however, the soldier's art flourishes more strongly than ever. No doubt England could be a mass of rubble and Widmerpool and Hogbourne-Johnson, the staff officer who represents General Liddament, would still be playing their childish games of military oneupmanship. Meanwhile a variety of recognizable army types--Officers and Other Ranks--pass before our eyes. There is Mr. Diplock, Hogbourne-Johnson's chief clerk for whom the filling in of forms is a religion and who becomes a valuable pawn in the machinations of the two officers. There is General Liddament who reads Trollope (can one imagine an American general, say, Curtis LeMay, reading Trollope?). There is Cocksidge, perpetually afire with fresh projects for self-abasement before the powerful. There is the unhappy Biggs, Staff Officer Physical Training, who takes his life "in the cricket pav of all places." The alcoholic Stringham makes an appearance as a waiter in the officers' mess. It is a tight-knit, cozy military establishment.

On leave in London, Nicholas Jenkins has dinner with
Chips Lovell and they are joined by the musician Hugh
Moreland and Audrey Maclintick. Lovell leaves early to
attend a party at the Madrid in honor of Bijou Ardglass.
(Hours later a bomb scores a direct hit on the Madrid and
Chips Lovell, Bijou Ardglass and their party are all instantly killed.) After his departure Lovell's wife Priscilla
enters the restaurant escorted by Odo Stevens. The war's
violent readjustments are reflected in the various pairings
of husbands and wives and ex-husbands and ex-wives. When
Nicholas asks Lovell if there is any question of a divorce,
the latter replies with typical British understatement: "It
isn't going to be much fun living with a woman who's in
love with someone else." Stringham sums up the general
state of affairs on the domestic front when he says, "What
lax morals people have these days. The war, I suppose."

In Edmund Wilson's literary chronicle of 1950-1965
entitled The Bit Between My Teeth, there is an imaginary
interview in which the noted critic is asked, "And Anthony
Powell -- have you read him?" "I don't see why you make
so much fuss about him," Wilson replies. "He's just entertaining enough to read in bed late at night in summer,
when his books usually reach me. If Evelyn Waugh is the
Shakespeare of this school, Powell is the Middleton or the
Day. It's a pity he ever dipped into Proust..." This
seems to be a fair assessment. At his best Anthony Powell
can be extremely funny. At his worst he still writes
superior gossip.

THE SONS OF MARTHA AND OTHER STORIES

By Richard McKenna (Harper and Row, 1967).

At the time of his death in November of 1964, Richard McKenna, the author of the prizewinning first novel, The Sand Pebbles, had completed about a third of the first draft of his second novel, The Sons of Martha. This unfinished novel has now been published along with three short stories based on the author's naval experience under the title, The Sons of Martha and Other Stories. "A dozen or more short stories, one superb novel and one third of a first draft of a second is a small body of work by which to judge a writer," Richard McKenna's editor, M. S. Wyeth, Jr., says in his introduction to the book, "but in McKenna's case it is an impressive legacy."

McKenna derived his title from a poem by Rudyard Kipling which describes the division of the world into two camps, the Sons of Mary and the Sons of Martha, and explains the role each must play. The Sons of Mary "have inherited that good part," but because Martha lost her temper once and was rude to the Lord, her sons must wait upon Mary's sons, "world without end, reprieve, or rest." Richard McKenna enlisted in the Navy during the Depression. He had spent one year at college but found it impossible to continue his education or obtain a job. As Mr. Wyeth points out, at that time the Navy was divided into two distinct groups, the "college men" and the "career men." Each group tended to avoid and disapprove of the other. Both groups claimed McKenna's allegiance and posed a difficult decision for him about his future: whether to stay in the Navy and make it his career, or go back to civilian life at the earliest opportunity. It is this conflict that he planned to develop in the novel as the major theme.

The protagonist of The Sons of Martha is Reed Kinburn, a former hospital corpsman, who is transferred to the Navy supply ship, Stella Maris, an unarmed vessel which regularly cruises between the island of Levenoa (Guam), Yokohama, Shanghai and other ports in the Far East. The first episode describes Kinburn's "trying out" as a fireman by Flangeface Hogan, water tender first-class

in charge of the fireroom. The second episode describes
shore leave in Yokohama and Kinburn's discovery of Japan
and the charming and artless Aiko. This is a warm and
sensitive vignette which clearly demonstrates McKenna's
ability to write convincingly about something besides machinery. In the third episode Kinburn is promoted to the
ship's ice plant which contains the complex refrigerator
machinery. The episode ends in a Manilla courtroom where
Kinburn is exonerated of negligence in a boiler explosion.

Of the three stories, the best is "Fool Errand," a hu-
orous account of a feud between two warrant officers aboard
the USS Polaris in which a left-handed monkey wrench and
a lady anthropologist figure prominently. "Kings Horseman"
is about a new man aboard a Yangtze River gunboat who
upsets the traditional Navy "pecking order." "A Chronicle
of a Five-Day Walking Tour Inland on the Southern Portion
of Guam," McKenna's earliest known story, is an un-
abashedly romantic adventure story in the vein of Robinson
Crusoe and Melville's Typee.

In a speech before the University Women's Club of
Chapel Hill, North Carolina, Richard McKenna told about
his ambition to become a writer and how he nurtured and
developed the small talent he possessed until it blossomed
forth into the spectacular triumph of The Sand Pebbles.
It is a story of hard work and dedication to the writer's
craft. The outstanding characteristic of McKenna's work
is its absolute authenticity. He wrote about what he knew
best, and what he knew best was the United States Navy in
the Far East and, in particular, the engine rooms and refrigerator plants of numerous naval vessels.

ROSEMARY'S BABY

By Ira Levin (Random House, 1967).

No less a personage than Truman Capote, that
modern-day devil's advocate, has commented favorably on
Ira Levin's Rosemary's Baby. "A darkly brilliant tale of
modern deviltry," Capote is quoted as saying, "that, like
James' Turn of the Screw, induces the reader to believe
the unbelievable. I believed it and was altogether enthralled. "

Guy and Rosemary Woodhouse are a young married
couple who move into the Bramford on Seventh Avenue in
New York City. Old, black and elephantine, the Bramford
is a warren of high-ceilinged apartments prized for their
fireplaces and Victorian detail. A friend of theirs, Edward
Hutchins, had tried to talk them out of moving into the
Bramford because of its unsavory reputation. It seems
that early in the century the Bramford housed such notorious
personages as the Trench sisters (two proper Victorian
ladies who cooked and ate several young children including
a niece), Keith Kennedy (his parties were infamous), and
Adrian Marcato who practiced witchcraft. After announcing
in the 1890's that he had succeeded in conjuring up the
living Satan, he was attacked by a mob and nearly killed
outside the hotel. The hotel became known as Black Bramford. Hutch speaks of it as a "danger zone."

Of course not many people believe in ghosts or
witchcraft and yet even in this country there are congre-
gations or assemblies of witches known as covens that take
themselves very seriously indeed and perform strange rites.
Rosemary Woodhouse has unwittingly stumbled on just such
a coven of witches in the Bramford. Moreover, she is
expecting a baby and it is a known fact that witches practically devour new-born infants for the fresh blood they contain. The title of the book, remember, is Rosemary's
Baby, and when Rosemary Woodhouse enters this particular
"danger zone" not even Dr. Spock can help her. Rosemary's husband isn't much help either. The Black Bramford begins to live up to its reputation for evil. An actor
named Donald Baumgart misplaces a glove and then suddenly goes blind. Hutch develops a mysterious malady.

Rosemary is presented with a book called All of Them
Witches by J. R. Hanslet which contains an anagram.   Elaborate and unspeakable evil is in the air.

        Or is Rosemary imagining it all?   Is she dreaming
or waking?   Is she actually beginning to crack under the
strain of her eagerly awaited pregnancy?   "As for the
desirability of cheerfulness during pregnancy," says Nicholas J. Eastman, M. D., in Expectant Motherhood, this
should follow naturally from the fact that you are well and
are approaching what will prove to be (although you may
not appreciate it now) the most permanently satisfying
event in your life.   Do not think, however, though you devote all your days to laughter, or all your nights to symphony concerts, that your child will be one bit cheerier or
one whit more musical because of it.   No, his mental char-
acteristics are more deeply rooted than that..."

        Like Truman Capote, this reviewer was induced to
believe the unbelievable and was altogether enthralled.   What
makes it so easy to believe is the fact that Rosemary and
Guy Woodhouse are such a believable young couple - bright,
witty, au courant.   He is an actor by profession who seems
almost as wholesome as Dick Van Dyke.   She might have
just stepped out of the pages of American Home magazine.
She gets a Vidal Sassoon haircut, finishes with the dentist,
votes on Election Day, crouches on her heels to talk to
small children, and smiles me too to pregnant women.   And
then the story takes place against the background of a very
live and dynamic New York City and of such memorable
events as the Pope's visit in the Fall of 1965.

        Rosemary's Baby is sheer verbal sorcery.

THE OLD MAN DIES

By Georges Simenon (Harcourt, Brace and World, 1967).

Georges Simenon, the famed creator of the Inspector
Maigret series, is one of the most prolific novelists of our
time. At the age of sixty-four, having written literally hundreds of novels, he shows no sign of slackening. The Old
Man Dies, translated from the French by Bernard Frecht-
man, must surely rank with the best work Simenon has
ever done.

The novel begins with the death of the old man in his
restaurant at Les Halles, the central market of Paris. The
son of a day laborer from Saint-Hippolyte, Auguste Mature
has made a success of his restaurant, but remained a peasant at heart, stubborn. hard-working and secretive. He
is especially cunning and reticent in money matters.

Auguste Mature is survived by three sons. Ferdinand,
the eldest, is a hard-working civil magistrate, a person of
some importance, who is living beyond his means. Bernard,
the youngest son, is something of a ne'er-do-well, who
is constantly getting involved in shady business ventures.
On top of this he is a problem drinker. The third son,
Antoine, has stayed home to help his father run the restaurant. For many years he has been a full-time partner in
the business. Now still in his forties, Antoine is a rich
man.

The brothers had indeed not realized how rich Antoine
was until their father's death when they learned that Antoine
had given him close to a million francs as his share of the
business. But what has become of the million francs? Now
that they are so near to inheriting a small fortune, Ferdin-
and and Bernard become very nervous about their father's
financial arrangements which not even Antoine can throw
much light on. "Until then," Simenon writes, "everyone
present had lived his life without great hopes of its ever
changing. They knew, of course, that they would inherit
something and that they were entitled to a greater or lesser
share of the restaurant in which they had become strangers
...But everything had changed since the night before. Antoine had mentioned a magical figure, a figure that made

people dream, on which the government had built its national lottery.   A million!"

      The Old Man Dies is a remarkable study of greed and what it does to people.   It is not a very happy story because it describes in ironic detail (Simenon can summon up a whole world simply by describing the contents of the old man's pocket) the disintegration of a once proud and united family, the family of Auguste Victor André Mature, born in Saint-Hippolyte on July 25, 1887, the same Auguste Mature who carried in his wallet a faded photograph of his wife when she was very young, as well as photographs of his three sons as children and young men.   In a sense this is what happens to all men and to all families, although not all families act as badly as this one.   The Old Man Dies offers a revealing glimpse into our common fate.

THE MAN IN THE GLASS BOOTH

By Robert Shaw (Harcourt, Brace and World, 1967).

   Born in Lancashire, England, in 1927, Robert Shaw
is a distinguished actor in addition to being the author of
four novels. Besides starring in the Broadway production
of Friedrich Durrenmatt's The Physicists, he has had important roles in such motion pictures as From Russia
with Love, The Luck of Ginger Coffey and A Man for
All Seasons.

   Robert Shaw's latest novel is called The Man in the
Glass Booth. It will be remembered that Adolf Eichmann
was put on trial in a bullet-proof glass booth. This novel
ends melodramatically in the same or similar courtroom
in Israel where an alleged colonel in the S.S., Adolf Karl
Dorff, is being tried for crimes against the Jewish people.
Dorff expresses deep loathing for Eichmann whom he refers to contemptuously as the Clerk. Dorff refuses to
base his defense on the plea that he was only carrying out
the orders of his superiors. Instead he flaunts his guilt
before the shocked courtroom. "I killed Jews," he boasts.
"I killed thousands. Turn back the clock and I'd do it
again...I am a living testament of the health-giving powers
of sin."

   Dorff has ostensibly been posing as a Jew named
Arthur Goldman who has amassed a fortune in the real
estate business in New York. Goldman is a mysterious
figure who moves quixotically among servants and art
treasures. "You will find me full of meaningless jokes,
metaphors, images and allusions," he tells his guests at a
lavish dinner party in his town house. "These you cannot
understand, for you are not historians, but my burden you
may feel, and afterwards remember."

   Goldman has been carrying this heavy burden since
his internment in a Nazi concentration camp where he was
allowed to live while his Jewish brethern died. Now Arthur
Goldman puts into effect a bold and outrageous (perhaps
insane) plan in order to personally suffer for having contributed to the misery of his people. He also considers
it his unique duty to demonstrate to the world the guilt of

Nazi Germany and destroy once and for all the excuse of
Eichmann and his cohorts that they were merely "cogs"
in the machinery of death, minor functionaries obeying the
orders of their superiors.   The Man in the Glass Booth
is a kind of fictional challenge to Hannah Arendt's portrait
of Eichmann in Eichmann in Jerusalem; the Banality of
Evil.

It seems to this reviewer that both Mr. Shaw and
Mr. Goldman (alias Colonel Dorff), fail to make their
point.   The idea is outrageous enough, but does it really
prove anything at all except that Arthur Goldman is insane?   The idea is not only outrageous; it is the height
of banality.   If Arthur Goldman truly desires to atone for
his past misdeeds, why doesn't he use his enormous wealth
to promote the cause of peace on earth, good will toward
man?   The trouble with Arthur Goldman -- and perhaps
with Robert Shaw as well -- is that he remains an actor
performing in a glass booth when much more is required
of him.

WHEN SHE WAS GOOD

By Philip Roth (Random House, 1967).

When She Was Good is a kind of morality play about twentieth century America by the award-winning author of Goodbye, Columbus and Letting Go. The novel begins where Frank Norris, Theodore Dreiser and Sinclair Lewis left off a half century or more ago. No matter what one thinks of the results, one must admire Philip Roth's courage in attempting to prove that the old-fashioned realistic novel is not dead.

A novel that attempts to restore Chicago as the literary capital of the nation has to be set in the Midwest. The heroine of When She Was Good is Lucy Nelson, a Midwestern girl from Lincoln Center, who has everything to live for but who eventually destroys herself and those close to her. Lucy is a parody of the girl next store and Liberty Center represents the enormous possibilities of American life. When Lucy's grandfather settled there in 1903, he was impressed by its quiet beauty, its serene order, its gentle summery calm. If ever there was a place where a man could find fulfillment and live at peace with himself and his neighbors, it was here.

It isn't long before life begins to close in on the dream. This particular girl next door has an alcoholic for a father, a man who cannot keep a regular job. Lucy despises her father and ultimately manages to destroy him. She has no intention of ever being made to feel inferior again. She considers herself to be a beacon of light in a dark, evil and hostile world.

For such a high-minded young woman, Lucy Nelson is not exactly a paragon of virtue. After going away to college at nearby Fort Kean, Lucy is suddenly confronted with the realization that what only happened to farm girls, to girls who didn't study, who quit school and ran away from home, has actually happened to her. The young man is Roy Bassart and they settle down to married life in Fort Kean where Roy has enrolled in a photographic school. Roy is a perfect foil for Lucy's endeavors to do good. He is a boyish, good-natured, not overly bright young man, who never quite understands what is expected of him. He is a truer, more brilliantly realized character than Lucy Nelson whose efforts to make a man of him -- a good man -- end in tragedy.

Lucy's efforts end in tragedy as stark and irrevocable as anything in Dreiser, and this is a major flaw in a novel that seemed to promise so much. Until the end the author maintains a certain detachment. He uses the raw material of American life ("During the fall he would usually walk back to the high school late in the afternoon to watch the football team practice, and stay on until it was practically dark, moving up and down the sidelines with the play ...") to extract irony, like a sourdough panning for gold. In the overwritten and heavy-handed denouement, however, the author -- no longer the detached, ironic observer -- throws away all that he has so patiently and skillfully built up. Frank Norris, the father of American naturalism, did the same thing in The Octopus.

WAR MEMORIAL

By Martin Russ (Atheneum, 1967).

     Martin Russ will be remembered as the author of an extraordinarily vivid journal describing his wartime experiences as a twenty-year-old Marine in Korea, The Last Parallel. The late John P. Marquand was so impressed that he compared it with Stephen Crane's The Red Badge of Courage, even rating it as a higher achievement in some respects.

     Martin Russ is not a very prolific writer and now, ten years after his initial triumph, he has published his third book, War Memorial. Seven years to produce a novel of barely 185 pages! But what a novel! Martin Russ has proven how right he was to bide his time and work carefully toward the fulfillment of his own unique view of the world. War Memorial is that most rare and special phenomenon in the book world, an original novel.

     The hero of War Memorial is Joe Shasta, 158 pounds of wild Indian from Gallup, New Mexico. Shasta turns up in Moduc City, Oregon, in August of 1950, looking for Barney Metraw, his former commanding officer in the Marine Corps, with whom he survived the bloody battle of Tarawa (November 20-23, 1943) in the South Pacific during the Second World War. Joe Shasta looks up to Barney Metraw as "the great one," the leader.

     For seven years Joe Shasta has looked forward to the day when he would be reunited with his old comrade-in-arms. In these seven years they have both changed considerably.

     For Joe Shasta, an economic dropout from the Great Society, the Marine Corps mystique ("Wehee fight our country's batulls in the air, on land and sea...") looms larger and larger until it completely dominates his life. In retrospect the Battle of Tarawa has become the most glorious chapter of his life. Barney Metraw, however, doesn't want to be reminded of the war. He is a paunchy, harassed proprietor of a store selling sewing machines

and vacuum cleaners.   In place of the glorious swift leader
of Marines is a peevish small businessman lost in a petty
world of commerce.

Joe Shasta goes to work for Barney Metraw as a
door-to-door salesman and thus becomes involved in a
hilarious campaign to place a Suckmaster vacuum cleaner
in every home in Modoc City.   The more ludicrous these
battles on the domestic front become (Shasta, who only
feels comfortable with cheap, made-up blondes, is mer-
cilessly pursued by Metraw's amorous sister, Sally Mary-
lou), the more he reminisces about the glorious past as
a Marine on Tarawa.   Ironically, Private Joe Shasta was
not exactly a hero.

War Memorial (what an apt title!) is a biting satirical novel in the vein of Voltaire's Candide.   The narrative
is like a chess board on which the counters of war and
peace confront each other in ironic juxtaposition.   Stark
and harrowing vignettes of the bloody fighting on Tarawa
in which 1,029 Americans and 4,690 Japanese were killed
alternate with comic misadventures on the home front.
The result is a war novel as vividly anti-war as anything
since Aristophanes' Lysistrata.

STONECLIFF

By Robert Nathan (Knopf, 1967).

Robert Nathan is the popular author of fifty volumes
of poetry and prose. He is the possessor of a beautiful
prose style and, to this reviewer's knowledge, has never
been accused of being obscure. Robert Nathan's latest
novel, Stonecliff, is written in his usual vein of ironic fantasy. His prose never sang more limpidly nor sweetly.
Yet, in spite of this, this reviewer must admit that he
doesn't have the foggiest notion what the "mystery" surrounding Stonecliff is all about.

Stonecliff is the home of Edward Granville, the
famous novelist, who lives in virtual seclusion high above
the sea on the rocky, fogbound coast of California.   To
Stonecliff comes young Michael Robb.   Robb has been commissioned by Granville's publishers to write the definitive
biography of the great man.   To say Robb finds the aging
novelist something of an enigma is pure understatement.
Nevertheless, Granville reluctantly agrees to cooperate with
his young biographer. Michael Robb settles down in this
Shangri-la on the West Coast for a protracted stay as Granville's house guest.

The deeper Michael Robb probes into Granville's life,
the more puzzled he becomes. Questions arise only to
remain unanswered. What, for example, has happened to
Granville's wife, inexplicably absent from Stonecliff? Who
is the beautiful young girl living on the estate and what is
her relationship to Granville? What are the strange voices
that haunt the corridors at night? What is the meaning of
the pelican, the mountain lion, the coil of rope that suddenly becomes a snake? What is illusion, what is real,
in this strange country of the heart?

Evidently Edward Granville, a contemporary of Edna
St. Vincent Millay and Stephen Vincent Benét, is the last of
the old Druids with the power to do things with the human
heart. He casts a spell on everyone at Stonecliff -- this
is his creative gift as a writer -- and they immediately become young and beautiful in Camelot-by-the-Sea. Meanwhile,
from his lofty pedestal overlooking the Pacific, Sir Edward

constantly lectures his young guest on the shortcomings of
the younger generation. "There are no beautiful places
left any more," he says despairingly. He suggests that anyone who hasn't heard Paul Whiteman's saxophone hasn't
lived. He sounds like a peevish old man.

When Michael Robb leaves Stonecliff he doesn't seem
to know any more than we do. "I have been sitting here
at my desk with the last page of my book in front of me,"
he remarks. "...And yet in a real sense it is not done at
all, for I know that the life of the book itself has escaped
me; the mystery that baffled me then eludes me still."

Even he begins to suspect that the mystery surrounding Edward Granville and Stonecliff is pure moonshine.

A MOST PRIVATE INTRIGUE

By Leo Rosten (Atheneum, 1967).

Leo Rosten is an extremely versatile writer. Besides being the creator of the immortal Hyman Kaplan, he has written books on such diverse subjects as Hollywood, painting, newspaper correspondents, religion and the French. He writes a feature page for Look and his name frequently appears on the movie screen. He has written mysteries under the pseudonym of Leonard Ross. Now this gifted Ph.D. from the University of Chicago (he is a distinguished teacher and lecturer in the social sciences) has tried his hand at the novel of suspense which is enjoying such a vogue these days.

The hero of A Most Private Intrigue is Peter Hazlett Galton, a former secret agent, now employed by a private agency called International Aids to Victims of Communism. Galton's boss at IAVC is approached by a bald, fat, perspiring Turk or Greek (Sydney Greenstreet with an accent) named Sulenkian who offers to deliver three important scientists, working against their will in the Soviet Union, for the neat sum of one million dollars. "Gentlement," says Sulenkian, "You are not children; I am not fool...I offer three world-known, first-ranking scientist...History swings on such brains, no?...So. The Russians have them; you Americans must want them. This, I arrange. These three I shall deliver--in Istanbul. The price is surely reasonable...To develop some puny gadget for space can cost more, no?"

The scene shifts to Istanbul where Peter Galton, a man with a mysterious past, goes into action. It seems that when he was working for Intelligence in Berlin, Galton had been involved in a rescue project called 'White Star.' He had gone into East Berlin to bring nine people out, but was betrayed and dumped, more dead than alive, in the American zone. There is a link between Operation White Star and this current adventure in the person of an Italian-German beauty, Baroness Margritta von Aschenfeld. When Sulenkian is unable to deliver the three scientists, Galton goes into the Soviet Union to get them out. He has a double mission: to save three lives and to avenge the past.

Despite the exotic setting and superb characterization, the novel is ultimately disappointing. Not only is it far-fetched and unconvincing, but the separate parts simply refuse to gel into a cohesive whole. In this most private intrigue, Leo Rosten wanders haphazardly over half the civilized world, from Washington to London, from Istanbul to Odessa. Sometimes it is not too clear why we are in a particular place at a particular time.

Primarily, however, A Most Private Intrigue is a novel of Istanbul--a refreshing change from Berlin, the unofficial capital of the spy thriller. Leo Rosten obviously knows Istanbul and is captivated by it. "Paris at daybreak," he writes, "Rome in the afternoon sun, New York at night--then these miracles of man turn their most romantic facets to the airborne. Istanbul? Twilight is the bewitched moment for the ancient Queen of Byzantium: dusk, when the sun sinks into the Marmara Sea and its misty fingers sweep the Golden Horn, turning countless mosques' cascading domes to gilt, flame-tipping the lances of a thousand minarets."

A MEETING BY THE RIVER

By Christopher Isherwood (Simon and Schuster, 1967).

The two protagonists of Christopher Isherwood's A Meeting by the River would seem to represent two sides of the author himself. We know that he was associated for several years with the American Friends Service Committee and in 1943 became a resident student of the Vedanta Society of Southern California in Hollywood and helped Swami Probhavananda edit the Society's magazine, Vedanta and the West. Isherwood has been employed as a Hollywood film writer. The man whom W. Somerset Maugham considered as far back as the 1930's to be the most promising writer of his generation has been an American citizen since 1946.

Oliver and Patrick are brothers, but about as different as any two persons could be. After a long silence, Oliver writes to his elder brother and informs him that he has entered a Hindu monastery near Calcutta on the bank of the Ganges River and is about to take his final monastic vows called sannyas after which he will become a full-fledged swami. Oliver has gone through a period of dedication to social service with the Quakers and Red Cross and now feels this is no longer sufficient. He must completely renounce all wordly concerns for a life of meditation.

Patrick is a successful London publisher who isn't too particular about the kind of books he publishes so long as they make money. Patrick is a charming rogue, as superficial and outgoing as Oliver is deep and introspective. He is married to Pénelope with whom Oliver was once in love, but this does not deter him from forming an attachment to a young man named Tom while on a business trip to Los Angeles. In short, he is a totally amoral individual whose sins encompass practically all of the Ten Commandments and then some.

It is perhaps preordained that these two so different brothers should confront each other on the bank of the Ganges. Patrick exerts all his considerable powers of persuasion to tempt Oliver to return to the life of the world. For his part, Oliver realizes that he must accept his elder brother with all his arts and tricks, all the good, all the

bad, everything. "What's the use of me, if I can't pass
this test?" he thinks. "What kind of a swami am I going
to be?"

Actually this meeting by the river is not exactly
earth-shattering. Perhaps the biggest surprise of the novel
is that neither brother succeeds in converting the other by
word or deed to his way of thinking (what is the point of
the confrontation if nothing is going to happen?), but each
goes his separate way almost as though nothing has indeed
happened. This is a subtle novel which refuses to proclaim the obvious. As a matter of fact, the novel is so
subtle that it took this reviewer some time to realize that
the point of the novel is that there is no point.

If the meeting between the two brothers is not very
productive, it is still quite illuminating. A Meeting by the
River is not so much a novel as a mild, good-natured spoof
of the Hindu religion as practiced by Westerners (of which
we learn a great deal) and of the mores and morals of the
English. Christopher Isherwood is really poking malicious
fun at himself and the two sides of his own nature.

THE CONFESSIONS OF NAT TURNER

By William Styron (Random House, 1967)

In the summer of 1831 something happened on American soil that had never happened before. In Virginia a
small band of slaves led by Nat Turner took up ax and gun
and sword in a desperate bid for freedom. The objective
was a bloody sweep through the countryside, the capture
of the arsenal at Jerusalem, and a safe flight into the
Dismal Swamp where no white man could follow them. The
rebellion did not succeed but before it was crushed fifty-
five white people were killed and a score or more seriously wounded. For three days and nights Nat Turner and his
men cut a swath through the countryside, spreading fear
and consternation throughout the South.

A native of the Tidewater region of Virginia, William
Styron grew up not far from Southhampton County where the
revolt took place. The story of Nat Turner always fas-
cinated him and was the first novel the author of Lie Down
in Darkness wanted to write. Now that it has been published, The Confessions of Nat Turner is already being acclaimed as a classic of our literature. Undoubtedly it will
be considered with Uncle Tom's Cabin as one of the two
greatest books ever written on the institution of slavery in
the United States.

The Confessions of Nat Turner is a kind of nonfiction novel in the tradition of Truman Capote's In Cold
Blood. Nat Turner's own confessions, a pamphlet of some
twenty pages, was published in Richmond early in 1832
and William Styron has incorporated parts of it in his novel.
"During the narrative that follows," Styron writes in a pref-
atory note, "I have rarely departed from the known facts
about Nat Turner and the revolt of which he was the leader.
However, in those areas where there is little knowledge in
regard to Nat, his early life, and the motivations for the
revolt (and such knowledge is lacking most of the time), I
have allowed myself the utmost freedom of imagination in
reconstructing events -- yet I trust remaining within the
bounds of what meager enlightenment history has left us
about the institution of slavery. The relativity of time
allows us elastic definitions: the year 1831 was, simul-

taneously, a long time ago and only yesterday.   Perhaps
the reader will wish to draw a moral from this narrative,
but it has been my own intention to try to re-create a
man and his era, and produce a work that is less an 'historical novel' in conventional terms than a meditation
on history."

Styron has beautifully and poetically and fully realized
his intention of re-creating a man and his era.   This novel
glows with the pulse of an era that is, simultaneously, a
long time ago and only yesterday.   It glows with a soft
musical murmuration in which can be heard the "chink-
chinking of hoes in the distant cornfields, sheep bleating on
the lawn and a Negro's sudden rich laughter, an anvil
banging in the blacksmith's shop, a snatch of song from one
of the remotest cabins, the faint crashing in the woods of a
felled tree, a stirring within the big house, a fidget and a
buzz, a soft musical murmuration. "

Despite the author's demurrer, it would be a mistake
not to draw a profound moral from this superb book.   In
August of 1831, in a remote region of southeastern Virginia, "the seemingly impossible" did, in truth, eventuate.
And it was wrought not by a "fiend beyond any parallel,"
but by an intelligent, gentle and sensitive Negro who was
known far and wide as a preacher of great skill and learning.   The words of the defendant's counsel, T. R. Gray,
echo in our ears to this very day: "How did it happen?
From what dark wellspring did it flow?   Will it ever happen again?"

IMAGINARY FRIENDS

By Alison Lurie (Coward-McCann, 1967).

In The Nowhere City Alison Lurie brilliantly delineated the bizarre confrontation between staid and conservative New England and kooky, way-out Southern California.
As this reviewer wrote about Miss Lurie's previous novel,
"the plot takes some surprising twists and turns, like L.A.
itself; the partners change hands as in some kooky ballet,
and when they are reunited, they are no longer what they
were."

Imaginary Friends, Alison Lurie's third novel, also
takes some surprising twists and turns, but the result is
nowhere near as successful as The Nowhere City. In attempting to repeat the formula of her critically acclaimed
second novel the author clearly demonstrates that the novel
form is not something that can be manipulated as easily
as George Romney's brain. One suspects that Alison Lurie
has learned a great deal from this ill-fated voyage into
outer space. Since she is a writer of extraordinary gifts,
this is no ordinary debacle.

Katherine Cattleman of The Nowhere City, a prissy
young lady from New England, becomes converted to the
California way of life and the L.A. scene. Professor
Thomas McMann of Imaginary Friends, a brilliant sociologist and the author of We and They: Role Conflict in
River City, a classic of descriptive sociology, becomes
converted to a spiritualist cult called "The Truth Seekers"
who believe in flying saucers and interplanetary communication.

It all begins when Professor McMann and his young
assistant, Roger Zimmern, travel to the small town of
Sophis in upstate New York, some thirty miles from the
university, to begin an in-depth sociological study of the
Truth Seekers, a collection of small-town eccentrics, whose
ideology is "a mixture of Calvinism, Christian Science,
spiritualism and straight science-fiction."

After several months on the project, Roger Zimmern,

a sophisticated, cynical social scientist from Columbia, an athiest and a Jew, finds himself falling in love with Virginia Roberts, a beautiful but unbalanced teenager, who is in urgent communication with a being on another planet, Ro of Varna. As if this were not enough, we are also asked to believe that a group of rural religious cranks are able to drive a famous sociologist engaged in an important study out of his mind. Before it is all over, Professor McMann believes that Ro of Varna has touched him personally with his magic wand. Or does he? Somehow it doesn't seem to matter. As Roger Zimmern puts it, "It's a sociological truism that you become the role you play, but it's not supposed to happen that fast."

In Imaginary Friends Alison Lurie tries to express some important truths about human behavior (science is a sacred cow), but the whole thing is too obviously stage-managed, too clumsily handled, too outrageous and yet not outrageous enough. Moreover, she does not write as confidently and convincingly about Sophis, New York, and its small-town types -- she almost seems to be intimidated by them -- as she did about Southern California in The Nowhere City, which was, among other things, a dazzling tour, a genuine spectacular of the L.A. scene, from Bohemian Venice to Beverly Hills, from the U.C.L.A. campus to the corner of Hollywood and Vine.

THE SONG OF DAVID FREED

By Abraham Rothberg (Putnam, 1968).

Abraham Rothberg's third novel, The Song of David Freed, joins that very select group of novels about Jewish childhood in New York City which includes Henry Roth's Call It Sleep and Chaim Potock's The Chosen. One might also add Alfred Kazin's A Walker in the City, but that is autobiography, not fiction.

The novel takes place during the Depression, that period of our history which seems in retrospect almost to be a golden age, at least in terms of its impact on creative minds. Although a time of adversity for just about everyone else, young David Freed is singled out as the possessor of a marvelous gift. He has a beautiful soprano voice and is soon singing as a soloist for Cantor Barrt on the Sabbath and High Holy Days and at weddings. He becomes known far and wide as "the little chazan," the golden voice of Beth Sholom Synagogue.

Just as his beautiful voice reaches its apogee, David begins to discover ominous cracks in the foundation of his moral universe. To his astonishment he learns that Chazan Barrt has been cheating him of money that is rightfully his. After this initial shock, his whole world begins to crumble. Stripped of his illusions, he sees the world as it really is and not as he would like it to be. The older generation is too rigid and uncompromising in its attitudes and this parochialism makes it vulnerable. The young people have no moral values at all and are easily led into a life of crime.

"Everything would be all right," David tells himself. "...His father would get regular work again...and the house would be as it used to be. They would both know and tell him that someone else had taken the pishka money. Toni would have the baby and Johnny Strigari would be all right. Pop Vecchione wouldn't have to peddle lemon ice anymore, but he'd have his old job as a carpenter back, and Joe would be able to marry Regina. The police would finally catch up with Georgie Harvard's gang and with the

Forty Thieves, and then Vito and Maxie and Nadie and all the rest of the boys Mr. McLean was worried about would be fine. Everything would turn out. God would hear his voice; God would not hide His ear at his cry." But everything doesn't turn out all right. When tragedy strikes, David comes to a final awareness. His golden voice, his innocence, is gone forever. He is no longer a child.

If The Song of David Freed is not up to the level of Call It Sleep and The Chosen, it is because David Freed is not as sympathetic a character as his counterparts in the other novels. For a teen-age boy, he is extremely holier-than-thou. Some of the words Abraham Rothberg puts in his mouth are simply unbelievable. "There's nothing to say," David upbraids Cantor Barrt. "You took money for work I did. You milked this cow long enough. It's enough. You cheated me, you used me. I don't owe you anything, not even an apology."

What this reviewer liked best about this rather somber novel is that it is full of local color depicting the melting pot that was New York in the 1930's, where Italian, Irish and Jewish immigrants and sons of immigrants lived side by side on the teeming, pushcart streets, sometimes in harmony and friendship, sometimes in violence and despair. At a time when, as the President's National Advisory Commission on Civil Disorders has recently noted, our major cities are in danger of becoming Negro ghettoes, it is refreshing to read about the friendship between a Jewish boy and a large Italian family in a bygone era and to see how each is enriched and broadened by the customs and mores of the other. Perhaps this is the ultimate test of a democracy.

BLADE OF LIGHT

By Don Carpenter (Harcourt, Brace and World, 1968).

Don Carpenter says more in the titles of his novels
than most novelists say in their entire books.   His first
novel, Hard Rain Falling, a brutal study in naturalism,
was described by one reviewer as "tough and vital, built
with slabs of hard prose."   Blade of Light is another naturalistic tour de force tempered by a somber and compassionate sympathy.   If William Faulkner has an heir
apparent, it is Don Carpenter.   Blade of Light is reminiscent of Faulkner's sensational novel, Sanctuary.   But.
though Faulkner admitted writing Sanctuary for money,
there can be no doubt that Blade of Light was written in
rage and loathing at the cruelty and injustice of a world
in which the good and simple can be grotesquely twisted
beyond all recognition.

After spending eighteen years in an institution for
the criminally insane, Irwin Semple is released.   It has
been years since he has done anything approaching violence
and the space is needed for others.   At the age of thirty-
five, a strange, ugly, inarticulate creature who in eighteen
years has learned only to be patient, Semple returns by
bus to a city now twice as large as the one he had left,
his only memories still so raw and powerful that he can
not even bring them to the surface.

What terrible crime has Semple committed to be
incarcerated for eighteen years?   (If he had been better
looking society probably would not have allowed him to
live.)   In a flashback to a remote time and place, we learn
what has happened to the adolescent boy -- the butt of
everyone's jokes -- to cause him to do what he has done.
He is drawn to Harold Hunt, good looking, arrogant and
tough, and tries to find acceptance in Harold Hunt's gang.
Harold Hunt spurns him, as does Harold's girl friend,
Carole.   Inside the shack, she whispers, "Don't you touch
me."   That is all she had to say.

Now eighteen years later, Irwin Semple, having learned patience, is trying to start all over again.   Following a

brief transition period in a halfway house, he moves into
his own apartment.   Gainfully employed in a furniture
factory, Semple has learned to take care of himself and to
attend to his simple needs.   Jackson Dilford, the psychiatric
social worker, is encouraged and buys Semple a typewriter.
"There's a man in there somewhere," he thinks, "if only
there was some way to get him out." He suspects that
there is a human being beneath the shell of all the poor
creatures held "incommunicado by their stupidity or the
stupidity of the society that created them, needed them,
used them, and let them die..."

Certainly Irwin Semple's new life would seem to
exemplify the basic goodness of man and the dignity of the
individual.   Even in prison he had found beauty from the
windows of the violent ward.   He had found beauty in the
changing sky, in the truck gardens and the white fences
and the small herds of red-and-white dairy cattle, in the
men in dark blue pants and light blue shirts hoeing or
leading the cows or sometimes just standing around doing
nothing.

Only a chance encounter with Harold Hunt brings the
past back in all its burning intensity and provides the
gruesome setting for the undoing of the man in Irwin Semple
striving so desperately to get out.

THE IMPOSSIBLE PROOF

By Hans Erich Nossack (Farrar, Straus and Giroux, 1968).

Hans Erich Nossack's The Impossible Proof, translated from the German by Michael Lebeck, has been called
by the noted German critic, Hans Schwab-Felisch, "the
most magnificent work of prose that postwar German literature has produced." As far back as 1948, Jean-Paul
Sartre called him "the most interesting contemporary German writer." Nossack won the Buchner Prize in 1961 and
recently held the chair for Poetics at the Goethe University in Frankfurt.

The Impossible Proof is an allegory -- a kind of
dream allegory -- in the tradition of Kafka's The Trial
and Camus' The Stranger. "Something which happened to
a man is keeping him awake," the novel begins. "He
attempts to think his life through -- backward to its be-
ginnings, forward to its end. He tries his own case,
taking all the parts; accuses, defends, and asks pardon,
to find rest at last. Yet each time his spiraling thoughts
seem on the verge of going under in sleep, they strike
a new fragment of his life, and once again they rise up
into the merciless twilight of insomnia."

The dreamer (known simply as the Defendant) is a
man whose business is insurance. He is widely respected
as "an honest broker and a dependable advisor." The
defendant has been married for seven years. To all outward appearances, his life is a model of bourgeois re-
spectability. There is only one difficulty. His wife of
seven years has disappeared without a trace. Although
there is no proof of foul play, the man is put on trial.
The Court addresses itself to the following questions:
Why had this disappearance occurred? Where had it led?
How closely implicated was the defendant? Was it to be
considered a crime or an accident? And, in the latter
case, why should the exact circumstances of this accident
have been covered up? Or was this a case of suicide?
And, if so, was the defendant an accessory, having driven
his wife to it? And where was the body? And, last of
all, was this a case of a real disappearance or only a
mock disappearance?

Although the defendant sincerely desires to cooperate
with the Court (whether he is guilty or not, he <u>feels</u> guilty),
he and the Court constantly misunderstand each <u>other</u>. The
Court is interested in the facts of the case, whereas the
defendant tends to depart from the facts to explore the in-
comprehensible or what he describes as "the uninsurable."
The Court rebukes the defendant for speaking in enigmas.
The defendant feels that the Court is futilely attempting to
reconstruct logically a situation that lay outside the confines of logic.

"Really, your Honor," the defendant remarks, "am
I never going to be able to make use of a metaphor without being taken literally? Not everything can be translated into legal terminology; and if we insist on attempting
it, we will only misunderstand each other. Language
wasn't made for such contingencies, and words are nothing but pills against a headache." One is reminded of
T.S. Eliot who wrote that each new venture in the use of
words is "a new beginning, a raid on the inarticulate with
shabby equipment always deteriorating in the general mess
of imprecision of feeling, undisciplined squads of emotion."

What is the author trying to say in this allegorical
novel? No doubt there are many levels of meaning, meaning within meaning. Perhaps it is a religious allegory.
When the defendant uses the term "departure into the uninsurable," it may be that he is referring to faith in God.
The crime is to look back and that is why he is on trial.
The defendant last saw his wife at night outside in a snowstorm. When the Judge asks him how he could <u>see</u> it was
snowing when it must have been pitch dark, the <u>defendant</u>
replies: "Please, your Honor, just consider this point for
a moment. Where does that light come from by which we
see our dreams? No one knows, and yet in dreams we
see clearly -- sometimes even clearer than by day."

THE MAN WHO CRIED I AM

By John A. Williams (Little, Brown, 1967).

This is the novel about which John V. Lindsay, Vice Chairman of the President's Commission on Civil Disorders, said: "If this book is to remain fiction, it must be read." Certainly The Man Who Cried I Am is John A. Williams' most sensational novel to date. What the blurb writer calls its "startling denouement" makes it suspect in this reviewer's eyes. Startling denouements such as this are more typical of Irving Wallace than of Richard Wright or James Baldwin. A novel that draws comparison with Irving Wallace's The Man in its sensational aspects is more reactionary than radical.

Max Reddick, the man who cries "I am," must constantly struggle to earn acceptance as a man among men rather than as a Negro intellectual among whites. He despises all those so-called liberals who would try to use him for their own selfish ends. Despite the falseness and hypocrisy of a racist society, he determinedly pursues his career. For more than thirty years he remains in the vanguard of the "Negro Revolution" in America. The author of several highly praised novels, he becomes the first Negro writer to be hired by a major news magazine. His career leads all the way to the White House where he becomes a speech writer for the President.

In depicting the social climate of America from the late 1930's to the 1960's, the author is at his best. Max Reddick emerges as a man struggling with the same hopes and aspirations as other men. The matter of color is only incidental. He enjoys hunting in the Catskills as much as any white man. Having fought with the 92nd Division in Italy during the war, he was subject to the same dangers and temptations as white G.I.'s. From post-war Europe his friend and mentor, Harry Ames, "the father of all contemporary Negro writers," jockeys in vain for the Nobel Prize. Max goes back and forth between America, Europe and Africa, all the time crying, "Give me my share! I am a man. Don't make me take it in this anger!"

It isn't until he gets to the White House, however, that he becomes totally disillusioned. Max learns that the President has deliberately subverted the lawful attempt of a Negro citizen to enroll in the educational institution of his choice. This is a deliberate misreading of history by the author and it must be considered in the realm of fantasy. In any event, Max leaves Washington in disgust, as well he might.

The biggest revelation is yet to come. In his travels between three Continents, Max stumbles upon a sinister plot known as King Alfred to be put in effect by the President in the event of widespread racial disorder. Among the participating federal agencies are the National Security Council, the Central Intelligence Agency and the Federal Bureau of Investigation. Operation King Alfred would result in the quick apprehension and detention of twenty-two million non-whites. It would be the ultimate fascist act for which there is ample precedent in the murder of six million Jews by Nazi Germany and the detention of American citizens of Japanese descent in World War II.

The message of this novel is "eat, drink and be murderous, for tomorrow I may be among the murdered." In this novel there is a maligned Civil Rights leader who is a caricature of Martin Luther King. In this novel the Martin Luther Kings are reviled by their Negro brothers. Mayor Lindsay said, "If this book is to remain fiction, it must be read." This writer humbly predicts that this book will remain fiction whether it is read or not. Fiction or fantasy.

ANOTHER HELEN

By Lane Kauffmann (Lippincott, 1968).

In Another Helen Lane Kauffmann, the author of An Honorable Estate, has taken the story of Helen of Troy and adapted it to a modern-day setting in Suburbia, U. S. A.

The author himself has furnished the following synopsis of his novel: "Eleanor Davenport is as lovely as her legendary counterpart, and equally wayward. Six years ago she had thrown over her responsibilities as wife and mother and eloped to France. Now that episode has ended tragically, and she comes home -- To the still-loving husband whose illusions have been sadly mauled. To the son who has grown from youth to manhood in her absence, and his fiancée who is unused to rivalry. To an outraged mother-in-law, who takes to her bed, and the gossip-loving neighbors in Bradley's Bluff, who take to their telephones. A delicate situation, fraught with awkwardness? For others, perhaps, but not for the Davenports -- who face up to all embarrassments with the unself-consciousness of high comedy."

Put like this, Another Helen sounds like one of those delightful comedies that the English do so well. Unfortunately, Lane Kauffmann is no Henry Green or Anthony Powell. The latter never make the mistake of taking their fictions too seriously; there is always an element of the preposterous to keep the whole thing in perspective. Mr. Kauffmann, however, gives the impression of one who actually believes his own fabrications. He asks more of us than we are willing to give. The result is a novel that crackles with witty dialogue, but remains basically without the saving grace of humor.

Instead of being funny, the novel verges on the banal. "The awkwardnesses appeared exactly as I expected they would," Eleanor confides to her son's fiancée Jessie. "As soon as I got home my position became ambiguous: was I a properly chastened wife or an impenitent hussy? George's intentions were of the best, he wanted to blot out the past, but the six years of my absence were

bound to stick in his craw because he couldn't tell how I
felt about them.   Did I repent my adventure or regret that
it had ended?   Was I still secretly in mourning for Pierre,
had I loved Pierre more than I could love him?   Had I
been happy there -- and, if not, then why had I stayed so
long?   And George's nagging curiosity kept alive the injustice of my going unpunished for his sufferings.   George
is far too decent to think in terms of punishing me -- he
would deny the charge indignantly -- yet he kept punishing
me despite himself, with little barbed reminders of the
past.   He couldn't leave it alone."   This is comedy?   It
sounds rather like any number of daytime television serials.

"You've introduced an epic quality into our life in
Bradley's Bluff which I'd not noticed before," Ken Davenport's uncle remarks when Ken compares his mother to
Helen of Troy.   The trouble is Bradley's Bluff, in its
blandness, its smugness, its provinciality, remains as
impervious as ever to rebellion in its midst as well as to
outside currents.   The Davenports are an eccentric family
by suburban standards, but in the end suburbia triumphs
over wayward Helen and King Menelaus, the commuting
stockbroker.   Helen, alias Eleanor Davenport, becomes
reconciled to suburbia and her stockbroker husband and
looks forward to settling down at 14 Elmwood Drive and becoming that most prosaic of all institutions, a suburban
grandmother.

THE CONFESSIONAL

By Georges Simenon (Harcourt, Brace and World, 1968).

Georges Simenon's The Confessional, translated from the French by Jean Stewart, is a somber and moving story of the initiation of a sheltered and idealistic youth of sixteen into the responsibilities of adulthood. It is a familiar theme and yet such is the genius of Simenon that he is able to take this familiar theme and, in a bare 150 pages, imbue it with so much mystery and significance that it almost seems to represent the human condition.

André Bar lives with his doting, well-to-do parents in a villa at Cannes on the Côte d'Azur. André jealously guards his privacy and likes nothing better than to take refuge in his attic room where he has his books, records and an electric auto racing track. His chief concern is to remain free, uncommitted, always making only such concessions to family life as were indispensable.

For the first time in his life, André has a girl friend, Francine, the daughter of his parents' friends from nearby Nice, the Boisdieus. André rides his motorbike to Nice and meets Francine. As they walk along the sunlit street, Francine observes André's mother hurrying out of a yellow house and going over to her red convertible a little way down the street. Just as she starts up the engine, André gets the distinct impression that their glances meet in the driver's mirror. This chance encounter changes André's whole life.

"No man is an island, entire of itself," John Donne wrote. André begins to realize that he is not free, however much he wants to be, that there are threads binding him against his will, not only to his parents but to his grandparents, and to other people who, although less important, nonetheless still play a part in his life. For some time André has known that his parents' marriage has not been a happy one, but he always took the position that it was of no concern to him. Now he can no longer simply withdraw to his attic sanctuary, for his parents, first one and then the other, seek him out in order to give vent to their grievances and to justify their own behavior. André becomes their confessional and is forced to listen to what he does not wish to hear. In the end, to preserve his sanity and integrity as a person, André in turn unburdens himself to Francine.

Georges Simenon has never written with more compassion and human understanding than he does in this short novel. The kinship of people, one to the other, has seldom been more movingly conveyed. Simenon has such a profound understanding of people and what motivates them that he can make a commonplace remark such as "ask her to remember me to her parents " actually palpitate with meaning. And this kinship of people which is the real theme of The Confessional encompasses more than the members of the Bar family; it encompasses all the people who constitute the human family. As André's mother remarks, "Everything that goes on around us has its importance in our lives."

THE ARMIES OF THE NIGHT

By Norman Mailer (New American Library, 1968).

Whoever would have thought Norman Mailer, the self-confessed "warrior, presumptive general, ex-political candidate, embattled aging enfant terrible of the literary world," capable of writing a dull book? To this reviewer, the biggest surprise of the year in the book world is that Mailer's The Armies of the Night, already being proclaimed in some quarters as a masterpiece, is essentially dull, lifeless, empty, a pathetic example of a once gifted writer frantically manufacturing tens of thousands of words to say very little.

The Armies of the Night is a chronicle of the anti-Vietnam demonstrations in Washington last October, culminating in the historic March on the Pentagon. Since Mailer took an active part in the demonstrations (and indeed ended up in jail), the book is a personal history. "Yet in writing his personal history of these four days," Mailer writes, "he was delivered a discovery of what the March on the Pentagon had finally meant, and what had been won, and what had been lost, and so found himself ready at last to write a most concise Short History, a veritable précis of a collective novel, which here now, in the remaining pages, will seek as History, no, rather, as some Novel of History, to elucidate the mysterious character of the quintessentially American event."

Thus the book is divided into two parts. The first part (which comprises most of the book) is called "History as a Novel: the Steps of the Pentagon." The second part is called "The Novel as History: the Battle of the Pentagon." In the first part, Mailer recounts his personal involvement in the peace demonstrations and calls it "history in the guise of a novel," whatever that means. In the second part, he writes a more or less objective history of the Battle of the Pentagon, including the bloody Battle of the Wedge in which the Army finally broke the back of the demonstration with M-14 rifles, bayonets and clubs. This second part Mailer calls a "collective novel ... written in the cloak of an historic style," whatever that means. Ever since Truman Capote's first nonfiction

novel, In Cold Blood, it has become fashionable to blur
the distinctions between the novel and other genres, and
this game has reached ludicrous dimensions with The Armies
of the Night.

Why isn't this book, which promises so much and
which has such a tremendous theme, better than it is?
Perhaps the answer lies in the character of the author.   He
tells us point-blank that he is "a ludicrous figure with
mock-heroic associations," a "vaudeville clown," a "comic
hero." He is the Don Quixote of American literature and
the Pentagon is his windmill.   Conceivably this book could
have been a comic masterpiece if Mailer had the genius
of Cervantes.   But that is a big "if." Mailer does not.
He is too contradictory a personality.   For all his outrage-
ousness, there is still in his makeup the spoiled Mama's
boy from Brooklyn who comes from a good family.   Nothing quite seems to gel.

The Armies of the Night does not gel either.   For
hundreds of pages nothing seems to happen except that
Mailer has an irreverent need to make a speech, any
speech, and if he is not given the opportunity he sulks.
The momentous weekend which for Mailer began with a
phone call from Mitchell Goodman and ended in jail is overshadowed by Mailer's desire to get back to New York in
time for a party.   It is overshadowed by his ambiguous
feeling for the poet Robert Lowell, a patrician figure
whom Mailer seems to admire, envy and despise in about
equal proportions.   Mailer gives the impression of not
even having his heart in the proceedings and yet he pre-
sumes to elucidate the "mysterious character of that quintessentially American event."

If the first part of the book is too trivial, the second part is too banal.   Toward the end, Mailer's prose
style breaks down completely, perhaps under the strain of
trying to support such a paucity of content.   Thus "the
phones were probably tapped" becomes in Mailer's inflated
prose, "Hundreds of phone calls had been made all over
the country, however, and it is not easily believable that
no one of the lines suffered from wire tap."

Mailer says of himself, "Mailer as an intellectual
always had something of the usurperer about him -- something in his voice revealed that he likely knew less than
he pretended." That is, alas, probably an accurate statement, judging from The Armies of the Night.

THE THREE SUITORS

By Richard Jones (Little, Brown, 1968).

The Three Suitors, Richard Jones' first published
novel, is a love story about the triumph of old age in the
hostile, alien world of the 1960's. More specifically, it
is "the absurd epic of one of the last survivors of the
great British Liberal tradition in her efforts to turn herself
and her family into marketable objects for the consumer
society of the 1960's. In a strange mid-century world,
where almost every institution holds a decayed interior,
Mignon was able to vindicate herself and her family."

Mignon is Lady Benson-Williams who lives alone in
a decaying Welsh farmhouse called Swanquarter with her
ineffectual brother Freddy, surrounded by the jottings and
clippings and amassings of fifty years. Lady Benson-
Williams' father was Daniel Samuel Roberts, for forty years
the M.P. for Caerifor and known there as the "People's
Friend." Her husband, the late Sir Arthur Benson-Williams,
was a distinguished public servant. But all of that is in
the past. Hard times have come for Mignon and her devoted brother Freddy, an old bachelor who devotes his
time to writing mediocre verse for the local paper. Mignon
is desperate for ready cash with which to repair her
ancient homestead.

"Don't you ever wish for something big and generous
to happen, Freddy?" Mignon asks plaintively. "Something
that would change us, transform us?" With the arrival of
Mignon's nephew, Edward Lloyd-Ballantyne, for a long
overdue visit to Swanquarter with his new bride, something big and generous does happen. A historian by profession, Edward suggests that the papers and journals of
her late husband might be of interest to a publisher. There
might even be some money in it. He promises to speak
to his publisher about the matter.

This is how it happens that the first suitor, Charles
Mulford, a foppish young assistant editor, arrives at
Swanquarter to examine Sir Arthur's papers. Charles
Mulford is not impressed with the papers and Mignon is
not impressed with him. Her struggle to pull herself out

of her predicament has only begun.   It is further complicated by the opposition of her daughter, Nesta, and other
members of the family ("They must be scraping the barrel
if they want to publish Father's ramblings," Nesta says.
"He was such a bore always.   Searching for hours for the
predictable thing to say.").

The second suitor is a rogue, but indirectly is
responsible for the final happy disposition of the papers and
journals of Sir Arthur Benson-Williams to Matthiesen College in Pennsylvania which has "money to burn."   This
novel, like a good Victorian medodrama, ends happily and
Mignon and Freddy are indeed transformed.   There is a
general reconciliation in which the dignity and worth of old
age and tradition are upheld while at the same time the
demands of youth and the future are discreetly made way
for.   "I have spent two rapturous evenings wolfing it," ex-
claimed Rebecca West, "and I will now read it again ...
It's made my life."

TRUE GRIT

By Charles Portis (Simon and Schuster, 1968).

True Grit, by the author of Norwood, Charles Portis, unceremoniously dispels whatever illusions we may have had concerning the Wild West of song and story, but it does nothing to dispel the idea that it took firmness of character, indomitable courage and pluck to settle the West in the years following the Civil War. 'Grit' is a peculiarly American word and these old-timers had it in abundance. If any one quality made America great, it was 'true grit.'

Certainly Mattie Ross, a fourteen-year-old girl from Dardenelle, Arkansas, has 'true grit.' One day in the 1870's Mattie sets out in the middle of winter to avenge the murder of her father. Papa Ross was shot in cold blood by a drunken outlaw named Tom Chaney at Fort Smith, Arkansas. Accompanying Mattie are "Rooster" Cogburn, U.S. Marshall for the Western District of Arkansas ("They say he has grit," said I. "I wanted a man with grit"), and a Sergeant of Texas Rangers named La Boeuf who is also on Tom Chaney's trail for having killed a state senator in Waco, Texas.

Mattie and the two law officers pursue Chaney and a band of robbers led by Lucky Ned Pepper into the Indian Territory, a refuge for desperadoes from all over. "Your headstrong ways will lead you into a tight corner one day," Lawyer Daggett, the family solicitor, predicts ominously, and his dire prediction is soon borne out. In pursuit of justice and Tom Chaney, poor Mattie falls into a deep pit literally crawling with rattlesnakes. Also keeping her company are bats and the skeleton of a man. "This, thought I, is a pretty fix," Mattie observes in her quaint way. Only 'true grit' enables her to survive her grisly ordeal.

The story is told a half a century later by the indomitable Mattie Ross who, though never married, has risen to prominence in Dardenelle as a leading banker and member of the Presbyterian Church. In the ensuing narrative we become witness to the contribution of that most formidable of nation builders, the American woman.

Mattie Ross is absolutely unflinching in adversity; her voice is as authentic as buffalo grass. Despite her wild adventures, she is a very prim and proper lady who modestly encloses words such as 'dickens' in quotation marks.

J.J. McAlester's store, where Mattie and her two comrades deposit four corpses of armed robbers and stock thieves, is now "part of the modern little city of McAlester, Oklahoma," Mattie tells us, "where for a long time 'coal was king.' McAlester is also the international headquarters of the Order of the Rainbow for Girls." This is how civilization came to the West! But the modern little city of McAlester and indeed the whole country was built on violence and 'true grit.' Horse thieves and train robbers, the Younger brothers and the James brothers, dominated the landscape. Even the U.S. Marshall's credentials are suspect. He is an ex-Buffalo skinner, wolf killer and bushwhacker, who has done everything but keep school. But he does have 'grit.'

LOVE AND WORK

By Reynolds Price (Atheneum, 1968).

Reynolds Price's third novel, Love and Work, although extremely short, is undoubtedly his most ambitious and philosophical work. It is as intricately put together as a poem by one of the metaphysical poets. It is not surprising that a poet -- none other than Allen Tate -- should call the author "the most sensitive prose stylist of his generation." In Love and Work Reynolds Price carries his elliptical, metaphorical style to greater lengths than ever before.

The danger of course is that in compressing meaning to the dimensions of metaphor the author will slight his characters who then become shadow figures rather than real flesh-and-blood people. This is what happens in Love and Work. The characters never do come to life. In a novel this can be disastrous. Real people do not speak in riddles.

The main character is a young college teacher and writer named Thomas Eborn. Tom and his wife are childless after seven years of marriage. With the death of his mother, Tom must face the possibility that he represents the end of his family. There are two alternatives to this death-in-life; namely, love and work. Love is represented by the example of his parents' otherwise meager lives. Work is the moving force in Tom Eborn's own life. "A craft, a skill may -- given good health -- last a man all his life," Tom philosophizes. "Very few friends, wives, sons, daughters will prove as enduring. Age, disease, death -- and worst, disloyalty -- exist and will in time win all that we love. The hardest shield for ourselves will be our work, if we have troubled to discover and master and commit ourselves to some absorbing and yielding work."

There are some fine scenes in this short novel, especially the scene at the hospital where Tom's mother lies dying. The scene is written in straightforward prose. What makes it effective is the talent for observation that it exhibits, not the fanciness of the writing. And Reynolds

Price can rival John Updike in fancy writing; e.g., "Eyes open in the room (on the table, on three forms), he saw only pressure, black against his face; felt no care for these people who cared for him; felt only clenched terror -- invisible spore locked in frigid mineral of meteor, alive and potent for larger life but trapped and hurtling with only two hopes: impact and explosion or perpetual fall."

This is a somber novel in which fancy writing (or sensitive prose) must substitute for wit and vivacity. It is a philosophical novel heavily freighted with metaphor, but the philosophical message (tinged at the end with a kind of mystical experience) is too heavy for the characters -- mere shadow figures -- to support.

THE SPORTING CLUB

By Thomas McGuane (Simon and Schuster, 1968).

This brilliantly written first novel is set in the Northern Peninsula of Michigan, not far from the place immortalized by Ernest Hemingway in his famous short story, "Up in Michigan." With the possible exception of Vance Bourjaily (who has enthusiastically recommended this novel and who in turn was once praised by Hemingway), Thomas McGuane writes with greater artistry about the simple pleasures of fishing and the outdoor life than anyone since Hemingway himself.

"Quinn held the rod high," McGuane writes. "He felt the curve of it lose rigidity. The fish broke and so began to lose ground. When it broke again it was splashy and without violence and came slowly to the net. At the net, it bolted once more and swung around behind but a moment later was in hand, a trout of two pounds that Quinn, with his thumb securely under the gill covers, held first against the trees and then against the sky before he put it in his creel. He rinsed the crushed fly in the water to rid it of slime which would sink it, blew hard on it until its hackles were upright and the false wings of feather stood out from the hook."

The sporting club of the title is the Centennial Club, grandest of the original sporting clubs of the Northern Lower Peninsula. The events of the novel take place during the summer centennial celebration of the club's founding on July 4, 1868. Two young men renew a friendship that goes back many years and has been marked by intense rivalry when they spend their vacation at the club. They are temperamental opposites. Quinn, a successful Detroit businessman, models himself after the sportsmen of gentlemanly cast, the old trout fishermen of the Catskills and Adirondacks. Stanton, an aristocratic renegade of Bunyanesque proportions, takes pleasure in doing nothing constructive. An incorrigible practical joker of diabolical energy and cunning, one of his favorite pastimes is to challenge his enemies, both real and imaginary, to elaborate duels with exquisite French pistols that fire wax pellets.

There is much more to The Sporting Club (such an
apt title!) than fishing and dueling.   What a stroke of genius
it was for this very talented writer to conceive the idea of
underscoring the tension and violence of American life
through the seemingly innocuous diversions of a sporting
club!   For into this wilderness paradise, already palpitating
with tension between the two chief protagonists, now enters
an uncouth local bumpkin named Earl Olive (the club has
been trying to hold the surrounding riffraff at bay for a
hundred years), a purveyor of live bait no less, to take
over the management of the club!   This is too much for
Stanton, the aristocrat par excellence, who provokes a
confrontation with the Snopesian newcomer and his friends,
a group of loutish motorcyclists with long sideburns and
degenerate tastes.

The denouement is as wild and Rabelaisian as anything in recent literature.   The Centennial Club is ravaged
and destroyed.   When the time capsule is opened on July
4th, a major (and, it must be acknowledged, not quite convincing) scandal is revealed.   Soon afterward, the club is
put up for sale as a "Gentlemen's Sporting Club with a
past"!   Stanton, now "heroic and at one with his illusions,"
has aged perceptively, his features clarified by madness
and loss of weight.   He no longer has his French dueling
pistols, only plywood cutouts.   Instead of using the wax
pellets which raise ugly red welts, he and Quinn merely
pace off, turn and say "Bang, bang!" at each other, po-
litely and soberly.   So in these hilarious pages the Wild
West bites the dust, finally and irrevocably.

HORN

By D. Keith Mano (Houghton Mifflin, 1969).

A scholarly, incorrigibly shy, middle-aged Episcopal priest named Calvin Beecher Pratt, who has led a sheltered life teaching in a seminary not far from his idyllic birthplace of Greensprings in upstate New York, assumes the pastorate of a huge, dilapidated church in Harlem. The Reverend Pratt has been inspired by George Horn Smith's powerful autobiography, My Head Lies Heavy, to involve himself in Christian work in the ghetto. "I had come as a pilgrim," he recalls, "to find the man of the autobiography."

The time is the 1970's and Harlem is in the midst of an economic, political and social revolution under the leadership of Horn Smith. Horn's Place is the capital of Black America. Horn Power represents "the death knell of white supremacy." George Horn Smith, ex-middleweight boxing champion of the world, was born with a horn, three long cylindrical barrels welded together and converging at a single point. Eleven inches long, it rises up from his forehead like the "span of an arched bridge from the shore." It is the symbol of his extraordinary power.

St. Bartholomew's Church has had a proud history, but now stands virtually abandoned by the church fathers. No attempt has been made to preserve it and it is only a matter of time before it will be demolished. Nevertheless, Pratt is determined to make the most of his opportunity. In less than half a year he is forced to the conclusion that the situation is hopeless. "I had come to be involved," he laments, "and I was less involved than I had ever been. I had come to do, and I had done nothing. I had come to evidence Christian love, and no one seemed to care."

A prisoner in his own church, Pratt is subjected to the most terrifying mental and physical abuse. In a series of bizarre happenings, he is brutally assaulted by a white colleague, is forced to participate in a drunken orgy which overflows a six-story building, and is made hostage to an incredible assassination attempt. Throughout he is under the constant threat of death.

Ironically, Pratt does make the acquaintance of Horn Smith and, for a brief time, lives under the illusion that he might still "make it" in Harlem. In a fiery denouement, however, these hopes are turned to ashes in his mouth. Horn Smith delivers a sermon to the white priest who has come to preach love and brotherhood. According to Horn Smith, there is no such thing as love or hate, prejudice or bigotry, but only fear. The white man fears the black man because he is different. He fears him because he maketh property values to go down.

"First, my friend," Horn Smith says, "get rid of the dirty words. The words that mean nothing. Racial prejudice. Brotherhood. Bigotry. And those stupid four-letter words, love and hate. They must go. We can't think clearly unless they go."

Surely the moral at the end is reactionary nonsense. D. Keith Mano is a tremendously talented writer, but his thinking is suspect. Has there ever been a more pains-takingly written novel with such a narrow-minded, simplis-tic conclusion? Surely hatred, prejudice and bigotry are all bound up with fear to produce racisn. We meet bigots almost every day. Mr. Mano may say there is no such thing, but we know better.

In the end, the Reverend Pratt gets out of Harlem, a thoroughly chastened and wiser man. Pratt's assailant, the Reverend John Meeker, who represents--even more than Pratt--the stupid, guilty, liberal Christian, ends up in a mental institution. According to the Messrs. Mano and Smith, that is the path of love.

SLAUGHTERHOUSE-FIVE, OR THE CHILDREN'S CRUSADE

By Kurt Vonnegut, Jr. (Delacorte Press, 1969).

Several months before the end of World War II,
British and American bombers attacked the city of Dresden
and 135,000 people (almost twice as many as had been
killed at Hiroshima) lost their lives in the bombing and subsequent fire storm. "It wasn't a famous air raid back
then," Kurt Vonnegut, who was once categorized as a
writer of science fiction, recalls sardonically. "Not many
Americans knew how much worse it had been than Hiroshima, for instance. I didn't know that, either. There
hadn't been much publicity."

Incongruously, Kurt Vonnegut was himself a prisoner
of war in Dresden at the time of the air raid. His prison
happened to be a slaughterhouse, a one-story, cement-block
cube built as a shelter for pigs about to be butchered.
Vonnegut was one of a hundred Americans captured in the
Battle of the Bulge and transported all the way to Dresden.

Slaughterhouse-Five is the famous book about Dresden
that Kurt Vonnegut has been trying to get out of his system
for the past twenty years. It comes forearmed with an
apology-of-sorts, but we should not be deceived by it. "It
is so short and jumbled and jangled...," Vonnegut confesses,
"because there is nothing intelligent to say about a massacre.
Everybody is supposed to be dead, to never say anything
or want anything ever again. Everybody is supposed to
be very quiet after a massacre, and it always is, except
for the birds."

Vonnegut creates an unlikely hero, a non-hero,
Billy Pilgrim, to tell us how it feels to have survived the
fire bombing of Dresden. Like Vonnegut, Billy Pilgrim
survived the massacre. There the resemblance ends.
Kurt Vonnegut can use his artistic genius as an outlet,
but poor Billy Pilgrim has no such talent. Billy becomes
unstuck in time. An optometrist from Ilium, New York,
Billy is rich. He has two children, Barbara and Robert.
Barbara marries another optometrist and Billy sets him
up in business. Robert joins the famous Green Berets
and fights in Vietnam. Billy survives an airplane crash

in 1968. Everybody else is killed. While recuperating in
a hospital in Vermont, his wife dies accidentally of carbon-
monoxide poisoning. So it goes.

And then, without any warning, Billy goes to New
York City where he appears on an all-night radio talk
program. He tells how he had been kidnapped by a flying
saucer back in 1967. The saucer was from the planet
Tralfamadore. He was taken to Tralfamadore and dis-
played naked in a zoo. He was mated there with a former
Earthling movie star named Montana Wildhack. So it goes.

Slaughterhouse-Five is satire of an almost Swiftian
ferocity. There is nothing funny about this book. It is
not really about Dresden, but about a world that allows
such tragedies to happen. It is about a world in which
halitosis is unforgivable, but the senseless destruction of
a beautiful city, with the loss of 135,000 lives in a matter
of hours, can pass almost unnoticed. It is about a world
that can create a monster like Hitler and allow him full
reign to do his diabolical work, yet cuts down in the prime
of life a Robert Kennedy or a Martin Luther King. And
of course it is about Vietnam, too.

And what do the birds say? All there is to say
about a massacre, things like "Poo-tee-weet?"

WHAT I'M GOING TO DO, I THINK

By L. Woiwode (Farrar, Straus and Giroux, 1969).

The title of L. Woiwode's (pronounced Why-wood-ee) beautifully written first novel reflects the uncertainty and even fear the young, newly married protagonist feels about his role as husband and prospective father. The climax of the novel occurs when Christofer Van Eenanam composes a mental letter to his wife. It is simultaneously a declaration of love, a confession of personal inadequacy and an ominous threat to life. "Dear El, love, my wife," it begins. "You're the only person I've ever been able to talk to and this is something I can't say... My feelings for you have grown every year, and that's good, that's how it should be -- but I've always felt there was something lacking in me, something held back or not there. A dead spot. It hasn't grown, but it hasn't gone away either... So what -- so what I'm going to do -- So --"

Chris and his bride Ellen have known each other for three years. They have been putting off marriage, ostensibly in order to finish college. It is also apparent that they do not feel themselves ready for the responsibilities of marriage. Ellen's grandparents (her parents were killed in an automobile accident) are opposed to the idea. Chris has reservations about marriage in general.

Now the couple can no longer put off the marriage, for Ellen is pregnant. In a scene of comic inspiration, Chris and Ellen are married in the First Presbyterian Church in Madison, Wisconsin, by the Reverend Nelson Hartis. It was not an easy wedding to arrange on short notice. Chris was brought up in the Catholic faith, but has since broken away. She is a Christian Scientist. "Well, here you are," the Reverend Hartis exclaims good-naturedly, "two young people of faiths that are hardly reciprocal, asking me, a minister of a third faith, a man in whom God's care has been entrusted and who my parishioners look to for guidance, asking me to marry you, total strangers, on the spot!" But he does marry them.

They spend their honeymoon at Ellen's grandparents'

hunting lodge in northern Michigan. It is here in this
idyllic setting ("the last symbol of the frontier") that Chris
and Ellen must learn to adjust to each other and to the
fact of marriage. "I'm elemental here," Ellen says in
a moment of happiness, and it is soon clear that what
the author intends to do is to examine an American marriage in private, as it were, away from the distractions
and encumbrances of civilization, to examine it in all its
uniqueness and complexity. This is an old-fashioned novel
in the sense that it creates believable characters. One is
reminded of some of the great novels of the past (before
critics lamented "the death of the novel"), An American
Tragedy or Tess of the D'Urbervilles. If What I'm Going
to Do, I Think is any criterion, the novel is far from
dead.

Such plot as there is is composed mainly of images that
express the psychological state of the protagonists, a dead
bird, the precarious cliff overlooking Lake Michigan, a
.22 caliber rifle, a sunken wreck, a lost wedding ring.
Apart from this, the novel beautifully captures the immediate experience of being young, of being in love, of doing
hard physical labor, of being hungry. There is another
superb comic scene in which Chris helps his neighbor, the
shrewd farmer Orin Clausen, with the haying for the
munificent sum of a dollar an hour. At the end of the
twelve-hour day, it is clear that the college boy has been
"taken" by his hick neighbor with the Stengelese syntax
who is undoubtedly one of the great comic creations of
recent fiction.

What I'm Going to Do, I Think is not a comic novel,
however, but an extraordinarily serious one in which
tragedy stalks the protagonists and in which a greater
tragedy -- represented by a .22 caliber carbine -- is narrowly averted.

REAL PEOPLE

By Alison Lurie (Random House, 1969).

Janet Belle Smith, forty-two-years old, mother of two teen-age children, author of sixteen and a half published stories, has returned for a brief stay to Illyria, a luxurious retreat in New England for artists, writers and musicians. Although feeling a twinge of guilt at leaving her insurance executive husband to fend for himself at home, she looks forward to a period of solitude and tranquility in the elegant surroundings of Illyra to resume productive work.

Of course part of the efficacy of a place like Illyria comes from the intellectual and creative stimulation generated when artists of varying kinds and backgrounds live in such close proximity to one another. Those currently in residence at Illyria include the elderly lady poet, H.H. Waters, L.D. Zimmerman, the literary critic, C. Ryan Baxter, the well-known novelist, the composer of international repute, Theodore Berg, and Nick Donato, a painter from New York. Janet Smith's best friend at Illyria, however, is Kenneth Foster, also a painter, whom Janet calls "my ideal reader." Although their conduct is above reproach, their feelings for each other are such as to suggest an unspoken love affair.

Once when a family of tourists came through the rose garden, a little boy saw some of the guests in residence through the arbor. "Are those artists, Mom, or are they real people?" he inquired ingenuously. When Janet Smith first arrives at Illyria she refers to it as "this small private Eden" where all practical problems and responsibilities vanish. "It's true, people are nicer here," she notes in her journal (Real People is written in the form of a journal). "Released from the strain of ordinary life...they relax and bloom like flowers...At Illyria one becomes one's real self, the person one would be in a decent world."

Before many weeks have passed, however, this small private Eden has turned into a kind of existentialist hell. The company of the elect who inhabited the premises like gods are now likened to children, madmen and demons. A simple-minded but pretty girl, the housemother's god-daughter, proceeds to make fools of the distinguished house guests. The artists, writers and musicians at Illyria are all too real. The well-known novelist is an alcoholic ex-Communist. The young poet is a long-haired hippie who takes drugs. The painter from New York is a crude, vulgar, loud-mouthed boor. And Kenneth Foster, Janet Smith's understanding friend, is apparently incapable of experiencing heterosexual love.

But most importantly of all, Janet Smith is finally forced to recognize that her whole life is a sham. Her work has become trivial, repetitive and boring simply because she wants to have the best of both worlds, the world of the pampered suburban housewife and the world of the artist. "What you're protecting, you see," Kenneth Foster tells her, "is the idea of this charming, intelligent, sensitive lady writer who lives in a nice house in the country with her nice family, and never makes any serious mistakes or has any real problems."

This novel by the perspicacious and witty author of The Nowhere City is somewhat disappointing. It affords Miss Lurie a convenient means for expressing the plight of the artist in society and there are many apt observations as well as some witty repartee. Perhaps it fails as a novel to the extent that it succeeds as a journal. Char-acterization is not Miss Lurie's forte, and yet so much depends on the reader's taking Nick Donato (who finally breaks through Janet Smith's polite mask of the sensitive lady writer) seriously. Unfortunately, Nick Donato is a caricature. Much is made of the role of Anna May in the novel, but she really doesn't contribute very much. And finally there are numerous dead spots. "I just went down to the kitchen to make myself some iced coffee," Janet Smith confides in her journal, "and found H.H. Waters there boiling water for tea." Sometimes Illyria is a deadly bore.

THE GIRL IN MELANIE KLEIN

By Ronald Harwood (Holt, Rinehart and Winston, 1969)

"I am sitting at the moment in Occupational Therapy before a typewriter circa 1066," Hugo remarks. "Mrs. Baverstock-Cohen, the therapist, radiates encouragement from every wrinkle of her enameled face and takes great pains to give each of us exactly the same amount of her time. She has just looked over my shoulder, read what I have typed, smiled, and said: 'Hugo dear, you have the fingers of Schnabel.' "

Hugo, ex-ballet dancer and inveterate composer of limericks, is an inmate of a luxurious asylum on the outskirts of London called The Nest. Under the terms of the trust, the atmosphere at The Nest should be "as much like a country house as possible. The patients should be made to feel like weekend guests." Hugo and the other two patients, Nora, who envisions herself Queen of England, and Wing Commander Wassler, still actively fighting World War II, are determined not to have their cozy little world disturbed. They are content to play Nest Tennis, a game in which the player hits a stone over a net with a hockey stick. The object of the game is to hit the stone as slowly as possible to give the player time to jump over the net and reach the other side before the stone does. "It is extremely difficult," Hugo acknowledges, "and has never, to my knowledge, been managed." When not playing Nest Tennis, Hugo and the others are usually trying to outwit the medical superintendent of the establishment, Dr. Ivan Lipschitz, better known as Heer Kommandant.

The arrival of a new patient, the girl in Melanie Klein, creates a crisis at The Nest. Niobe Grynne, alias Naomi Green, is young and beautiful and suffers from an extreme form of schizophrenia brought on by a terrifying experience in which she was deceived by a murderer posing as a policeman. Hugo, Nora and Wassler fear that the girl in Melanie Klein will disturb the tranquil tenor of their days at The Nest. After all, Nora exclaims, she obviously isn't royal! Niobe keeps insisting that it is all a mistake and that she should not be there at all.

Ever methodical in their madness, Hugo and his two

comrades-in-arms devise a diabolical scheme to clear up
the mystery of the girl in Melanie Klein. Not only will
they help to free her from The Nest, they will also prove
that, instead of Niobe Grynne, it is Dr. Lipschitz who is
insane. Is it not true that he gestures constantly to conceal tremors in his hand? "Our beloved Kommandant is
himself around the bend," Wing Commander Wassler remarks, "loony, dippy, goofy, whatever they say nowadays.
If anyone has fantasies it is he."

In The Girl in Melanie Klein Ronald Harwood explores
the shadowy and delicate no-man's land between sanity and
insanity. He does it with so much loving tenderness and
gentle humor that in the end he makes us realize that perhaps we are all a bit touched in the head (or whatever
they say nowadays) and no less human for that.

THE CHAIR

By Joel Lieber (McKay, 1969).

Sidney Reuben Pfeiffer is a forty-two-year-old dentist who lives in a nice house on a tree-shaded street in the town of Oakdale, about a five-hour drive from New York. A native of New York City, Sidney Pfeiffer moved to Oakdale after completing dental school. He thought it would be a good place to set up practice and raise a family. Now fifteen years have passed and Sidney Pfeiffer would seem to have everything to live for. He is happily married, the father of two bright and charming children, and his practice is thriving as never before.

Suddenly everything goes wrong. Sidney Pfeiffer's downfall dates from about the time this exemplary expounder of liberal causes (including fluoridation) sends a check for a hundred dollars to an anti-war group and finds his name listed in a full-page ad in the New York Times under the heading, "Doctors, Dentists and Lawyers for Peace." Dr. Pfeiffer becomes the innocent victim of an anonymous smear campaign. An ugly rumor spreads around town that the good dentist has taken advantage of a young girl under anesthesia in the chair. A rumor like that isn't good for business and Dr. Pfeiffer's practice suffers drastically. Another rumor circulates that he creates cavities where none exist. In addition, he and his family become the recipients of nasty mail and obscene phone calls.

But who is the accuser? Where is the enemy? How can he fight back if he doesn't know whom to fight? Won't anybody listen? "We've got some strange people in this town," Sidney tells his wife, "lunatics who masquerade as human beings and somehow get away with it."

Then it turns out that, although he has lived there for fifteen years, he is condescending about Oakdale and never did care for the place very much. He chose it for the "physical properties involved" and as a nice place to raise a family. He also makes it clear that in order to live in Oakdale he has "gone along with a great many little things I didn't particularly care for." Ever since he can recall he has felt like an outsider in Oakdale.

Poor Sidney Pfeiffer is a liberal from the big city
and his neighbors are small-town ignoramuses whom he inwardly despises and no doubt they bear him no great affec-
tion either.   So the longstanding feud between Sidney and
his neighbors is out in the open.   They are spreading vicious
lies about him and he retaliates by calling them a "human
garbage dump."   "We're living in the midst of a human
garbage dump," he adds for emphasis.   (Sidney Pfeiffer is
a gentle, wry, witty man.)

For such a gentle, wry, witty man, Sidney Pfeiffer
is a thoroughly obnoxious character.   He has such a super-
iority complex.   (In this respect he is reminiscent of some
of the current crop of college rebels, many of whom were
born knowing exactly what is wrong with the world.)   Sidney
Pfeiffer is contemptuous of Oakdale and all that it represents,
but when he goes to New York City for a weekend fling with
an old girl friend (Oh you rogue, Sidney!)   he automatically
starts carping about how New York City isn't what it used
to be.   Even God isn't exempt from his perennial faultfind-
ing.   "In the words of Gauguin," he exclaims melodramatically, "I say, God.   I charge you with injustice and malice."

This reviewer has a theory about Sidney Pfeiffer.
He is not a gentle, wry, witty man after all.   On the contrary, he is sick.   He suffers from a sickness of the mind
called a persecution complex.   All those ugly Oakdale rumors
about Sidney Pfeiffer are the product of his own sick and
tortured imagination.   Ezra Goodman never said, "They're
out to get you, Sid.   They want to drive you out of this
town."   Sidney imagined it.   "Okay," Sidney Pfeiffer says,
"I am the victim of a conspiracy..."   Now there's a word
for sick minds.

COWBOYS DON'T CRY

By L. J. Davis (Viking Press, 1969).

When Clark Kantavski was born in Brooklyn in 1937 his mother decided to change his name to Kent. In the America of her immigrant's imagination, successful and prosperous men were never called Kantavski. In 1938 the first Superman comic adventure appeared and Kent's fate was sealed. Every day of his life had been a battleground where he strove to make people believe his name and take it seriously. At the age of twenty-one he thought of changing it back to Kantavski, but that would have left a twenty-one-year hole in his life. Cowboys don't cry. The brave win.

Despite his name, Clark Kent somehow manages to forge an academic career for himself as an instructor of theoretical physics in California. He marries a pretty girl named Judy, and sees as few people as possible, all of them with their heads full of numbers. Then one day he and Judy have a quarrel (he'd wanted hollandaise sauce on his asparagus, and she hadn't felt like making it) and the next thing he knows he is on an airplane headed home for Brooklyn, obstreperously drunk, and in mindless flight from his wife, his home, and his career.

The theme of this bizarre fantasy is "You Can't Go Home Again," especially if your home is New York City in the 1960's. In Mr. Davis' perfervid imagination, New York is anything but Fun City, U.S.A. To begin with, Clark finds that Penn Station is a pile of rubble. This is unnerving enough, but when he visits his sister and her junkie boy friend on the Lower East Side, they rob him of all his money. He walks across the Brooklyn Bridge and arrives home. His parents haven't changed. His mother is "squat, blondish, sleazy, stubborn -- and stupid -- looking," with a waist that comes all the way up to her armpits. His father is a craven weakling who somehow managed to get rich during the Depression. They are no help to Clark, financial or otherwise.

But good cowboys don't lose. Clark Kent decides to earn some money donating blood to the Myrtle Avenue blood

bank.   There he runs into a blood bank quack and is convinced that donkey blood has been injected into his veins.
Then a Negro impersonating a policeman hits him over the
head and steals his money and identification.   Now nobody
will ever believe he is really Clark Kent. Cowboys don't
cry.   The brave win.

It goes on like that (there is an episode featuring a
podiatrist's pot-smoking daughter) until Clark is able to
call his wife and begin the trip safely back to California.
L. J. Davis can hold his own with Joseph Heller and James
Purdy.   If he has a weakness, it is a tendency in the early
chapters to stand back from his bizarre handiwork and summarize the salient points, as if to say, "Isn't this wild!"
In a lesser writer this self-congratulatory note would be
fatal.   Davis is able to survive these momentary lapses,
however, because he can write a passage such as this:
"The nearest blood bank was up on Myrtle Avenue, beneath
the El... The same sockless derelicts slept among the
broken bottles on the sidewalks in the same Salvation Army
suits... Daylight fell through the girders in a tangle of
shapes, and as Kent approached, a train roared overhead,
sifting a new layer of soot down over the parked cars like
the fine gray rain at the bottom of the sea, stirring the
sleeping men into new postures and different dreams."

"Up to now," Clark Kent ponders, "his former life
had been present in his thoughts like a sort of superior
reality, something that continued to exist on the other side
of the continent, waiting for him to return and take it up
like a bundle of clothes."   Perhaps this is a clue to an
understanding of what the author is up to.   Not only Clark
Kent's name but his "adventures of mud and falling" in the
urban wastes of New York are symbolic of the schizophrenia
that afflicts our country and savagely rends it apart.   If
L. J. Davis seems to lack compassion for the lonely people
who inhabit this tortured landscape, perhaps it is because
he has an idealistic vision of a greater, more compassionate America, an America that is one society rather than
two, where it is truly possible to go home again.

PICTURES OF FIDELMAN

By Bernard Malamud (Farrar, Straus and Giroux, 1969).

Fat, fortyish and foolish, Arthur Fidelman of the
Bronx, a self-proclaimed failure as a painter, has come to
Italy to prepare a critical study of Giotto. Thanks to his
sister Bessie, he has enough money for a year or two of
independent study. Well, actually, Fidelman came to Italy
a long time ago. Fidelman first made his appearance in
Partisan Review in a short story entitled "The Last Mohican."
In 1963 "The Last Mohican" was reprinted in the author's prizewinning collection of short stories, The Magic Barrel.

As a matter of fact, three of the six chapters that
comprise Pictures of Fidelman appeared in somewhat different form in The Magic Barrel and Idiots First. Like
his quixotic hero, Malamud is also an artist. He too must
"keep his finger in." (Fidelman's crowning glory is that
despite everything that happens to him, he keeps his finger
in art.) "Without art there's no life to speak of," says
Fidelman, "at least for me. If I'm not an artist, then
I'm nothing." One way to "keep your finger in" is to re-
furbish old stories, add a couple of new ones, and call
the whole package "a new entity, a picaresque novel."
Pictures of Fidelman is definitely not a novel, but if the
publisher has his way it will probably pass for one. For
the gifted Malamud it is a way of marking time until a new
novel appears.

Fidelman's adventures begin in Rome and end in
Venice with stops in Milan and Florence. Rome is a revelation. Having read that the ruins of Ancient Rome lay
buried under his feet, our hero is thrilled to think that he,
Arthur Fidelman, born a Bronx boy, was actually "walking
around in all this history." In Rome Fidelman encounters
the refugee Shimon Susskind and his "endless demands."
Inquiring about an advertisement in the American language
newspaper in Rome ("Studio to share, cheap, many ad-
vantages, etc., A. Oliovino"), he learns that the occupant
is not a pittore, as expected, but a pittrice, Annamarie
Oliovino. Fidelman falls in love with Annamarie. Fidelman is always falling in love.

Fidelman, "ever a sucker for beauty and all sorts of experiences," comes upon hard times. Adrift and penniless in the stony gray streets of Milan, he picks the pocket of an American tourist. The tourist bellows murder and Fidelman only manages to escape by holing up in the Hotel du Ville, a joint for prostitutes. There he is held captive by art thieves who plan to use him in a daring theft of Tiziano's "Venus of Urbino." Fidelman's role is to make a copy which will be substituted for the original.

Three other pictures comprise an exhibition. Bawdy, irreverent, uncertain in tone and execution, sometimes profound but more often pretentious, the exhibition is called <u>Pictures of Fidelman</u>. Throughout Fidelman pursues his eccentric course among the riff-raff of Italy as the complete artist. Whether painting pictures, sculpting, studying Giotto, digging holes in the ground and calling it a new art form or blowing glass on the island of Murano, Fidelman keeps his finger in.

THE EXTERMINATOR

By Patrick Skene Catling (Trident Press, 1969).

Residents of the East Side recently discovered that
New York City has a burgeoning rat population. As Major
Bradley Farson, President of Sanikill, Inc., explains,
"It's undermined and rotten and diseased with them. They
are gnawing at our very vitals...In New York right now,
in this enlightened day and age, there are more rats than
people, and I'm not only talking about the waterfront slums
and Harlem. There are rats everywhere."

Christopher Weston, a young pharmacist from the
country, has accepted a position with Sanikill as an exterminator. Christopher is a very bright and personable young
man indeed and why anyone in his position would go into
the exterminating business is a question the author, despite
all his glibness, doesn't answer very satisfactorily. Christopher is newly married and an expectant father. Maybe
the job represents security.

It certainly isn't a dull job. And Sanikill needs all
the competent help it can get. Christopher is soon going
out on assignments with Sam Rathbone, a senior pest-control operator. Sam's cynicism is exceeded only by his
loquaciousness. He is married to a wealthy heiress and
lives in a luxurious penthouse apartment. Sam Rathbone
quite obviously doesn't need the money. Apparently it is
sheer love of adventure that keeps him on the job. For
all his cynicism, Sam is a delightful character. He is a
charming and civilized man who refuses to live like an
automaton. As a senior pest-control operator he has entrée
into all the best places. It is quite apparent that he is the
author's alter ego. Compared to Sam Rathbone, Christopher
is innocence personified.

The two exterminators have more on their minds than
rats. They are concerned about the human population explosion ("The world population today is three and a half
billion...The way it's increasing, it'll be up to four and a
half billion before 1985. Four and a half billion human
beings on this pitifully shrinking, eroding old planet!"),
the space race, chemical and biological warfare, Vietnam

(according to Major Farson, the rats have a major sanctuary in Central Park, so he proposes to defoliate it!), child raising, poverty, modern architecture ("Architects had obviously abandoned the human module...the scale and proportions were now quite candidly overwhelmingly colossally mechanical, and people were rapidly diminishing in stature and individual significance"), suicide and even bowling ("automatons...rolling balls to automatons").

The Exterminator is not so much a novel as a fable for our times. There is a theme (man is trapped in the modern city like a rat in a maze), but nothing so cohesive as to constitute a plot. The author valiantly tries to conceal this fact by inventing one preposterous scene after another. It is all marvelously entertaining, a vaudeville feast, but in achieving this kind of limited success, Mr. Catling has sacrificed credibility. The credibility gap is wider than Lyndon Johnson's. As in Rosemary's Baby, which this novel superficially resembles, the denounement is supposed to build up to a genuine pitch of horror. It does not. The witty Patrick Skene Catling has chosen to play the buffoon and he is stuck with the role.

THE SEMPINSKI AFFAIR

By W. S. Kuniczak (Doubleday, 1969).

The Polish-born author of The Thousand Hour Day has now written a novel of suspense which he wisely calls "An Entertainment." This is a polite way of saying, "Don't take this nonsense seriously!" This reviewer began The Sempinski Affair under the illusion that, nonsensical or not, it would turn out to be a superior novel of its kind. It definitely is not a superior novel of any kind. The Sempinski Affair is even more ridiculous than most so-called spy thrillers.

The main protagonist is a forty-two-year-old consultant on Eastern antiquities, "the foremost authority on the Trebizond illuminations," Dr. Oliver Hazard Shippe, better known as O. H. A wealthy client hires O. H. to travel to a nameless European country (apparently Poland) in order to authenticate the most fantastic find of this or any century, the Pontic Tribunals, which are the actual records of the trial and death of Jesus. They form part of the legendary Romanowski Library which fell into the hands of General Danilow, the leader of the Polish resistance movement, near the end of World War II. After the Tribunals have been authenticated, they are to be smuggled out of Poland by boat across the Baltic to Sweden and thence will find their way to O. H.'s rich client in America.

One would think that the Pontic Tribunals would be subject matter enough for one book. Mr. Kuniczak is not a modest man when it comes to fashioning a stirring plot, however. The real subject of the novel is "the Sempinski affair" which concerns quite another matter. Through his assignment on the Tribunals and also through his slight acquaintance with Julian Sempinski, the Nobel Prize winner and distinguished man of letters, who has survived the wars and social upheavals that have turned Central and Eastern Europe upside down, O. H. becomes involved in an incredible plot to assassinate the Chairman of the Soviet Union while that gentleman is making an important policy speech in the nameless capital of the nameless country (apparently Warsaw). The United States government and the free world will be implicated in the plot. With the

Chairman's assassination, the stage will be set for Armageddon.

"Foreign intrigue is out of my depth," O. H. admits sheepishly at one point. This is the understatement of the whole book. O. H. stumbles from one misadventure to another and finally ends up in the hands of the conspirators led by the notorious General Rauss, the national security director of the nameless country, and Herr Professor Karpovitch, the master spy, who has earned the appellation of the Magician even though he is even more stupid than O. H. himself. The only thing that saves O. H. and Kristin Napoji, our hero's newly found love, from certain death on innumerable occasions is his fantastic luck. Indeed, O. H. is so lucky that he and Kristin actually joke about it when enjoying a respite from the hazards of howling wolf packs and rats in narrow tunnels, fire and ice, locked doors in the castle of Hetmanska Gora and wild automobile rides through the bitter cold Polish countryside.

Certainly O. H.'s luck is W. S. Kuniczak's. Without it, how would the author's bumbling hero survive long enough to make a single chapter, let alone a novel -- excuse me, an entertainment. Or as old General Danilow says, "I've survived a great many plots and conspiracies but this Sempinski business is too much."

THE BIRDS

By Tarjei Vesaas (Morrow, 1969).

Tarjei Vesaas, the seventy-one-year-old Norwegian poet and novelist, is regarded by many as Scandinavia's greatest living author. For the past twenty years Vesaas has been prominently mentioned as a candidate for the Nobel Prize for literature, but as yet this honor has not been accorded him. Translated from the original by Torbjorn Stoverud and Michael Barnes, The Birds was originally published in 1957 under the title Foglane. Tarjei Vesaas is also the author of Palace of Ice (1963).

This simple but memorable story revolves around an unusual triangle consisting of a brother and sister, Mattis and Hege, and Hege's lover, the lumberjack, Jorgen. Mattis and Hege are no ordinary brother and sister. Thirty-seven years of age, Mattis is mentally retarded and incapable of earning his own living. He is cared for by his sister, three years his elder, who ekes out a frugal existence knitting sweaters at home. They live alone in an idyllic cottage at the edge of the forest. Nearby stretches a broad lake upon which Mattis occasionally sets out in a dilapidated rowboat to try his luck at fishing. Sometimes he seeks odd jobs on neighboring farms.

One day a woodcock flies right over Mattis' house and it changes his whole life. It returns again and again. Mattis is filled with a nameless joy, the "soft, dark touch of something beyond understanding." The more Mattis thinks about the woodcock, the more he feels sure something good is going to happen. "Things are going to be different from now on," he says to himself. Even though the woodcock is killed by a fowler, things do change for the better. For one thing, Mattis discovers that he has a vocation as a ferryman. "I must have been born to row on a lake," he thinks. "Fancy wasting so much of my time on all sorts of other things." The only drawback is that Mattis doesn't have any customers, but this doesn't bother him too much. He sun bathes lazily in the bottom of the boat. He stretches, happy and content. "And I'm fully employed as well!" he exults. "Lying here and loafing about." He can't help laughing.

One day Mattis does have a customer who not only changes his life but Hege's as well. The customer is a lumberjack whom Mattis ferries across the lake from the other side. The lumberjack is named Jorgen. It seems that Jorgen is looking for a place to stay. Hege is glad to offer him the attic room and he accepts. Every day Jorgen goes out into the forest and fells trees. He even tries to teach Mattis the rudiments of his trade, but Mattis prefers the life of a ferryman. Mattis sees instantly that Jorgen is one of the "clever people." Although Mattis is not one of them, he is clever enough to see that Jorgen's entrance into their lives has changed the relationship between him and his sister. He knows that Hege and Jorgen are in love. He worries that Hege will leave him.

Mattis has mixed feelings about the new person in his life. He is happy for Hege but afraid of what the future holds for him. He remembers the woodcock and how it brought happiness and then died. He knows that he has brought happiness to his sister. Should he die too? Suddenly he realizes what he has to do. "Inwardly he was in a state of turmoil as he carried out this stage of his plan," we are told. "But everything worked satisfactorily, he said the right things, the things he realized it was safe to say, and he knew exactly what these were. Isn't it odd that you only become clever when it's too late? he thought."

"I'm not a pessimist," Mr. Vesaas said recently in a rare interview. "I think you have to be a little optimistic to live. Writing a book is a sort of optimism. But my books are very sad. There's a lot of sorrow and horrible things in my books. I cannot read a glad book." Although the ending is sad, The Birds is not a sad book. There is too much love and understanding and compassion in it for it to be sad. The author knows that all people -- the simple-minded as well as the clever -- have a deep and compelling need to be needed, even if that need finds expression in ferrying nonexistent passengers across a secluded lake. He knows that people don't need words to communicate with one another. He knows that in general people are kind. Such knowledge is surely deserving of the Novel Prize.

FAT CITY

By Leonard Gardner (Farrar, Straus and Giroux, 1969).

The fat city of the title refers to Stockton, California. Leonard Gardner is not one of those novelists who feels required to make up place names. He writes in the naturalistic tradition of Frank Norris and Jack London which stresses realism and the scientific method of observation and experiment in the treatment of character. The stunning success of this extraordinary first novel is proof that the naturalistic method first promulgated in the nineteenth century still has validity today.

Actually in his choice of title the author is being ironic as well as realistic. A commercial and manufacturing center with a population of eighty thousand, a port city and chief distributing point for the agricultural products of the San Joaquin Valley, Stockton is indeed a "fat city." In the midst of all this material wealth, however, the three protagonists of Fat City, two boxers and their manager, lead impoverished lives.

Not yet thirty years of age, Billy Tully is a prize fighter whose best years are already behind him. A leading lightweight contender in the 1950's, Tully expected to go all the way to the top. Now his manager, Ruben Luna, refers to him optimistically (a fight manager has to be optimistic) as "the most colorful lightweight in Northern California." Tully's downfall began when he was badly cut in an out-of-town fight and Ruben wasn't even in his corner. Tully blames Ruben for what happened to him. Not long after that, Tully's wife left him. Without her he cannot even find the strength to get up in the morning.

Tully's life is a dreary succession of jobs, from fry cook in a Main Street lunchroom to laborer in a box factory to driving a truck. The final indignity for Tully is when he has no alternative but to go out on the labor bus and do menial, backbreaking farm work, thinning tomatoes for ninety cents an hour. Moving from one cheap hotel to another (Fat City is a sad itinerary of hotels, from the Hotel Como to the Azores Hotel near the channel where "over the rippled wallpaper on the ceiling were large stains the color of tobacco juice"), drunk most of the time, Tully makes one halfhearted attempt to rise above the "monumental misery of the present." He forms an attachment with Oma Lee Greer, a middle-aged habitué of the Harbor Inn, the widow of a full-blooded Cherokee and paramour of a Negro named Earl, now serving time in prison.

Tully has visions of making a comeback in the ring. While working out in the Y.M.C.A. gym, he spars with an eighteen-year-old gas station attendant, Ernie Munger, and is so impressed with the youth's ability that he urges him to see Ruben Luna. Ruben takes Ernie under his wing and again dreams of casting off the "hopeless folly of his life" by producing a champion. Ernie dates an impassive girl named Fay Murdock and out of sheer inertia finally wins her. In <u>Fat City</u> love is not something to be celebrated, but rather a melancholy rite performed mechanically and without joy.

The lives of Ernie Munger and Billy Tully -- the one on the way up, the other on the way down -- intersect briefly, but it is clear that Leonard Gardner, this twentieth-century exponent of naturalism, is suggesting that both they and their manager are victims of the same uncontrollable exterior forces. Ernie Munger is destined to recapitulate in his own life the fate of Billy Tully. Ruben Luna is destined to sell out Ernie Munger as he did his older white hope. In Fat City, U.S.A., the sun shines dully through the gray haze like the lid of a can.

THE FLAW

By Antonis Samarakis (Weybright and Talley, 1969).

Antonis Samarakis is the noted Greek novelist whose
work has been praised by Graham Greene and Arthur Koest-
ler.   Translated by Peter Mansfield and Richard Burns,
The Flaw is set in a nameless police state.   The citizens
of this state are divided into two categories: those who
are with the Regime and those who are not.   To be considered an enemy of the Regime it isn't necessary to be
actively opposed to the Regime.   It is enough simply not to
have done anything positive in behalf of the Regime.   The
philosophical premise on which the Regime is based is "he
that is not with me is against me."

Of course in such an Orwellian world of terror and
intrigue the National Security Department or NSD plays a
very important role.   Two of the three main protagonists
of The Flaw are members of the NSD.   One is known as
the Interrogator; the other is called simply the Manager.
The third protagonist is a man suspected of crimes against
the state.   He is known as the Café Sport man since it was
in the Café Sport that he was apprehended.   The case is
referred to as the Café Sport Case.

As the novel begins, the NSD men are escorting
their suspect by automobile to the nation's capital where
he will be interrogated in depth at Central Headquarters.
The situtation is this: The NSD does not have any concrete
evidence against the Café Sport man, but such is the nature
of that organization that he is presumed guilty until found
otherwise.   What they really hope is that, in desperation,
the Café Sport man will attempt to escape, thereby proving
his guilt beyond a shadow of doubt.   If he does not attempt
to escape they anticipate that he will break down and confess
under rigorous interrogation.   It scarcely occurs to them
that he could be innocent.   Actually the Café Sport man is
guilty (he belongs to an anti-Regime organization), but he
doesn't know if the NSD has any real evidence against him
or not.   He suspects that they may be bluffing.   He is
determined to remain calm at all cost and not to give anything away.

Before starting out for the Capital, the NSD agents
have been instructed by Central to put into execution a plan
("masterly in its conception, unique in its flawlessness"),
a form of brainwashing designed to extract a confession of
guilt from the suspect.   In accordance with the Plan, the
NSD agents will "exploit the abrupt changes of temperature
to which the prisoner will be subjected."   Just as a piece
of tubing subjected to successive sudden changes of temperature -- from cold to hot and back to cold again -- will
eventually crack, so will the Café Sport man.   The crux of
the Plan is a pleasant four-hour walk that the Interrogator
and his prisoner take through a small town while their car
is ostensibly being repaired in a nearby garage.   The atmosphere is relaxed and congenial, all according to plan.
They get a haircut.   They idly windowshop along the main
thoroughfare.   They exchange good-natured banter with
various passers-by.   They stop for refreshment at a café.
They casually pick up two girls and accompany them to the
beach.   They attend a small carnival on the edge of town,
a carnival characterized by "a warmth, a familiarity, a
friendliness well suited to the poor part of the town it was
in."   "I was beguiled by the whole atmosphere," the Interrogator acknowledges, "the games of every description, the
lovely beat of the place, the vitality, the hundreds of people,
mothers and children and everybody, all having a good
time, enjoying themselves, shouting happily, laughing."

There is a flaw in the Plan, a basic flaw, and it
must be apparent by now just what it is.   "I can't hand
him over," the Interrogator cries out in despair,   "the Plan,
the perfect flawless Plan is like a perfect crime which isn't
perfect, we had worked everything out in advance down to
the last detail, we had calculated everything with mathematical accuracy, we had carried everything out in masterly fashion, but there is a flaw...no, men are not divided
into those who are with the Regime, and those who are not
with the Regime, a flaw, a mistake, we've made a mistake,
there's a basic flaw, the Regime is riddled with it, undermined, a mistake that will blow us sky high..."

This is a witty and accomplished novel with an important message to convey, but it has one basic flaw.   If
the Regime is as repressive as the author says it is, why
are the townspeople so spontaneous, free and joyous?

THE DAY OF THE DOLPHIN

By Robert Merle (Simon and Schuster, 1969).

This is a novel about the immanence of Armageddon in which the world is saved (if indeed it is saved) not by man but by a couple of dolphins. The dolphin is an amazing animal -- there is no question about that -- but Robert Merle tells us more about dolphins than most people probably care to know. He does for the dolphin, in fact, what Herman Melville did for the whale, but The Day of the Dolphin is no Moby Dick.

Professor Henry Sevilla, a world-renowned authority on dolphins, is working on a project for the U.S. Government in a laboratory in Florida. Known as Operation Logos, Professor Sevilla and his dedicated staff are attempting to establish communication between man and dolphin. As can be imagined, the implications of Operation Logos are enormous. If man can train dolphins to obey orders, it will virtually make obsolete naval warfare as practiced by graduates of the Naval Academy. Professor Sevilla is rather naïve politically and does not at first understand the frightening implications of his own research.

The excitement comes late in the book, however. The first couple of hundred pages are devoted to Operation Logos itself and to the little personal triumphs and tragedies of the research staff. A confirmed bachelor, Sevilla even falls in love with one of his assistants. Together they patiently pursue their task of getting two dolphins to talk. They eventually succeed and the two dolphins hold an historic press conference. "Fa, how old are you?" a reporter asks. "Five," replies Fa. "Bi, how old are you?" the reporter asks the other dolphin. "I do not know," Bi says. "Why?" asks the reporter. Fa answers for Bi. "Bi was born in the sea." "Fa, why are you answering for Bi?" asks the reporter. "Bi is my wife," replies Fa. There is much laughter. Dolphins even have a sense of humor!

Of course all of this represents a great scientific advance, but as far as the average novel reader is concerned there is nothing quite so boring as page after page

of dialogue between man and dolphin! The dolphin is a good
and gentle creature (man is a vile and oafish beast by comparison), but he will never take David Susskind's place on
TV. I guarantee you that.

Time passes. Sevilla is no longer working for the
U.S. Government. Fa and Bi have been taken away from
him to work on a highly secret project. Sevilla publishes
a book on his work with dolphins. It is translated into
twenty-three languages and condensed in the Reader's Digest. Sevilla earns a total of three million dollars in
royalties and retires to a small island off the coast of
Florida to continue his research with two new dolphins.

The year is 1973. The U.S. is still at war with
North Vietnam. On January 4 the U.S. Cruiser Little Rock
is destroyed by atomic explosion off Haiphong. All hands
are lost. War hysteria sweeps the country (and with it the
author's style degenerates badly). It is assumed that the
Chinese are responsible. The President issues an ultimatum
to the Chinese. But could reactionary forces within the
U.S. Government have planned the attack to force a show-
down with Red China? What was the secret mission that Fa
and Bi were entrusted with by the Secret Service? Can
the good guys get Fa and Bi to talk before it is too late?
Before the bad guys get them?

The dolphins have the last word. The dolphin is a
good and gentle creature.

THE GUILT MERCHANTS

By Ronald Harwood (Holt, Rinehart and Winston, 1969)

In his third novel the author of the zany and touching The Girl in Melanie Klein has attempted to do something different. Not content to repeat his previous triumph, he has written a "serious" book in an unrelievedly flat and colorless prose. One must admire Ronald Harwood's courage in attempting to write "against the grain" as it were, but he has stumbled badly. The plot of The Guilt Merchants is as ludicrous as the style is wooden.

The novel is set in the small South American town of El Pueblo. The chief protagonist is a quiet, hardworking man of Jewish descent who has assumed the name of Carlos Andreas. After the war Andreas emigrated to South America from Germany. Andreas is a mysterious figure about whom little is known except that he survived the infamous Weisering concentration camp.

El Pueblo is a stagnant and indolent backwater in which the few Europeans who have gravitated there for one reason or another form a small, closely knit colony. There is Andreas' boss in the tannery where Andreas works as chief export clerk, the wealthy Jewish merchant Cordonez. There is Cordonez' promiscuous wife, Anna. There is the local doctor, Ludwig Zeiger, an ex-Nazi with a passion for Brahms. And of course there is Andreas himself. Andreas' wife is bedridden with an incurable disease. His son is a homosexual. Andreas rents a small windowless room in the center of town near the refrigeration plant and for years the talk of El Pueblo centers around Andreas' strange visits to this mysterious room. Andreas has been heard shouting and screaming in German. There is much speculation that he keeps a prisoner there.

Actually all of these people are the guilt merchants of the title. They trade in guilt and human misery just as surely as Cordonez trades in leather. Each one is guilty of something. No one is innocent. Into this festering community of guilt merchants arrives a stranger from Israel named Sidnitz. Sidnitz is an Israeli agent. For sixteen years he has been searching for the notorious

Wilhelm Brullach, commandant of Weisering, and the trail
has led him to El Pueblo.

       Now this is where things begin to get slightly ridicu-
lous. Sidnitz does catch up with Brullach, but suddenly
decides he no longer wants him. The author asks us to
believe that, after searching for Brullach for sixteen years,
Sidnitz would suddenly develop qualms about apprehending
him! It seems that Sidnitz is himself one of the guilt merchants. The only reason he decided to become an Israeli
agent in the first place and track down Brullach was to get
out of Israel. He has never gotten over his feelings of
guilt about what his countrymen have done to the Arabs.
Poor confused Sidnitz somehow equates the dispossessing
of the Arabs in the Middle East with the murder of thousands of men, women and children in the infamous Weisering death camp! Since they are all guilty, Brullach should
be set scot free!

       When Cordonez expresses understandable alarm at
these developments, Sidnitz says wearily, "I'm not a knight
in shining armour."

TWO, THREE, MANY MORE

By Nicholas Von Hoffman (Quadrangle, 1969).

Since reporting on the free-speech controversy at Berkeley, Nicholas Von Hoffman has written several non-fiction books on the college scene and generation gap including We Are the People Our Parents Warned Us Against and The Multiversity. One, Two, Many More is his first novel, but it still reads like nonfiction. Von Hoffman is always relevant and that is an admirable quality. What he seems to lack is a novelists' imagination.

The author takes his title from a remark by Tom Hayden, the militant leader of the New Left: "Create two, three, many Columbias." Two, Three, Many More describes in documentary form the student revolt at a great American university. Although the university remains nameless, there is absolutely no doubt that it is Columbia. Von Hoffman doesn't leave too much to the imagination.

The trouble on campus begins over University Regulation XXVII which prohibits any form of demonstration, theatricals, speech, song or music by anyone except registered students, faculty, teaching assistants, or other university employees, without prior approval from one of the deans. The lines are immediately drawn between the SDS and the administration. The SDS is itself split into three factions, the radical or Maoist faction led by Roger Elias, the conservative or "Russian" faction led by Raymond Shapiro and the anarchist faction led by "Sil."

On the other side of the barricades is the administration represented by the President, Martin Hungerford, a fund-raising type who according to the rebels has sold out the university to the military-industrial complex. There is Chancellor A. A. McVey, a sensible moderate who tries desperately to effect a solution but is destined to fail. There are Blackie McTavish, Associate Dean of Students, and Vernon Yaldell, an assistant dean whose office is in the Student Union where he operates as a kind of forward observation post. And there is Myron Mirsky of the Faculty Emergency Committee whose amnesty formula is rejected by the administration.

Roger Elias of SDS sets the tone of the confrontation.
"I don't want a test," he shouts. "I want a declaration of
war. I want another Pentagon here. I want people like
Jerry Rubin to say dirty words and take off their clothes.
I want to put 'em up tight, that's what I want. I'm not
interested in busting Regulation **XXVII**. I want to bust it
and the 26 that come before it. Break open the whole
place."

The rest of course is history. The radical students
occupy Fletcher Hall, the main administration building, and
Philosophy. In a parallel development, the blacks occupy
Ripon after being refused permission to celebrate Afro Day
in contravention of Regulation **XXVII**. The police are finally
called in after a bomb damages the University gym building.
Violence and death are the final legacy.

The author uses newspaper accounts, miscellaneous
documents, letters and lengthy excerpts from a Verbal
History Project to give a sense of immediacy to the fast-
changing events. A sort of literary Charlie McCarthy, he
is extremely skillful in representing all sides and points
of view in the conflict, from Myron Mirsky (" What is
wrong with our system of thinking? Millions of poor people
and black people in this country, and we didn't see them.
It took these meshugganah, these true-believing fanatics,
these crazy young people to find them..."), to Vernon Yaldell
("If that's the wave of the future, I'm baffled certainly.
Mostly I wish I was born thirty years earlier, because I
don't want to be around when that crowd takes over").

Unfortunately, this mass of documentation remains
just that. It would require a novelist's imagination to
ignite it and make it blaze. Vernon Yaldell is right when
he says resignedly (Verbal History Project), "We played
it out like the Easter Story. There was not one moment of
real suspense."

THE ANDROMEDA STRAIN

By Michael Crichton (Knopf, 1969).

Why is a sixty-nine-year-old Sterno drinker with an ulcer like a two-month-old baby? The answer to this riddle is sought desperately by a group of scientists, including Nobel Prize winner Dr. Jeremy Stone, deep under the earth at the Wildfire Laboratory in Flatrock, Nevada. It is the clue to the puzzling mystery of the Andromeda Strain.

The Andromeda Strain is a new breed of organism introduced to earth from outer space following the landing of a small unmanned satellite (Project Scoop) in Piedmont, Arizona. Within eight hours of the landing, fifty people die horrible deaths in Piedmont. Some died instantly, their blood turned to stone. Others went stark raving mad and killed themselves in bizarre fashion. Michael Crichton seems to take perverse, ghoulish delight in describing the gory details. Of course in his clumsy and naïve way he is describing the first biologic crisis on earth. He obviously doesn't want anyone to miss the significance of the events he describes.

The Wildfire group goes on immediate alert. In their special isolation suits, they are dropped by helicopter into Piedmont where they collect the satellite and the only two survivors of the disaster. They are then flown to the secret Wildfire Laboratory in Utah to begin their investigation of the extraterrestrial life form. It is imperative that the organism be kept from spreading.

The Wildfire scientists are under the impression that Directive 7-12 has been put into effect by the President, resulting in the destruction of Piedmont by atomic bomb. Actually there has been a rather elementary breakdown in communications and the Wildfire group misses two important teleprinter messages. It seems that the President has postponed Directive 7-12. A good thing too because it is discovered later that the ornery little critter would simply thrive on an atomic explosion. Such an explosion would spread the darn thing from Las Vegas to San Bernardino. It would be just a matter of time before Los

Angeles was totally annihilated, topless dancers and all.

So the Wildfire group goes back to trying to solve the basic question, the clue to the riddle of the Andromeda Strain: Why is a sixty-nine-year-old Sterno drinker with an ulcer like a two-month-old baby? Before they arrive at an answer, a great deal of excitement occurs at the Wildfire Laboratory. One of the scientists has a grand-mal seizure induced by looking at a red light that blinks at the rate of three times per second. Despite all their safeguards, nobody knew he had a history of epilepsy. And what a time to have an attack! Another scientist becomes sealed in the laboratory when it becomes contaminated and the doors automatically close.

The other scientists manage to keep him alive, but then a new emergency arises. The Andromeda Strain has mysteriously changed to a mutant form that is harmless to man but eats rubber gaskets! The whole Wildfire building is rapidly becoming contaminated and is on automatic self-destruct. In three minutes the bomb will go off and spread the organism all over the surface of the earth. There will be a thousand mutations, each killing in a different way. The only hope is that the Odd Man ("the key to all this") can reach a substation through the central core and abort the automatic self-destruct by turning a key in the lock. To accomplish this he must dodge poisonous darts fired by automatic guns. These guns were originally intended to prevent the escape of lab animals. In The Andromeda Strain everyone is a lab animal. There are no human beings.

In this worst of all possible worlds for computers and lab animals, all ends happily. The Andromeda Strain has apparently mutated to a benign form. The Wildfire scientists are fairly confident that the organism will move into the upper atmosphere without causing further difficulty on earth. The author, who writes in boring technical detail about everything else, is a bit vague about this, but I guess we can take his word for it. Good riddance to the Andromeda Strain!

Now you know why a sixty-nine-year-old Sterno drinker with an ulcer is like a two-month-old-baby. Or do you?

PART TWO

ENTERTAINMENTS

All reviews in Parts II and III originally appeared in Library Journal and are reprinted
here by permission of the R. R. Bowker
Company. One review--of Harris Greene's
The Thieves of Tumbutu (page 365)--was
written for LJ but was never published there.

SON OF THE GAMBLIN' MAN

By Mari Sandoz (Clarkson N. Potter, 1960).

Mari Sandoz has been writing for more than twenty-five years and her work has won unstinted praise from Edward Weeks, W. R. Burnett and Oliver La Farge. This reputation is based largely on her biography of her father, Old Jules; but Son of the Gamblin' Man is an incredibly amateurish piece of writing about John J. Cozad, who founded a community in the Platte River region of Nebraska in the 1870's. Nothing about this fictionized biography of a Nebraska gambler turns out quite right. Cozad, a gambler who piled up huge winnings before becoming a "community builder," is evidently supposed to be a picturesque character, but he seems instead to be merely grasping and mercenary. The young settlement's struggles to survive prairie fires, lynchings, grasshopper plagues and cattlemen are the familiar stuff of countless Hollywood and TV westerns. And the author's style ("Growth brought problems to Cozad," one paragraph flatly begins), without a semblance of wit, humor or irony, is best described as disingenuous. For popular collections, as well as for those specializing in Americana, and for Cozad, Neb. (pop. 2,910).

THE ROLLICKING SHORE

By E. R. Karr (McDowell, Obolensky, 1960).

As the title suggests, this is supposed to be a big rollicking novel of carefree youth sowing their wild oats in Vino, Ohio ("Vino, Vino, Vino! How I loved you! How I love you now in retrospect! You are some of me, I am much of you. I will never forget you...for you are not just a place, but a people"), a small resort town on Lake Erie. As you may gather from the above sample, this book has to be read to be believed. It relates the picaresque adventures of Allie Curtis who from his fourteenth year spends his summer vacations at Ciro's Camp on the lake shore. Woefully naïve at first, Allie makes a complete fool of himself by pulling such goucheries as, for example,

trying to buy a "yellow wiggler, " a kind of fly, in a "sporting house " under the impression he is in a sporting goods
store.   The author is, as you can see, very fond of double
entendres, the cruder the better, and he will spin whole
interminable chapters for the sake of a single witless dirty
joke.   This book is a ghastly mistake.

PEACEABLE LANE

By Keith Wheeler (Simon and Schuster, 1960).

        Peaceable Lane is a street in an upper-middle-class
suburban community near New York which proves anything
but peaceable when a Negro artist worth "a thousand bucks
a painting and up" moves his family there from Harlem.
The author is undoubtedly sincere and strives earnestly to
bring out into the open the hates, fears and prejudices of
the people concerned.   The trouble is it all sounds so
feeble and banal.   The cliché-ridden style (afternoons become a nightmare, people are tense with nameless foreboding, rage tears at them and weariness sits on them like
a drug) and predictable characters all conveniently typed
contribute nothing to our understanding of the problems involved but simplify them out of existence.   Furthermore,
this book may very well be misleading in its appraisal of
the questions it raises.   The implication is (after the
artist gets conveniently killed in an auto accident) that the
Negro "problem" can only be resolved by the children.   It
is tempting to slough off one's responsiblities onto the
shoulders of children, but in this case it is probably too
pessimistic, if blessedly vague, a view.   The world is
obviously moving faster than Mr. Wheeler.   Incidentally, the
dialogue in this book is absolutely insane.   On Peaceable
Lane one doesn't cut the grass but "barbers the lawn."   A
juicy steak is a "handsome hunk of cow."   More than three
hundred pages of this can get on one's nerves.   Peaceable
Lane is the Book-of-the-Month club choice for December
and presumably meets with the approval of Gilbert Highet
and other distinguished members of the Board.

THE TOWERS OF LOVE

By Stephen Birmingham (Little, Brown, 1961).

If this book wasn't first published serially in the Ladies' Home Journal it should have been. All the ingredients are there. Hugh Carey, an advertising executive in his early thirties, returns for an extended visit to the ancestral estate in Connecticut. His wife is in the process of divorcing him, and he has come home to reassess his life and to plan for the future. Coincidentally, Edrita Smith (nee Everett), a childhood friend whom Hugh has not seen for more than ten years, has also come home under similar circumstances. Hugh and Edrita renew their friendship ("Would you like me to come over and fix something for you?") and there is the inevitable seduction scene. Hugh's domineering mother lurks ominously in the background. There is even a homosexual interior decorator named Titi. The Towers of Love, Titi and all, is sheer tutti-frutti. It will end up in many rental collections and feel right at home.

LORD LOVE A DUCK

By Al Hine (Atheneum, 1961).

In a recent article in Esquire magazine, Mr. Hiram Haydn of Atheneum is quoted as saying, "I like to make my own mistakes." This is one of them. For sheer vulgarity it would be hard to surpass this book. Of course it is all supposed to be good clean fun, a raffish satire on American mindlessness, the cult of youth, Hollywood, sex, permissive education, ad infinitum. Barbara Anne Greene, an aspiring cheerleader type from Nichols Corners, Iowa, is the epitome of all this. She has her heart set on a career in the movies, and with the help of Alan (Gooney Bird) Musgrave, a warped genius, actually succeeds in making her dreams come true. Not exactly the Tab Hunter type himself, Gooney Bird apparently takes a perverse pleasure in manipulating and controlling Barbara Anne. He takes her to Fort Lauderdale, Florida, where she meets a Hollywood scout. He introduces her to Bob (Bobby Bear) Barnard and persuades her to marry Bobby Bear. At the height of his power, he tracks down the newlyweds on their

wedding night and surreptitiously tape records the event
for later playback alone with Barbara Anne. In a zany denouement, Gooney Bird gets his comeuppance. Mr. Hine
is entitled to his little joke if he thinks it's funny, but
libraries are cautioned to read carefully and not let old
Gooney Bird hypnotize them as well as Barbara Anne.

A GAY AND MELANCHOLY SOUND

By Merle Miller (Sloane, 1961).

This long, tedious novel by the author of That Winter
and Reunion examines the life and times of Joshua Bland,
ex-child prodigy, World War II veteran and theatrical
producer. Joshua, disillusioned by all the minor grievances
of life (a bolder spirit wouldn't deign to notice most of what
troubles him), decides to do away with himself. While
awaiting the end he conceives the gruesome idea of tape
recording his reminiscences. A Gay and Melancholy Sound
(the accent is on the melancholy) is the result of all this
soul-searching on tape. The author's pseudo-cynical
philosophy, his pre-packaged Madison Avenue prose (Hollywood is "Out There," Washington is "Wonderland" and Charlotte is "Charley") and his general inability to create a
genuine emotion out of all those short staccato-like para-
graphs do not add up to a very impressive performance.
Still, most libraries which have the author's other books
will probably want to add this one. Incidentally, the
current fad of having a prodigy or ex-prodigy for a hero
is surely a mistake. In order to make a character with
an I.Q. of 188 halfway convincing the author would himself
have to have a comparable I.Q. , n'est-ce pas? Unfortunately, Joshua Bland's intellect is most ordinary, even if
he did read a Burma Shave ad before the age of three.

JENNY BY NATURE

By Erskine Caldwell (Farrar, Straus, 1961).

"I'm Jenny by name and Jenny by nature," Erskine
Caldwell's latest heroine keeps affirming throughout this
not very good novel. Like Claudelle Inglish before her,

she is still another version of the author's favorite female whose place is in the home, especially in the bedroom. This is not exactly true as Jenny, who is about fifty, is now a "respectable retired lady." Her main pastime is taking in boarders. These include a recently jilted "Good Bad Girl" (as Leslie Fiedler would say) and a circus midget whom Jenny keeps around in the off-season as a sort of pet. In a typically kindhearted gesture, Jenny befriends a young Negro girl. As it turns out, this is not such a good idea since poor Lawana's life is thanklessly snuffed out in what must be the least awe-inspiring fire in modern literature. It is all entertaining enough no doubt. There is no substance to any of it, unfortunately, but only a kind of good-natured salaciousness which the author probably mistakes for robust humor. The sad truth is Mr. Caldwell has nothing very important to say and keeps repeating it. Certainly not essential, though if you have thirty copies of Peyton Place stored away in the basement, what harm can it do?

THE LAST OF THE SOUTHERN WINDS

By David Loovis (Scribner, 1961).

The Southern Winds is a restaurant and bar in Key West, Florida. Jake Romano, the owner, needs twenty thousand dollars to keep it going. He asks an old college friend in New York, the Reverend Benjamin T. Hoyt, to lend him the money. Carl Solon, sent down by the Reverend Hoyt to look things over, is immediately caught up in the diabolical atmosphere of Key West. "What was it on the island," he wonders, "that undid one's civilized reconciliations, that caused one to exist, defensively and offensively, in the center of perhaps more primary life forces?" After 350 turgid pages this profound question is still not satisfactorily answered. The tumult, one suspects, is mostly in Carl's head. Things go from bad to worse and the Southern Winds catches on fire and burns to the ground. (It is really the only solution.) His civilized reconciliations now completely undone, Carl decides to marry Charlotte Tully, who not only is old enough to be his mother but is stone deaf besides. Their first goal, Carl announces, will be to restore Charlotte's hearing. On this hopeful note the novel closes.

THE CARPETBAGGERS

By Harold Robbins (Trident Press, 1961).

One doesn't have to be an Edmund Wilson to know
that this is pulp fiction on the level of Mickey Spillane.
Like The Dream Merchants, it is ostensibly about the motion
picture industry, though this is open to dispute. The narrative covers the years from 1925 to 1945. The principal
carpetbaggers are: (1) Rina Marlowe, bosomy Hollywood
actress who can't seem to decide whether she's a Lesbian
or a nymphomaniac, (2) Jonas Cord, manufacturer of something called plastics, (3) Nevada Smith, ex-outlaw turned
cowboy star, and (4) Jennie Denton, fabulous call girl who,
having "used up her ration of love" (but not before page
627!), seeks to atone for her sins by taking holy vows.
And let's not omit the author, perhaps the biggest carpet-
bagger of all! The thought of respected and well-meaning
libraries methodically ordering, cataloging and shelving
trash like this completely boggles the imagination. Let's
say "No" and keep our self-respect.

OLD LIBERTY

By Marshall Terry, Jr. (Viking Press, 1961).

Redwine Walker, an ebullient young man from Java-
lina, Texas, enrolls at his Daddy's Alma Mater, Liberty
College in Pennsylvania. Old Liberty, the reader should be
forewarned, no more resembles a college than the Co-
existence Bagel Shop. The author's style is a peculiar
blend of Beatnik and Texas Colloquial with absurd snatches
of The Catcher in the Rye thrown in for good measure. It
is a completely indigestible brew. The climax of the school
year is the Spring Retreat to which our hero brings the
town whore, chivalrously known as the Whale. Before the
night is over, Old Liberty burns to the ground, thus en-
abling the author to extricate himself after a fashion from
the unholy mess he has made. "This has been a kind of
raggedy, strange story, I know," Redwine ruefully admits
at the very end, "and I am sorry for that. It has merged
together for me now, so it hardly makes sense." My sentiments exactly.

TO LIVE AND DIE IN DIXIE

By Theodore Roscoe (Scribner, 1961).

Is this book a practical joke? This reviewer has never read a more atrociously written book and yet Theodore Roscoe is, as the blurb writers say, a writer of wide experience. In any event, To Live and Die in Dixie is about a murder that takes place in a small southern town around the turn of the century. It is probably based on a real case of murder as no one could possibly have made it up. A prominent citizen's wife is scalded to death in a bathtub ("a boiling and terrible tub"). "At 10:00 P.M. on the last Sunday of August, 1902," Mr. Roscoe writes with characteristic naïveté, "Amityburg had been a somnolent American town dutifully engaged in concluding Sabbath observances. . . " "Thirty minutes later," he continues, "Amityburg was a Donnybrook -- a bedlam wrapped in the clamor of pandemonium. Shouts. Cries. Running footfalls. Galloping hoofs. The penetrant shrilling of a police whistle answered by whistling from distant precincts. The gong-gong-gong of the patrol wagon. The frantic bell of the ambulance cart. Fire bells joining in. And then the bell over City Hall -- Boong- Brang! Boong-Brang -- the baleful disaster tocsin." Anything I might add to that would be superfluous indeed.

CATCH-22

By Joseph Heller (Simon and Schuster, 1961).

Catch-22 is about a bombardier named Yossarian stationed with an American bomber squadron on a small island off Italy during the closing months of World War II. Yossarian, who has a "morbid aversion to dying," is determined to live out the war. Two main drawbacks stand in his path: (1) Colonel Cathcart who keeps raising the number of missions the men must fly, and (2) catch-22 which specifies that a concern for one's own safety in the face of dangers that are real and immediate is the process of a rational mind. In other words, Yossarian would be "crazy to fly more missions and sane if he didn't, but if he was sane he had to fly them." If this sounds complicated, it is. Catch-22 is pure burlesque, a zany concoction rem-

iniscent of nothing so much as Abbott and Costello's "Who's
on first" routine.   I confess the whole thing seemed tedious
to me, especially the author's incessant paradoxes of which
catch-22 is a fair sample.

GOING AWAY: A REPORT, A MEMOIR

By Clancy Sigal (Houghton Mifflin, 1962).

This very earnest, very immature work by the author
of Weekend in Dinlock seems to be written on the naïve assumption that if one asks enough ordinary people between Los
Angeles and New York how they are going to vote one will
somehow penetrate to the very heart of America.   Mr.
Sigal's private poll-taking becomes tedious, but at least he
cannot be accused of shirking the grand summing up.   "Everything in me cries out that we are meaningless pieces of
paste," he announces mournfully, "everything in me hopes
that this is not the end of the story.   For there is something in the atmosphere of America which multiplies and en-
hances this basic nausea of experience while preventing, or
hindering, that which might counteract the inescapable,
papered-over vertiginousness: a direct apprehension of dis-
crete phenomenon, America straight."   This quotation gives
some idea of the pretentious quality of this book.   Indeed,
although the narrator, a former labor organizer, was only
fourteen in 1940, one gets the impression that he and
Samuel Gompers practically started the entire labor movement.   A Houghton Mifflin Literary Fellowship Book.

THE SPANGLED ROAD

By Borden Deal (Scribner, 1962).

This is the worst book I've read since The Carpetbaggers.   The famous clown, Domino, is on his way to
Florida to retire after an illustrious career as "the greatest
sideshow freak in the whole of the civilized world."   He
comes upon the Cosmos Brothers Great International Circus
and learns that it is about to go into bankruptcy.   Domino
invests all his savings in the stranded circus and puts it
on "the spangled road" under the name Circus Domino.

Everything goes wrong for Domino. An expensive lion gets loose and has to be shot. The great John Morales of the Flying Morales is seriously injured in a fall. The temperamental Skoda-Jones Troupe is forever quarreling. Things improve when Eva Skoda-Jones marries the elephant trainer Walt Ringo ("Life Goes To a Circus Wedding"), but not for long. Borden Deal belongs to the Fab Soap School of American Realism: "She weighed the laundry and stuffed it into a machine. She bought a small box of Fab because the stuff they supplied in laundromats was never any good, a dull green powder that wouldn't clean any better than sand." For rental collections.

MIGNON

By James M. Cain (Dial Press, 1962).

This is an unusually inept performance even for this day and age. (One is almost tempted to say marvelously inept, so ludicrous is it.) The action takes place in New Orleans during the Civil War. The dashing hero is William Cresap, who becomes involved in a plot to sell cotton to the Union Army (or is it shoes to the Confederate Army?) and survives an extraordinary number of adventures, not the least of which involve such exotic New Orleans types as the beautiful Mignon Fourent (who smells like Russian leather, incidentally) and Marie Tremaine. The entire Union and Confederate Armies combined don't give our hero half as much trouble as Mignon who, passionate creature that she is, spits in Cresap's eye at the slightest provocation. Mr. Cain has the quaintest way of describing people and things that I have ever encountered. One man has a "blue chin, fat stomach, and a New England way of talking." This is how the author describes a room: "... the halls had Axminster runners; in place of the mustard paint was decent wallpaper, with lords and ladies and dogs; in place of the Sunday-School smell was her smell [Russian leather], the smell of books, and the smell of ham frying. . ." Not ever for libraries that buy everything.

DRUM

By Kyle Onstott (Dial Press, 1962).

      This odious book could be subtitled "Adventures in the
Skin Trade." It begins early in the 1800's with Tamboura,
a majestic African, who is sold into slavery and taken to
Havana. Tamboura works in the sugar fields by day and
breeds new slaves by night. Needless to say, the author
of Mandingo concentrates on Tamboura's nocturnal pursuits
and we learn very little about how cane sugar is harvested.
(For a writer who appeals primarily to prurient interest,
what could be better than a stud farm?) Tamboura is an
ambitious youth and before long he is serving his master
as groom. As he advances up the social ladder his mis-
tresses (if that's the right word) become progressively
lighter in color. Finally he proves irresistible to his
owner's white mistress, the Comtesse Alix de Vaux. Alas,
the lovers are caught and Book One comes to an end with
the demise of our hero and the sudden departure of Alix de
Vaux for New Orleans. Book Two is a recapitulation of
Book One except read Drum in lieu of Tamboura. Drum
is, in fact, Tamboura's son, the offspring of his affair
with the Comtesse. Alix now presides over an establishment euphuistically called the Academy of Music. Drum
fathers a son called (what else?) Drumstick. And so it
goes. Onstott could keep it up for years and probably will.

FACE TO FACE

By Edward A. Rogers (Morrow, 1962).

      Inevitably someone had to write a book loosely based
on the Kennedy-Nixon debates. Only a very naïve and unimaginative writer would have required such a crutch and
indeed Face to Face is strictly on the level of such classics
of sub-literature as The Carpetbaggers and The Lion Pit.
The Presidential aspirants who meet face to face (the
book ends just as the momentous hour finally arrives) are
Secretary of State Andrew Conger, representing the incumbent party, and Governor Joseph Green. Charles Dale,
a young independent TV producer, foolishly leaves his
lucrative Denver business to conduct Andy Conger's television campaign. Somewhere the author has picked up the

idea that the better known candidate always stands to lose
in a TV debate.   By repeating this profound thought over
and over again he is able to pad a wordy two hundred page
book to well over twice that length.   Anyway, North American Broadcasting Company enters into a crooked deal with
Green whereby they will manipulate the debates in his favor
in return for which the President of North American will
become Secretary of Communications in Green's cabinet.
(Oh, these people are evil, evil!)   As you can see, it is
all very absurd and anyone who takes it seriously should be
made to eat Newton Minow's shirt, cuff links and all.

A SHADE OF DIFFERENCE

By Allen Drury (Doubleday, 1962).

        Allen Drury resembles nothing so much as a gigantic
computer that ingests old back issues of Time, Life and a
half dozen newspapers, and then spews them out again in
great indigestible chunks.   The scene of his new novel
shifts from Capitol Hill to United Nations Headquarters in
New York.   The principal characters are His Royal Highness the M'Bulu of Mbuele ("Terrible Terry"), Felix
Labaiya-Sofra ("La-buy-uh-Soaf-ra"), Ambassador of Pana-
ma, Cullee Hamilton, Negro Congressman from California,
and Senator Harold Fry, acting head of the U.S. Delegation.
The time is the post-Geneva period when East-West ten-
sions are at their height.   The M'Bulu of Mbuele, heir to
the African kingdom of Gorotoland, is pressing for immediate cessation of British rule.   His Highness is of course
a valuable pawn in the ideological struggle between East
and West.   At Charleston, South Carolina, he deliberately
creates an international uproar when he escorts a Negro
girl into a newly integrated all-white school.   A resolution
is introduced at the UN calling for an immediate investigation of racial practices in the United States.   The novel
swirls and eddies around this resolution, in which the U.S.
is "publicly attacked and humiliated before the world," for
over six hundred interminable pages.   Obviously this book
is going to be a best seller.   Why?   Perhaps the main
reason is that Mr. Drury has a message, albeit not a very
original one.   As Senator Fry remarks to the British Ambassador, "But chivvying the United States is fair fun for
all, is that it?"   This is really the theme of the book.   Mr.
Drury is basically conservative and narrowly chauvinistic,

though he tries to camouflage this under the guise of moderation. Should public libraries buy this book? Yes, and for the following reasons: Mr. Drury is a Pulitzer Prize-winning author; people who ordinarily do not read books or newspapers might learn something about the mechanics of the UN, and the library profession (for perhaps defensible reasons) has chosen to follow public taste rather than lead it.

BREAKING UP

By W. H. Manville (Simon and Schuster, 1962).

Breaking Up concerns the marital breakup of a young New York advertising man named Bill and his wife June. These two have a problem all right. June must feel needed, but Bill is essentially cold, indifferent. The only person who does make her feel needed is a beautiful homosexual, Ned Capane, who gets his kicks wielding a rhinestone whip. Bill, on the other hand, is attracted to Lesbians ("You turn to a woman the way a lush turns to drink," one tells him scornfully). As a matter of fact, Breaking Up is a kind of tourist's guide to New York low life, written without any attempt to understand, or even minimal ability to report. It is extraordinarily crude. At one point, June, who resents her husband's coldness, says poignantly, "It was like you were only watching me take the garbage out, when I left." The author, a columnist for The Village Voice, previously wrote Saloon Society.

ETERNAL FIRE

By Calder Willingham (Vanguard Press, 1962).

Ever since End As a Man (1947), Calder Willingham has been the enfant terrible of American fiction. In Eternal Fire he introduces another of those sadistic monsters à la Jocko De Paris for which he is famous (or should we say infamous?). This time his name is Harry Diadem. Harry's main function is to break up a pending marriage between wealthy Randolph Shepherdson III of Glenville, Georgia, and virtuous Laurie Mae Lytle. The mastermind behind all this is Randy's guardian, Judge Micah V. Ball, who wishes to maintain the status quo. (If his ward mar-

ries, he will no longer have access to Randolph's $800,000.)
The idea is to disgrace Laurie Mae by having Harry seduce
her or even rape her if necessary. How Harry carries out
this plan is meticulously delineated through nearly five hundred closely printed pages.   There is also a subplot involving incest between a demented ex-policeman and his daughter
Poppie.   As disgusting as all this sounds, Calder Willingham is a serious and in many ways a talented writer.   This
is satire or nothing.   (No one in his right mind would take
Eternal Fire seriously as a realistic portrayal of humanity.)
Not succeeding as satire, however, it remains merely disgusting.   It is a matter of style.   The author is too ver-
bose and heavy-handed.   There is literally too much gnash-
ing of teeth.   There is anger but no wit or humor to
make it palatable.

THE WINTER PEOPLE

By Gilbert Phelps (Simon and Schuster, 1964).

Colonel John Parr is an eccentric amateur arch-
aeologist whose explorations have earned him a small niche
in A History of the British Explorers by the Reverend
Amos Bullock, D.D., in twelve volumes.   In 1895 while
rummaging about in the Andes, he claims to have discovered
an ancient and hitherto unknown people of pre-Inca descent
who live in a remote, seventeen-thousand-foot-high valley,
a kind of Shangri-La of the Andes.   The Colonel refers to
them only as the "Winter People."   This fantastic claim is
dismissed as the hallucinations of a madman.   Thirty-five
years later the Colonel dies in virtual seclusion in England.
The full story of the Winter People is revealed in a journal
that he has bequeathed to his nephew David, who in turn
bequeaths it to us.   The journal is a weird account of
amnesia, ritual war, mass entombment (the Winter People
hibernate during the winter), and bells and doors that oper-
ate by temperature changes and mysterious vibrations.
David, who appends brief comments to his great-uncle's
manuscript, is at first skeptical about the existence of the
Winter People, but is finally won over.   This reviewer
was skeptical at the beginning and remained skeptical to
the very end.   A crudely conceived and executed, unabash-
edly romantic piece of escapism which has little to recommend it.

SKIN DEEP

By Ralph G. Martin (McKay, 1964).

Skin Deep is a very poor novel, about on the level
of The Carpetbaggers. It is about four American Negroes
living in Paris. They are a musician (Johnny), a writer
(Lester), an artist (Steve) and a psychologist (Herman),
but don't let the nomenclature discourage you. Mr. Martin isn't interested in their professional competence ("Pic-
asso never painted photographs," Steve muses, "and yet
when he drew a hand, it looked handy, and when he drew
a horse, it looked horsey ..."), but mostly on their sex
life which is, like the title of the book, only skin deep.
As Johnny says, sex is "like strawberry shortcake. Try
eating strawberry shortcake every day. After a while, it
turns your stomach. After a while you want something else.
You want pie or you want eclairs or you want only bread..."
This is about as profound as anybody ever gets in this first
novel.

A VOICE FROM THE WINGS

By Nancy Hallinan (Knopf, 1965).

Miss Hallinan's second novel will perhaps be of interest to psychiatrists, for each character in this book is
a little mad and a case for a mental institution. Long
after the rest of us have discovered this grim fact for ourselves, Carla Gorin's psychoanalyst tells her that she has
symptoms of schizophrenia, Korsakoff's psychosis, psy-
choneurotic hysteria. She belongs to the agitated depressive
type, and is manic, hebephrenic, catatonic. Put a character like this in a novel to stir things up and it must be
admitted that the result is not exactly dull. If only Carla's
thoughts did not lean so heavily toward the banal! Of
course she can't help it if she is the granddaughter of a
countess and has all that "rich foreign background," but
even the granddaughter of a countess should be able to
think occasionally in terms other than the romantic clichés
of soap opera. This book might be labeled soap opera
Greenwich Village style. Carla, whose father is the celebrated three-fingered guitarist Boris Gorin, seeks a career
as an actress. After many ups and downs (the low point

comes when she flees to Juarez, Mexico, to become a taxi
girl, "no longer Carla Gorin, but a slight, agile dancer
paid in pesos"), she finds a measure of success on the
stage. Certainly the stage is an ideal place for her to release her volatile emotions. Carla seeks a solution to the
problem of love through a non-monogamous marriage, but
this raises more problems than it solves. "I don't believe this scene," says a shrill voice from the wings of
this tour de force of histrionics. Neither will you.

BOOM!

By Leland Gralapp (Dutton, 1965).

This is the story of Ernst Pilger, who sails to
America from Hamburg, Germany, to seek fame and fortune
in dynamic America. "The West will be my land of promise," he decides. "There I'll get wealth. There I'll
find the power that I crave." In Rock Springs, Wyoming,
he meets his first real Indian, who turns out to be from
Dum-Dum, near Calcutta. In Elko, Nevada, he gets into
the vending machine business, selling insurance to gamblers.
Then he drifts on to California and really makes the big
time. In Riverside, Orange County, California, he starts
a Zen monastary and soon enrolls more novices than he
can accommodate. After the comic possibilities of this
have been exhausted (Exhausted? Bulldozed!), our questing
hero travels on to Los Angeles to seek his "rendezvous
with destiny." He founds an organization called Protest,
Incorporated, an agency for pickets. Before long he falls
in love with his secretary, Connie Mayfield, who suffers
from one disturbing little idiosyncrasy. She goes into a
sexual trance whenever she hears a sonic boom--a quite
frequent occurrence around L.A.! Perhaps this reviewer
had best spare his reader further details. As far as Mr.
Gralapp's dialogue is concerned, his characters all talk
like Senator Everett Dirkson. In short, Boom! is a bomb.

A HOUSE OF GLASS

By Harvey J. Howells (Appleton, 1965).

The house of glass is the twenty-five-story United

Products Building on New York's Fifth Avenue, the home of
United Products, Inc., a veritable "microcosm of civilization" with thousands of employees, a company cafeteria
seating nine hundred, a five-bed hospital, airplanes, and a
theater. J. Harvey Howells belongs to the Fab Soap School
of Realism and leaves nothing out. The company theater
boasts two full-time projectionists. The five-bed hospital is
staffed by two young doctors and three older nurses, or one
for each bed. The plot (if that's the proper word) is about
the power struggle that takes place in the upper echelons of
the company upon the resignation of President Warren Gale
("That's the first step, Will. Organize the man power in
this building from the top right down to the slob level"), a
struggle that spills over rather sloppily into the grubby private lives of the various executives. Purple passages are
strewn like overripe plums in the gray, impenetrable,
cement-mixer prose.

ELIXIR OF LIFE: AN HISTORICAL NOVEL OF NEW
                   ORLEANS

By A. E. Cowdrey (Doubleday, 1965).

          In the year 1851 an ambitious young man by the name
of John Samson Donnelly, a "country boy with a bit of
cash (twenty dollars), his carpetbag with a change of shirts
in it," arrives in New Orleans to seek his fortune. For a
while things look good. He meets a sweet wench from the
little upriver town of Carrollton. Marie Cousin is "country
French with a drop of Africa in her blood." In the summer
of 1853 the plague strikes New Orleans and the city is in
chaos. As John Samson gets out of bed one morning and,
"with many yawns and much slow-jointed movement," puts on
his stockings, drawers, pants, shoes, and coat, a thought
flashes through his mind. He will concoct and peddle a fever
cure ("What was the fever? Where did it come from? How
did it communicate?") and strike it rich. Is he not a "true
eclectic, a jack of all quackeries"? Alas, John Samson has
difficulty communicating with Ole Yellow Jack, for his fever
cure is a bust. Marie dies. Undaunted he joins the "odd
crew on Orange Street" and resorts to common blackleg
or dishonest gambling. Now with money in his pocket, he
rides off upriver where the wind is "winey, piney and tur-
pentiney." Many yawns and much slow-jointed movement
in this first novel.

BAZZARIS

By Don Tracy (Trident Press, 1965).

Until the blight in '47 Rovalla, Florida, was called the "Sponge Capital of the World " and the <u>Bazzaris</u> was the queen of the sponge fleet. Although Rovalla is no longer the sponge capital, the proud, tight-knit Greek community clings stubbornly to the old ways. They have never forgiven Fotis Giranopoulis for having deserted his good Greek wife, Eleni, to run off with a <u>Kseni</u> movie queen, Lorey King, filming <u>Pirate's Galleon</u> on location in Rovalla. Actually Lorey was just an excuse. Fetis hated being a sponge diver, but his uncle Kitsos, the boss of the Giranopoulis family, would not allow him to accept a football scholarship at the state university. Once free of Rovalla, Fotis changed his name to Pete Gerard and made a fortune in real estate. As the narrative begins, Eleni has died and Pete Gerard returns to Rovalla to say a last goodbye. The Greeks of Rovalla think he has come back to taunt them, however, and Pete is knifed in the shoulder. Apparently he is near death in Clearwater when Dimitries Samoris, accompanied by his pretty granddaughter, Sofia Tsingoros, attempts a reconciliation. "It would be ironic," Sofia muses, "if the first man I'd think of letting touch me should die a few hours after I met him." (Oh, those Greek muses!) Of course Pete doesn't die. It's too bad such a colorful locale is wasted in the hands of such an inept writer. Moreover, it would be ironic if this book should be purchased after the above.

CONDITION GREEN: TOKYO

By Neil Goble (Tuttle, 1966).

According to U.S. Intelligence the Japanese Communists plan to seize control of the government on May Day, 1970. The only thing that stands between them and their objective is good old Uncle Sam (naturally!) which maintains air bases on Japanese soil in accordance with the U.S.-Japan Security Treaty. In direct contravention of the treaty, Captain Joe Holiday and his buddies are scouting Russian and Chinese targets from secret bases in Japan. These unarmed reconnaissance planes are called "Black

Bats." On an eleven-hour mission in his trusty Bat, Captain Holiday dramatically turns the tide against the Communists and almost single-handedly makes Japan safe for democracy. When not violating other countries' air space, Joe Holiday and company are busy alienating the Japanese with their incredibly boorish behavior. Here is an example of just how ridiculous and banal this novel is: seven hours after her parents have been blown to bits by a Communist bomb, the Ambassador's daughter is exchanging quips with Joe Holiday about their little escapades ("Sally laughed, despite her misery"). Essentially a comic book in hard covers.

TENANTS OF THE HOUSE

By Heather Ross Miller (Harcourt, Brace and World, 1966).

Like Heather Ross Miller's first novel, The Edge of the Woods, which received praise from Granville Hicks and others, Tenants of the House is set in a small town in North Carolina. Johnsboro is a factory town that lives in the shadow of the huge Piedmont Aluminum Smelting Company. It is a honeycomb of monotonous row houses, softened by the roses and lobelia that grow in profusion and the "steady blossoming of children around the doorways and in the small green yards." From her lofty perch as omniscient author, Miss Miller views Johnsboro as a "doll town" far, far below. Obviously she has not attempted to write a story in the traditional sense, but has tried to breathe life into a whole town ("the town of Johnsboro lay still as a mouse in the dark of the mountains"), as though it were not just an assemblage of houses, but a living, breathing entity. Despite the author's heroic attempt at artificial resuscitation, the patient dies. In the rarefied atmosphere of her self-consciously "arty" style, there is simply not enough oxygen to sustain life.

MEMORIES OF THE FUTURE

By Paul Horgan (Farrar, Straus and Giroux, 1966).

It is hard to believe that this innocuous tale is by the distinguished author of Things As They Are. It is a

paean of praise to patriotism that is almost embarrassing
in its effusiveness.   In the process of celebrating the ex-
alted concepts of Love, Duty and Country, the author's usually subtle and discriminating style degenerates.   Duty begins at prewar Annapolis where "a generation of heroes" is
molded in the hallowed traditions of that august place (June
Week and all).   Duty is represented by the venerable Admiral Grace and by Mrs. Grace saying in her best hostess
voice to the Admiral's unmarried aide (a mere commander
in the naval reserve), "What is your Miss Cleveland like?"
Of course the Admiral's wife is the price we must all pay
to defend our country.   World War II with its terrible human sacrifices comes along just in time to make everyone
from the Admiral's lady to the lowliest midshipman feel
very pleased with himself.

OPINION OF THE COURT

By William Woolfolk (Doubleday, 1966).

Mr. Woolfolk has tried to do for the Supreme Court
what Allen Drury did for the Senate.   Like Advise and Con-
sent, the novel is long on research and short on merit--
literary or otherwise.   The protagonist is Paul Lincoln
Lowe, Governor of Nebraska, who is chosen by President
Lamont Howard to fill the vacancy on the Court created by
the retirement of Justice Frank Joyce.   Justice Lowe soon
makes it clear that he will be a great liberal justice in the
tradition of Justice Charles Edmunson, but as far as his
private life is concerned, he is just a common ordinary
adulterer.   When not delivering brilliant opinions, he is
carrying on an affair ("Hello, dear. I'm afraid I have to
work late again tonight") with an attractive young newspaper-
woman named Katherine Prescott whom he eventually marries.   Meanwhile revolution is brewing in Burma and President Howard sends our hero on a special assignment to see
what the Commies are up to in that part of the world.   On
his return the President orders the Seventh Fleet to steam
to Rangoon and the Supreme Court to crack down on sub-
versives at home ("We're going to have to deal with these
vermin at home at the same time we're fighting them over-
seas.")   Clearly President Lamont Howard is a dangerous
man, but the author shows no interest in pursuing this
thought.   Instead he returns abruptly to the solemn delib-

erations of the Court.   Oh, yes, Katherine dies and Justice
Lowe's patient, long-suffering wife of twenty-three years
offers her condolences.

UNDER THE EYE OF THE STORM

By John Hersey (Knopf, 1967).

      At the age of thirty-four Tom Medlar comes to a
crucial point in his life when he and the three passengers
aboard his yawl Harmony--his wife, Audrey, and a fun-
loving couple, Dottie and Flick Hamden -- are swept out
to sea in the path of a hurricane.   Under the eye of the
storm this "real marlinspike-seaman of a sailor" (a noted
hepatologist by profession) hopes to find the "dead center
of reality, the self."   Alas, the self is not so easily apprehended and the whole experience is a disillusioning one for
our intrepid voyager.   The truth is that men and boats
have secret flaws.   Harmony's flaw is a bad place around
the forward keel bolt where the builder used a piece of
cheap lumber.   Tom Medlar also has a secret flaw that
corresponds to the one in the Harmony.   Just as the Harmony has dry rot, so does John Hersey's prose.   He
piles meaningless cliché ("the teeth of the gale, " "the center
of chaos, " etc.) upon cliché to form a towering slag heap of
bad English.   John Hersey's literary barometer is falling
with each new book.   However, he does perform a useful
function as a kind of popularizer of current ideas.   He is
the Will Durant of the novel.

THE GOLD OF MALABAR

By Berkely Mather (Scribner, 1967).

      A few hundred miles south of Bombay, sixty million
pounds of Dutch gold lie buried off the Malabar Coast near
the tiny enclave of Goa.   The gold was appropriated by the
Japanese when they invaded the Dutch East Indies in 1941.
In attempting to ship it out of the country, the Japanese
were forced to ditch it off the Malabar Coast.   A quarter
of a century later, not many people know about the buried
treasure.   While serving a sentence for manslaughter in a
prison in Goa, a sailor-adventurer named Mike O'Reilly

learns about the gold from a fellow prisoner, Rokkjer. Rokkjer gives O'Reilly a medal and tells him to show it to a Buddhist monk in Bombay, Nu Pah, with the words, "Rokkjer said to keep the faith." Thus begins the fortune hunt. If it sounds like pulp fiction in the grand manner, that is exactly what it is. Whatever interest this absurd tale may have springs from Mr. Mather's apparent knowledge of every nook and cranny of the Far East. Although the story has a certain quaint charm, it is as dated as Tarzan of the Apes.

MISS MAMMA AIMEE

By Erskine Caldwell (New American Library, 1967).

Widowed in her fifties, Aimee Mangrum inherited all the family property consisting of the stately Mangrum mansion and nearly eighty thousand acres of valuable farm and timber land on the outskirts of Augusta, Georgia. In order to support herself and her numerous relatives, she has found it necessary to sell large parcels of land from time to time. Only a thousand acres of the original plantation remain. Besides her son, Graham, who is not right in the head, Aimee supports her daughter, Velma; Velma's guitar-playing husband, Woody Woodruff; her brother-in-law, Russell Mangrum; and Russell's complaining wife, Katie. Into this constantly bickering, inbred (Aimee was already a Mangrum when she married a Mangrum), demented ménage, the author slyly introduces an illiterate, penniless young preacher of the Supreme Being Missionary Church named Raley Purdy. Aimee considers him "the handsomest-looking manly man" she has ever seen and promptly offers him free room and board. When Aimee's daughter Connie arrives home from Savannah, Georgia, where she is a hostess at the Select Club, the stage is set for one of those titillating seduction scenes which Erskine Caldwell has perfected over the course of a half dozen recent mediocre and repetitious novels. As usual, Mr. Caldwell cannot seem to make up his mind whether he is writing low comedy or high tragedy and, in the absence of either, settles for easy ribaldry.

364 The Novel of the Sixties

HARTSPRING BLOWS HIS MIND

By Ernest Lockridge (New American Library, 1968).

These "random jottings toward an elementary treatise
on life" by the son of the late Ross Lockridge, Jr., tell
the story of a thirty-five-year-old graduate student and assistant instructor of English at a New England college who,
instead of working on his dissertation on Theodore Dreiser,
spends his free time ogling "a pair of embryonic Ann Corios"
who live in the girls' graduate dormitory some thirty yards
away. A voyeur's paradise, it is the only office in the
entire building that commands such an enticing view. The
girls put on quite a show for our oversexed hero, a self-
confessed "sentimentalist and pervert," who is finally moved
to reciprocate with a unique favor of his own. This is a
curious novel, even in this age, and I'm not sure what Mr.
Lockridge meant to accomplish by it. The kindest view
would be to say that it is a parody of the exhibitionist-type
novel which Mr. Bennett Cerf said he wouldn't touch with
a forty-foot pole. Although extremely scatalogical, it
isn't very funny. Mr. Lockridge possesses a Ph.D. in
English, but his humor tends toward the sophomoric; it
is immature, crude, and superficial. On the plus side,
he writes with considerable verve and style. He is obviously a talented writer. He knows how to put a story,
albeit a sordid one, together. There isn't a dull page in
the whole book. Ernest Lockridge has yet to write his
first novel, but when he does it will probably be a good
one.

LAST WORDS

By Alex Karmel (McGraw-Hill, 1968).

Apparently dying of cancer, Alan Stein's last words
are a series of seemingly endless letters to his late beloved who died in an automobile accident some ten years
before. Now a successful New York lawyer who lives in
a luxury apartment in the East Seventies with his wife and
children, Alan labors over these last words while pretend-
ing to be deeply engrossed in work from the office. His
wife does not know that "it is a date with an old girl friend,
even if it is posthumous and only on paper." "Darling,"
the first letter begins, "...what I will try to do is tell

you, and in telling you perhaps even manage to discover
for myself just who I was when you met me and just what
it was that you meant to me, meant for me, made of me
in that short time before you abandoned me..." Then our
lovesick hero who has been pining away for a decade tells
us all about himself, himself, himself, in excruciating
detail -- "I was sitting on the stone steps with a notebook
under my behind, bundled up in my mackinaw, trying to
keep the jelly from my cream cheese-and-jelly sandwich
from dropping on my corduroy knickers." This embarrass-
ingly naïve novel has bits and pieces of good realistic
writing, but the whole idea is so ludicrous that it is difficult to take the book seriously.

THE THIEVES OF TUMBUTU

By Harris Greene (Doubleday, 1968).

     The Sheikdom of Aragosta is a wretchedly poor
island in the Indian Ocean under the Horn of Africa. It
is administered by the British and Italians under the aegis
of the United Nations. The downtrodden but numerically
superior Bantus at the eastern end of the island ("the
part which resembles two claws and the head of a lobster")
threaten an uprising. Young Bill Sibley, desk officer for
Aragosta in Washington, is sent on TDY to the tiny country.
His mission is to see what he can do to protect the NASA
auxiliary tracking station at Sombooni and its complement
of fifty Americans. When the American Consul is forced
to leave the country, Sibley is made Acting Consul. There
is also an Acting Grand Sheik named Mulay Hadji and an
Acting British Resident, Miss Millicent Middleton from Mid-
dlesex with the rank of Minister. Sibley saves the situation
by having a black elephant, the sacred totem of the Tumbutu,
flown in from the mainland by helicopter ("Oh, no! Not
an elephant! No, Pete, it's too much"). The elephant
has UHURU painted on the sides and becomes known as
"The Elephant Who Led a Revolution." The Sheikdom of
Aragosta becomes the People's Republic of Tumbutu. Sibley
is decorated by the Deputy Assistant Secretary of State
and reassigned to Rabat. The Thieves of Aragosta is this
reviewer's candidate for Worst Novel of the Year. It's just
too much.

PROVIDENCE ISLAND

By Calder Willingham (Vanguard Press, 1969).

        Imagine being stranded on a tiny uninhabited island
in the Caribbean with a Lesbian writer and a missionary's
wife! This is what happens to Jim Kittering, a television
executive, who had sailed on the freighter Lorna Loone
bound for Bluefields, Nicaragua, to obtain background material for a new comedy-adventure series, "Tramp Steamer."
Hurricane Beulah blows the ship onto a reef where all
hands conveniently perish except Jim and the two charming
ladies. Undaunted they make themselves comfortable in a
cave and are immediately faced with deep philosophical
questions and moral imponderables ("Shall I put on my
trunks in case we decide to go swimming?"). They soon
lose their inhibitions, however. Although married, Jim
decides the only realistic thing to do under the circumstances
is to become common-law husband to Florence, the Lesbian
writer, and Melody, the missionary's wife. Florence is a
problem, since it is unclear whether she is a real Lesbian
or only a thirty-eight-year-old virgin terrified of men. In
an orgy that goes on for hundreds of tedious (that's what I
said) pages and includes a "nice" orgy and a "not-so-nice"
orgy, Florence finally "does it." She is not a Lesbian, after
all, but merely has Lesbian tendencies. After four months
and four days of love and games on Providence Island, Jim
and his two playmates are rescued. "I can't believe it,"
sums up Melody. "One minute we're on the island, the
next we're gone." As Jim says about his own profession,
the gluck is endless.

NATIONAL ANTHEM

By Richard Kluger (Harper, 1969).

        Christopher "Kit" Kwait is "a pillar of normality, a
dedicated family man...working regular hours for good pay
...a paragon of decorum, a consummately civilized man.
And dead." He decides to break out of his tranquil but humdrum existence by committing adultery, and committing a
spectacular crime. Certain indelicate complications prevent the fulfillment of the first objective, but the crime, a
$400,000 robbery, is a resounding success. If this novel

begins to sound like a spoof of Norman Mailer's An American
Dream, perhaps it is.   At any rate, our hero is beginning
to get over his hangup.   Now a millionaire, he joins Shag
Shaughnessy, "visionary saloonkeeper," at a training camp
in the Berkshires.   Together they unleash a "two-hundred-
man legion against the unrepentant villains who abound in
the land." Armed with paint, shells and napalm, this army
on wheels begins by attacking Huntington Hartford's Gallery
of Modern Art and ends in the New Mexico desert where it
comes to the aid of the Apachaho Indians in their "death
struggle with the deputies of the Great White Father."
Using a sledgehammer rather than a stiletto, the author
flails away recklessly at our national follies and foibles,
Norman Mailer included, but the result is not remarkable
for wit, insight, or subtlety and left this reviewer hopeless-
ly uptight.   My hangup is unfunny satire.

THE BUZZARDS

By Janet Burroway (Little, Brown, 1969).

In her third novel the author of Eyes and Dancer
from the Dance writes about a political campaign in which
the incumbent senator from Arizona is seeking reelection.
The senator is a States' rights advocate who sententiously
expounds on the "American way of life." "The family is the
mortar of the American dream," the senator announces
grandiloquently, "and it is with the family that America
must start rebuilding." So what happens? His twenty-eight-
year-old daughter, married unhappily in Weehawken, New
Jersey, runs off to Mexico to get an abortion. His wife
is a self-sacrificing, self-pitying martyr to his political
career. And his younger daughter ends up murdered in a
park. End of family. End of American Dream. All this
is apparently supposed to be ironic, but this reviewer found
it simply boring. The characters are so lackluster and uninteresting in themselves they hardly seem to merit the
author's heavy-handed introspection and soliloquizing. As
one of the senator's aides says, "Two years from now
nobody's going to come back and count the votes."

IMAGES

By Paul Young (Nash, 1969).

To begin with the very first sentence of this first novel, Michael Freeman is riding along Wilshire Boulevard as "the sun sets through the windshield of the car." An extraordinary phenomenon even for Los Angeles! Michael is a young personal manager who flips around a lot ("I can never keep my mind on one course for very long...it gets very distracted"). He is good at his job, but doesn't want his boss to think he was "just some guy who'd walked in off the street and decided to be a personal manager." He is also a great guitar player and signs a fabulous one-million-dollar contract. Michael has a nice cozy relationship with a forty-two-year-old secretary, Penny Colman, and her two daughters, Carol, twelve, and Diane, seventeen. They all love him, but he is in love with a beautiful actress, Wendy Martin. When Wendy is killed in an auto accident, Michael is overcome with grief (pages 156, 157 and 158 are intentionally left blank). Just as he begins to recover, Diane tries to seduce him. After he resists her advances, Diane tells her mother Michael is the one. Penny is furious. At this moment, Carol enters with a gun and shoots him. He comes to in a hospital and for the first time in his life is "forced to probe deeply to find where my substance lay, if any...to find out what I was made of or whether my life was shot at thirty." I liked the three blank pages best.

PART THREE

APPRECIATIONS

THE CALL TO MURRALLA

By George McMurry (Harper, 1960).

As a work of fiction this book undoubtedly has its
faults but considered simply as autobiography it is an
absolutely first-rate piece of writing.   Told in the first
person, The Call to Murralla is the story of a thirteen-
year-old Anglo-American boy's last year in India around
the turn of the century as a member of a dedicated missionary family (as the novel closes the Rughs are about
to sail for America).   It is difficult to know just what to
say about this evocative and beautifully written work.   It
is an excellent study of missionary life, of course, but
it is also a moving study of adolescence.   It is a study of
America as well as of India, though we never do set foot
on American soil.   Indeed, one of the most remarkable
aspects of the book is the dreamlike image of America
(copies of The American Boy, pressed maple leaves from
the cool Wisconsin woods, boxes from Montgomery Ward)
which young Paul cherishes as his birthright in an India
of extreme pestilence and cruelty.   If this one aspect of
The Call to Murralla were only set in slightly sharper focus
(the novel as a whole suffers somewhat from a tendency
toward diffuseness) there would be very little to complain
about.   Highly recommended generally.

A KIND OF FIGHTING

By Patrick Cruttwell (Macmillan, 1960).

This book must give its author considerable satisfaction.   Not only does he have a great deal to say on the
complex subject of nationalism in the Far East -- the
novel relates the story of Lin Soe, the liberator of Sagha,
a not-so-mythical country in Southeast Asia -- but he has
also written a superior work of fiction.   A Kind of Fighting is narrated by Professor Henry Little, a former
teacher of history in the capital of Sagha, who has had
occasion to observe Lin Soe at crucial moments in the
latter's career, from humble student chafing under British
rule to Dinzah, or Leader, of independent Sagha.   Setting

down his story as a corrective to the "official" legend, the narrator reveals the Dinzah to have been "a sentient, limited, changeable creature, simultaneously playing on, and being played on, by the forces around him." Actually A Kind of Fighting is not a novel in the usual sense of the word. Although it recapitulates the career of Lin Soe, it is not really a study of "character." It is quite explicitly a study of "history." And yet, though Mr. Cruttwell is occasionally repetitious, he is so skillful with words (his sentences carry weight, a weight imposed by style) that he literally makes history come alive. Recommended for all libraries.

CAPTAIN CAT

By Robert Holles (Macmillan, 1960).

       In England, where this novel of life in a boys' army training unit was published earlier this year, one reviewer called it a "perfect Salinger." To this reviewer, the book indeed bears such a startling resemblance to The Catcher in the Rye as to read almost like a deliberate parody. Consider this: "I kept pretending to be worried about where the darkness was going. 'Look, Gangst,' I said, 'what happens to the darkness when you walk straight into it and fill up a bit of the space where it was before. Where the hell does it go?'" In Salinger's novel this is of course the refrain, "Where do the ducks in Central Park go in the wintertime when the lagoon is frozen over?" The truth is Mr. Holles has not only written a devastating parody of The Catcher in the Rye but paradoxically he has composed (written is too crass a word) an excruciatingly convincing book in his own right. He is even more whimsical than Salinger, but his book gathers strength as it goes along, whereas Salinger's goes soft and slack at the end. What is Captain Cat about? It is about a Christ-like figure, Rex Boone, who struggles desperately to maintain his integrity despite the tyrannies of military life. Even more it is about his friend, protector and eventual betrayer, Harry Bell. It has pathos, sex, humor, tragedy and, yes, compassion. It is most assuredly a small masterpiece.

THE TRIAL BEGINS

By Abram Tertz (Pantheon, 1960).

This extraordinary novel was first published in Paris
after having been smuggled out of Russia by an unknown
Soviet writer using the pseudonym of Abram Tertz. It is
a wickedly satirical portrait of a Russia which bears little
resemblance to the "official" Russia prescribed by Socialist realism. This "official" Russia is represented in The
Trial Begins, however, by Vladimir Globov, the Public
Prosecutor. As the novel begins (the main action takes
place during the last year of Stalin's life), Globov is
prosecuting the case of Citizen Rabinovich, a gynecologist
who has unlawfully performed an abortion. Ironically
Globov's own wife, Marina, has had occasion to flout the
law in this regard, to the Public Prosecutor's complete
mortification. To make matters still worse, Globov's
son is taken into custody as a traitor to the cause. And
Marina, beautiful and self-indulgent, carries on an affair
with her husband's opposite number, the Counsel for the
Defense. The satire is extraordinarily comic and inventive.
In the Epilogue the narrator (we know him only as "the
writer"), his manuscript having fallen into the hands of the
authorities, facetiously remarks that in the course of the
interrogation "it was established that everything I had written was pure invention, the product of a morbid and ill-
intentioned mind." Using a brilliant surrealistic technique
that recalls the novels of Nathanael West and John Hawkes,
the author of The Trial Begins has written not only an
absorbing philosophical fable of our time but an excellent
novel in its own right.

FIRST FAMILY

By Christopher Davis (Coward-McCann, 1961).

This book with the exceedingly mundane title is what
this reviewer would scarcely have thought possible at this
date -- a moving, artistic and altogether first-rate novel
on the subject of white and colored families living side by
side in a suburban community. It may be recalled that
Keith Wheeler recently explored this same subject in
Peaceable Lane, a shrill, hackneyed piece of writing en-

dorsed by the Book-of-the-Month Club. In First Family a
Negro professor of classics moves with his wife and twelve-
year-old son into an all-white residential district. Mr.
Davis has had the happy idea of unfolding his narrative
mainly through the eyes of an imaginative, high-strung
child prodigy who happens also to be colored. By getting
beneath the skin of young Scotty McKinley (where there is
neither white nor colored) the author is able to describe
the terrifying events as they impinge on Scotty from the
outside and at the same time is able to add a human di-
mension to his narrative which makes all the difference.
The delicate relationship between the boy and a slightly
older girl is exquisitely and heartbreakingly handled. Mr.
Davis offers no easy solutions to the so-called Negro
"problem"; indeed, he is rather pessimistic. Nevertheless the mere fact that he has been able to write about it
in such human terms is itself cause for optimism. Several
years ago Martin Levin said of Christopher Davis' first
novel, Lost Summer, that what especially distinguished it
was "the way its author avoids either sanctimony or sen-
sationalism, and re-creates instead a finely texured bit
of the American social fabric." This can also be said of
First Family.

REVOLUTIONARY ROAD

By Richard Yates (Little, Brown, 1961).

Suburbia, that much maligned phenomenon, has at
last found its Zola. So much nonsense has been written on
suburban life and mores that it comes as a considerable
shock to read a book by someone who seems to have his
own ideas on the subject and who pursues them relentlessly
to the bitter end. On the surface the Wheelers would appear to be a typical suburban family. He commutes to
work to his above-average, white-collar job in the city.
She is active in community theater. Their children are
pretty much like everyone else's on Revolutionary Road.
The trouble is he detests his job, the play is a flop, and
the home the children inhabit is far from a happy one.
Unfortunately, Frank Wheeler is a moral weakling who
feels that he was made for better things. By constantly
deprecating his surroundings he spares himself the pain of
having to face reality. Seldom has the talk of a desperate,

ineffectual man been captured with such uncanny precision
as in this novel.   Frank literally talks himself to death.
This is not a pleasant book (it reminds this reviewer of
Katherine Shattuck's remarkable The Narrowest Circle of
a few seasons back), but such is the nature of life that some
of the most pathetic moments are also the most comical.
For quality fiction collections.

THE LIME TWIG

By John Hawkes (New Directions, 1961).

"Mr. Hawkes' writing is cold, brilliant and cryptic,"
the New Yorker said in its review of his first novel, The
Cannibal, "he writes like no one else at all." The Lime
Twig, Hawkes' fourth book, seems to represent, as Leslie
Fiedler suggests in his excellent introduction, a new departure for this remarkable writer.   On one level it is
what Graham Greene likes to call an "Entertainment," a
thriller that revolves about an ingenious plot to steal a
race horse named Rock Castle and enter it in an English
horse race, the Golden Bowl.   (As it turns out, a gang of
professional crooks muscle in on the operation and things
end disastrously for all concerned.)   On another level, and
more importantly, it is a twentieth-century journey through
the infernal regions, the "long downhill deathless gliding of
a dream" that will literally make your hair stand on end.
Mr. Fiedler entitles his introduction (somewhat perversely)
"The Pleasures of John Hawkes."   Obviously Fiedler's
pleasures are not everybody's and many readers will find
The Lime Twig a bit oppressive (oppressive in the way that,
say, Bergman's brilliant The Virgin Spring is oppressive).
What this reviewer hadn't noticed before in Hawkes' work
was his skill with dialogue -- and English dialogue at that.
The tension and excitement he creates in the counterpoise
between this sprightly dialogue and the dark, moody, introspective current of his prose are a constant source of
surprise and delight.   For all libraries that feel a responsibility to the future as well as to the passing moment.
Yes, buy, borrow or steal his other works too!

SATURDAY TO MONDAY

By Ruth Rehmann (Viking Press, 1961).

Many of us who review fiction occasionally have our little fun at the author's expense (sometimes it is the only consolation), but when a good novel comes along we know it and only want to sing its praises. Saturday to Monday, beautifully translated from the German by Catherine Hutter, is one of these all-too-rare books. Amazingly enough it is a first novel. Four office workers, a man and three women, employed by the firm of Wellis, leave their ultra-modern Office EA-39 at precisely 1:15 on Saturday afternoon to encounter their past selves and also to get through the "unbearable, interminable Sunday" ahead. There is Paul Westermann, chained to a domesticity he resents, whose dreams lie buried in the Sahara ("every 'a' magnified by a dream"). There is old Frau Schramm whose strong sense of duty to the firm underlies a terrible insecurity. There is Frau Schramm's successor-to-be, Carmen Viol, her beauty beginning to fade at forty. And finally there is Theresa Pfeiffer, a character out of a Françoise Sagan novel, already bored and indifferent at nineteen. The novel conveys a powerful impression of the generations treading one another down, while death in the guise of an obscene old man waits patiently at the gate. "Filled with a dreamlike light and overflowing with a dreamlike time" (to borrow the author's own words), Saturday to Monday is written in a poetic prose of extraordinary beauty and precision. No one interested in the modern novel should be denied the opportunity to read this remarkable work.

BY NATURE EQUAL

By Josep Maria Espinas (Pantheon, 1961).

This book, translated from the Catalan, joins a truly distinguished list of foreign novels recently brought out in this country. It reminds me in particular of Ruth Rehmann's Saturday to Monday. En Pere Jordana, an impoverished clerk in a woolen mill, is chosen to accompany the head of the firm, Senyor Joaquim, on a business trip, to act as chauffeur and general handy man. The

employer-employee relationship is rigorously maintained
until they become involved in an auto accident. Jordana
saves his employer's life by attending to his wounds and
carrying him to a lonely farmhouse. Thrown there into
unaccustomed intimacy and completely separated from his
past, Senyor Joaquim discovers not only that "all men are
brothers" but that "all men are men." This novel could
have been merely sentimental, but it is not. The author
writes with a sure sense of the complicated nature of the
human condition, of the subtle differences that separate
men as well as the similarities that bind them together.
His use of symbolism (the working man's café is on the
harsh level of the street, the rich man's three steps
down "below the level of life") is excellent. Furthermore,
he has humor and deep poetic insight. In short, By Nature Equal is that rare book (but not so rare as we might
think?) that touches something deep in all of us.

MASTER OF THIS VESSEL

By Gwyn Griffin (Holt, Rinehart and Winston, 1961).

     Mr. Griffin is that unfashionable phenomenon, a
serious novelist who believes that a novel should tell a good
rousing story. Accepting a temporary position as Chief
Officer on a small Italian ship bound for Australia, young
Serafino Ciccolanti reluctantly takes command of the San
Rogue upon the Captain's death en route. Trouble soon
breaks out between the English and Italian tourist-class
passengers. An altogether unsavory lot (Mr. Griffin has
a very low opinion of the human race in general and the
English race in particular), they are constantly at each
other's throats. There are also some exceedingly unpleas-
ant first-class passengers, including a still young English
ex-naval officer who attempts to seize control of the ship
during a severe storm. Frankly, I think the author has
tried to cram too much into this novel, with the result that
he sometimes tries our patience. Nor is he above resort-
ing to melodrama to achieve his ends. And yet if one is
reluctant to compare Master of This Vessel with Conrad, it
is still a very entertaining piece of fiction. Mr. Griffin
has a sharp eye for the phony and his characters, as
drab as most of them are, do ring true. Moreover, the
characterization of Serafino Ciccolanti, the overburdened

young ship's master with the lame foot, is extremely well
done.   Recommended for most libraries.

NIGHT

By Francis Pollini (Houghton Mifflin, 1961).

          This powerful novel about G.I. prisoners of war
does for the Korean conflict what A Farewell to Arms did
for World War I.   First published last year in Paris, Night
isn't nearly so "glamorous," but then the Korean War was
a very unglamorous war.   There are no Catherine Barkleys
in Night, only "Progressives," "Reactionaries" and the cunning Chinese who play one group against the other.   The
scene is a prisoner of war camp on the Yalu River.   The
chief protagonists are Sergeant Marty Landi of the U.S.
Army and a Chinese "Education Officer" known as Ching
who attempts to brainwash him.   The camp is divided into
two groups: the "Progressives" who cooperate with Ching
and are treated leniently and the "Reactionaries" led by the
almost legendary Phillips.   The tragedy is that the former
out-number the latter by almost eight to one.   It is Phillips
who succeeds in doing something about this unhappy situation.
"You're fighting two enemies here," Marty acknowledges,
"the Chinks--and the one right inside those guys."   This
novel, librarians are forewarned, is as obscene as war itself; it may very well become a classic.

THE SUN DOCTOR

By Robert Shaw (Harcourt, Brace and World, 1961).

          This fine novel by the English author of The Hiding
Place combines the exoticism of Conrad and the guilt of
Graham Greene.   Dr. Benjamin Halliday returns to England
after twenty-five years of service in a West African hospital.   Although about to be knighted, he is overwhelmed by
remorse and a profound sense of failure.   In Africa Dr.
Halliday had come upon a weird community situated in a
dense swamp where the diseased ruled the healthy.   Shut
off from the world and suffering from malnutrition, the
inhabitants of Manda continually douse themselves with

water (sweat being the symbol of death) and live in terror
of the sun.   The Sun Doctor leads many of these people
out of the swamp but his impatience and lack of humility
(as he gradually comes to realize) bring pain and disillusionment.   This is a very exciting and ambitious work,
though not a completely successful one.   It makes up in
originality and imagination, however, what it lacks in
technical control.   The author seems particularly obsessed
by the physiognomy of Africa and his descriptive passages
are positively stunning.

THE ACCIDENT

By Elie Wiesel (Hill and Wang, 1962)

        The author of this short, bitter novel is of course
the author of the widely acclaimed Night.   In that work
(which unhappily was not fiction) Mr. Wiesel told the hor-
rifying story of his and his family's personal tragedy in
the concentration camps of Nazi Germany and his resultant
loss of faith.   Everything he has since written has apparently been an attempt to come to terms with this searing
and catastrophic experience.   In The Accident Eliezer
_____, a correspondent for an Israeli newspaper and a
survivor of Auschwitz, is run over by a taxicab while
crossing a New York street.   For weeks Eliezer hovers
between life and death.   One of his frequent visitors in
the hospital is Kathleen with whom he has long had an
affair but without passion or commitment.   In a number of
skillful flashbacks the author sketches the history of this
affair against the background of Eliezer's tragic fate at
the hands of the Nazis.   Only toward the end of his con-
valescence does he realize that his "accident" was not an
accident at all but a deliberate attempt to do away with himself.   For all collections.

BILLIARDS AT HALF-PAST NINE

By Heinrich Böll (McGraw-Hill, 1962).

        This extremely fine novel must surely establish the
author as one of the most important German novelists to

emerge since the War. It tells the story of an aristocratic
family of architects, and covers the period from World
War I to the present. Dr. Robert Faehmel, a demolition
expert during the last war, has blown up famed St.
Anthony's Abbey which his own father had built thirty-five
years before, even though its demolition has no tactical or
strategic importance. Now thirteen years later, he plays
billiards with mathematical precision in his suite in the
Prince Heinrich Hotel and bares his soul to a hotel boy
who reminds him of loved ones sacrificed in the War. He
has erected monuments with dynamite as his father had
done with brick and mortar, monuments of "dust and rubble for those who had not been historical monuments and
whom no one had thought to spare." Written in an ironic
style and utilizing the interior monologue technique, the
novel is practically Joycean in scope. And just as the
subject of Ulysses is Joyce's Dublin, so the real subject
of Billiards at Half-Past Nine is Germany. The novel is
not easy reading in the beginning, ranging as it does backward and forward in time and from one consciousness to
another. The author never loses control, however, and
gradually the pieces fall beautifully and unerringly in place.
Recommended for all libraries.

THE SUMMER LAND

By Burke Davis (Random House, 1965).

        "Here's to the land of the longleaf pine," begins
the North Carolina State Toast, "the summer land where
the sun doth shine." In his fourteenth book, Mr. Davis,
the distinguished historian and novelist, "aided by a large
band of folklorists and renegade sociologists," has written
an affectionate and altogether charming narrative of life
in the Redwine Valley of North Carolina near the Virginia
border in the year 1916. This is tobacco country and
the very survival of the Starling family is dependent upon
getting a good price for their crop. The story unfolds
through the eyes of fifteen-year-old Fairfax Starling, the
shy, bookish member of the family (fourteen in all), who
turns out to be "the toughest knot of all" when he breaks
up an attempted barn burning by a couple of mean Indian
halfbreeds, Jess and Pembroke Sixkiller. The oldest
member of the clan (and a lovable old rogue) is grandpa
Starling, a Civil War veteran in his eighties. Grandpa's

"Confederate lies" are notorious throughout the Valley.
"Ah, Buddy, dammitall, I've lied so much about the War
that I've clean forgot what really happened." The good
people of John M. Virden County thrive on hunting, horse
trading and playing baseball with a rock wound tightly with
string. They attend a one-room schoolhouse presided over
by Miss Cassandra Carson, a graduate of Rappahannock
Female Institute. And they make occasional forays to
Tootsy Kinnamon's distillery located smack on the state
line. A rare and wonderful piece of Americana for all
collections, including YA.

A PURSUIT OF FURIES

By Janice Warnke (Random House, 1966).

The setting for this unusually rich and absorbing
novel is the Villa Kilchberg, a pleasant country house in
Switzerland. The Villa Kilchberg is presided over by
Gwendolyn Dartley, a "thrice-married and thrice-bereaved"
widow with an interesting past (Churchill, Stravinsky and
Toscanini are numbered among her acquaintances) whose
home is a gathering place for some of the leading artistic
and intellectual lights of Europe. The time is 1956 and
Mrs. Dartley's guests include Sylvia Grierson, a young
novelist, Ernest Campion, a disillusioned atomic scientist,
two American youngsters, Marshall and Posy, George Bing-
ham, an agent of the CIA, and Benjamin Knox, an American
TV personality who is at the Villa Kilchberg to film an
interview with Mrs. Dartley. The Villa Kilchberg is, in
fact, a microcosm of Europe. Gradually, as the outside
world begins to impinge on the villa, its guests depart.
The cruel suppression of the Freedom Fighters in Hungary
marks the final demise of the Villa Kilchberg and the Europe
it represents. With it the "crown of culture" goes spin-
ning into the pit, the "last gleams of its intricate gold fading." Highly recommended.

THE LAST GENTLEMAN

By Walker Percy (Farrar, Straus and Giroux, 1966).

This fine avant-garde, James Purdy-ish novel is
by the award-winning author of The Moviegoer. The nar-

rator is Williston Bibb Barrett, the last immediate survivor
of a fine old Southern family, who drops out of Princeton
in his junior year and comes to New York where he lives
at the Y.M.C.A.   With his last $1,900, Will buys a tele-
scope, the lenses of which (ground by German craftsmen
in the Harz Mountains) do not simply transmit light but
penetrate to the heart of things.   Will becomes acquainted
with the wealthy Vaught family.   As it turns out, Chandler
Vaught was a good friend of Will's uncle, a distinguished
Southern congressman.   Already in love with Kitty Vaught,
Will accepts a position as traveling companion to Kitty's
sixteen-year-old brother Jamie, who is dying of a strange
malady.   Together they go on a long hegira in a Trav-L-
Aire trailer home to Ithaca in the Mississippi Delta.   The
sentient engineer (as he is called) with the gift of divining
persons and situations suffers from a nervous condition and
sees for the first time the possibility of a happy, useful life.
Among his other accomplishments, Mr. Percy has etched a
vivid portrait of the modern South reminiscent of the long
fight so brilliantly depicted in Truman Capote's In Cold Blood.
Recommended generally.

THE PACT

By James Ambrose Brown (Putnam, 1966).

        Although James Ambrose Brown, a resident of
Johannesburg, is the author of four novels, The Pact is
the first to be published in the United States.   Chris Murray, a thirty-eight-year-old employee of the Johannesburg-
New York Gold combine, sets out on a journey to Maseru,
the capital of Basutoland, to avenge the terrorist murder
of his wife and her family while on a caravan holiday at
Koodoo Bridge.   One small bullet propelled into Makofane's
head from a length of grooved steel would destroy the brain
from which had emerged violence and a vaunting ambition
to leadership.   At the time that Murray sets out on his
journey, Jonathan Nkosi, a black schoolteacher, who has
recently joined the movement, receives instructions to
kill him.   Nkosi has taken the killing oath and has bound
himself to obedience.   The ensuing journey takes both
men on an exciting chase that ultimately leads to a monastery perched on a cliff in Basutoland ten thousand feet
up in the African mountains.   Murray finds that in choos-
ing to become the hunted he has become the hunted.   He
and his pursuer finally reach Maseru, but neither could

have survived the perilous journey without help from the
other. Once in Maseru they share a similar fate. This
is an extraordinarily terse, exciting and vivid novel. It
does what all good fiction must do--tells a story which is
at the same time an important commentary on the world
in which we live. The Pact will undoubtedly be one of
the best novels of the year. Don't miss it.

THE BROKEN PLACE

By Michael Shaara (New American Library, 1968).

In this well-written first novel Michael Shaara has
taken an ordinary, rather trite theme--a prizefighter kills
another man in the ring--and turned it into a moving allegory of man's search for belief in an unbelieving world.
Tom McClain is a Korean War hero who miraculously
escapes death on patrol. Returning to civilian life, he
renounces college in order to see the world with a buddy,
Tony Wilson. They get as far as the Himalayas when
Tony becomes delirious and dies. Death continues to
follow McClain when he returns home to become a professional prizefighter. He is known as "the finisher" a carry-
over from his college days. McClain has a great future
ahead of him, but he is a strange, philosophical young man.
"I got this one problem," he tells his friend Charley Rav-
enal. "I just can't stop believing...In all this world there
are no signs and no miracles and nobody watching over and
nobody caring. But I believe anyway." If there is such
a thing as a born writer, Michael Shaara is certainly that.
Although owing a good deal to Hemingway (no doubt he is
still young), he has a natural rhythm that is unmistakable.
He will probably have to curb a tendency to attempt too
much (war, love, travel, boxing) too glibly. Nevertheless,
he has written an impressive first novel. The Broken
Place is recommended for any library.

THE RED MACHINES

By F. D. Reeve (Morrow, 1968).

This is the story of one day in the lives of several
dozen men, members of an itinerant combine crew and their

families, who follow the ripening wheat from Texas to
Saskatchewan. (Mr. Reeve, who has previously written
Robert Frost in Russia and The Russian Novel, has himself been a farmhand and truck driver as well as actor,
waiter, longshoreman, and college teacher.) In the midst
of a typical day under the broiling South Dakota sun, an
old truck driver, Blue, dies and is given a makeshift
burial. The tenor of the day is rudely interrupted, but
only for a moment. Trapped in a world of gears and
jacks and forty-bushel hoppers, of wife, children, boss,
wheat, and men, there is little time for the workers to
mourn. The crew prepares to move on to Canada. Although one chapter is apparently modeled after the Night-
town scene in James Joyce's Ulysses, The Red Machines
would seem to owe much more to the naturalistic fiction
of Dreiser and Norris. It is curiously old fashioned, yet
very effective. There is a dark, brooding, mystical
quality that is particularly reminiscent of Norris. The
author is a poet and his vision is of the earth as a terrible
crucible where history is "a hundred years of darkness."
The crudities of style, the obscenities, flow naturally and
unselfconsciously from the blunted, inarticulate mouths of
men. As Paul Horgan has said of this work, "It is clearly
an act of literature."

INDEX OF AUTHORS

385

INDEX OF TITLES